Microsoft Azure for Java Developers

Deploying Java Applications through
Azure WebApp, Azure Kubernetes
Service, Azure Functions,
and Azure Spring Cloud

Abhishek Mishra

Apress®

Microsoft Azure for Java Developers: Deploying Java Applications through Azure WebApp, Azure Kubernetes Service, Azure Functions, and Azure Spring Cloud

Abhishek Mishra
Navi Mumbai, India

ISBN-13 (pbk): 978-1-4842-8250-2 ISBN-13 (electronic): 978-1-4842-8251-9
https://doi.org/10.1007/978-1-4842-8251-9

Managing Director, Apress Media LLC: Welmoed Spahr
Acquisitions Editor: Jonathan Gennick
Development Editor: Laura Berendson
Coordinating Editor: Jill Balzano

Cover designed by eStudioCalamar

Cover image designed by Freepik (www.freepik.com)

Distributed to the book trade worldwide by Springer Science+Business Media New York, 1 New York Plaza, Suite 4600, New York, NY 10004-1562, USA. Phone 1-800-SPRINGER, fax (201) 348-4505, e-mail orders-ny@ springer-sbm.com, or visit www.springeronline.com. Apress Media, LLC is a California LLC and the sole member (owner) is Springer Science + Business Media Finance Inc (SSBM Finance Inc). SSBM Finance Inc is a **Delaware** corporation.

For information on translations, please e-mail booktranslations@springernature.com; for reprint, paperback, or audio rights, please e-mail bookpermissions@springernature.com.

Apress titles may be purchased in bulk for academic, corporate, or promotional use. eBook versions and licenses are also available for most titles. For more information, reference our Print and eBook Bulk Sales web page at http://www.apress.com/bulk-sales.

Any source code or other supplementary material referenced by the author in this book is available to readers on GitHub (https://github.com/Apress). For more detailed information, please visit http://www. apress.com/source-code.

Printed on acid-free paper

This book is dedicated to my ever-supporting wife Suruchi and lovely daughter Aaria.

Table of Contents

About the Author

Abhishek Mishra is a Principal Cloud Architect at a leading organization and has more than 17 years of experience in building and architecting software solutions for large and complex enterprises across the globe. He has deep expertise in enabling digital transformation for his customers using the cloud and artificial intelligence. He speaks at conferences on Azure and has authored four books on Azure prior to writing this new book.

About the Technical Reviewer

Haixia Cheng is a software engineer for Java on Azure at Microsoft. She has three years of experience building products and supporting Java enterprise customers in embracing the cloud paradigm. Haixia has helped companies migrate (modernize) largely monolithic Java EE applications to Virtual Machines and Kubernetes on Azure.

Acknowledgments

I would like to thank Apress for giving me the opportunity to work on this book. Also thanks to the technical reviewer and the editor and the entire Apress team for supporting me in this journey.

Introduction

This book helps you build and run Java-based applications on Azure. You will get an understanding of available services on Azure that support Java-based applications and learn with practical demonstrations how to create these services and run the Java applications on these services. The book shows how to deploy your Java applications in Azure WebApp, Azure Kubernetes Service, Azure Functions, and Azure Spring Cloud. Also covered is integration with components such as Graph API, Azure Storage, Azure Redis Cache, and Azure SQL.

This book is for Java developers planning to build Azure-based Java applications and deploy them on Azure. Developers should be aware of the preliminary cloud fundamentals to help them understand the Java capability available on Azure. The developer need not be an expert in Azure to grasp the book's content and start building Java-based applications using the capability available on Azure. However, developers should have a good understanding of the Java programming language and frameworks.

The book starts with a brief discussion of cloud computing and an introduction to Java support on Azure. You'll then learn how to deploy Java applications using each of the deployment models, and you'll see examples of integrating with Azure services that are of particular interest to Java programmers. Security is an important aspect, and this book shows how to enable authentication and authorization for your Java applications using Azure Active Directory.

Implementing a DevOps strategy is essential in today's market when building any application. Examples in this book show how to build continuous integration and continuous deployment pipelines to build and deploy Java applications on Azure. The book focuses on the best practices one should follow while designing and implementing Java applications on Azure. The book also elaborates on monitoring and debugging Java applications running on Azure using Application Insights and Azure Monitor.

PART I

Building and Deploying Java Applications to Azure

CHAPTER 1

Getting Started with Java Development for Azure

Cloud is the new generation hosting environment. All modern applications developed using cutting-edge frameworks are hosted on the cloud. Cloud hosting helps you save cost and address concerns. You need not worry about building and managing the underlying infrastructure hosting your application. You build your application and host it on the cloud, thus easing the development and maintenance efforts. Microsoft Azure, Amazon Web Services, and Google Cloud Platform are the popular cloud vendors. However, there are a lot of other vendors providing cloud hosting.

A lot of large enterprises build their application using Java, and Azure provides excellent support for Java. These enterprises can run their Java applications on Azure with ease and build robust cloud-native Java solutions running on Azure.

Structure

In this chapter, we will discuss the following aspects of Azure for Java developers:

- What is Cloud Computing
- Introduction to Azure
- Java support on Azure

Objectives

After studying this chapter, you should be able to get the following learnings:

- Understand the fundamentals of cloud computing on Azure

© Abhishek Mishra 2022
A. Mishra, *Microsoft Azure for Java Developers*, https://doi.org/10.1007/978-1-4842-8251-9_1

- Identify Azure services that support Java applications

- Identify Java frameworks that can be hosted on Azure

What Is Cloud Computing

Cloud Computing Basics

We develop an application and host it on a server. We purchase the server infrastructure, install the Operating System, add it to the network, and install the necessary hosting software and application dependencies. And then, we host the application on the server. The entire process is time-consuming and incurs capital expenditure for purchasing the server infrastructure and necessary software required for the application to run.

Once we have hosted the application, we need to keep the server and the hosting environment up and running. We need to perform fixes for the hardware failures and even replace the hardware if needed. We may have to apply software patches for the Operating System and the application hosting software from time to time as needed. We may also need hardware experts to work along with the application developers to perform the maintenance activity. We would incur operational expenditure in maintaining the hardware. Also, once we purchase the server, then we will have to live with it. If we plan to retire the application, then we may not need the server infrastructure anymore. We are blocked with the server as we have purchased it.

To address these issues, enterprises started planning virtualized hosting environments. They started purchasing powerful data centers or server infrastructure and virtualized the underlying infrastructure as multiple Virtual Machines and started hosting the application on these Virtual Machines. They provisioned Virtual Machines to host new applications and decommissioned the Virtual Machines whenever the application retired. This process made the hosting environment to be available on demand. Large organizations like Amazon and Microsoft took inspiration from these virtualized environments and started building cloud infrastructure. They started running their applications on these cloud infrastructures and then commercialized their cloud services.

Cloud computing is all about renting computing services like hosting environments, databases, storage, and many more. You can build your application, rent a hosting environment from a cloud vendor like Microsoft Azure or Amazon Web Services, and host your application in the rented hosting environment. You need not worry about the underlying hosting infrastructure as the cloud vendor will manage it. You need to deploy your application in the cloud service provided by the cloud vendor. This approach will save you both capital and operational expenditure. You need not purchase any server to host your application and need not worry about keeping the server up and running. You need to rent the hosting environment on demand from the cloud vendor and host your application. The cloud vendor will maintain the infrastructure, and you can decommission the infrastructure whenever you do not need it. And not just the hosting environment, you can rent other services like databases, storage, network, and many more such services as per your application requirements.

Note   Cloud computing is all about renting cloud hosting services from a cloud vendor like Microsoft Azure, Amazon Web Services, or Google Cloud Platform.

Cloud Service Types

You may choose to rent the Virtual Machine service from the cloud vendor and host your application on the Virtual Machine. Before hosting your application, you will have to install and configure the hosting environment and all necessary application dependencies. For example, suppose you are hosting a Java application. In that case, you need to install the Java Runtime Environment (JRE) as the hosting software and other necessary application dependencies. You need to install the Operating System and the hosting environment patches from time to time as per the need. Even though you save on the ownership cost of the underlying hosting infrastructure, you still incur some operational expenditure and need to plan some dedicated efforts for maintenance tasks. However, you need not worry about hardware failures for the underlying infrastructure as they will be taken care of by the cloud vendor. This approach of renting the Virtual Machine and hosting your application is called Infrastructure as a Service (IaaS). Here in this hosting model, you get complete control of the hosting environment. You can install all necessary application dependencies as you need and configure the hosting environment. Hosting the application on a Virtual Machine gives you a similar experience of hosting it on an on-premises server.

Note   In the case of Infrastructure as a Service, you get greater control over the underlying hosting environment. However, this cloud hosting approach is expensive.

Infrastructure-as-a-Service hosting option incurs operational cost and effort. To make the process more efficient, the cloud vendors came up with another effective hosting model. In this new model, the cloud vendor would take care of all operational aspects of the hosting environment and the underlying hosting infrastructure. As a developer, you need to build your application, rent the hosting environment, and then host the application. You need not worry about creating the underlying infrastructure or the hosting environment. The cloud vendor will own all the maintenance activities for the underlying infrastructure, Operating System, and hosting software. This approach is a cost-effective option as you need not worry about purchasing the infrastructure and maintaining the infrastructure and the hosting environment. You need to focus on building the application and deploying it to the hosting environment running on the cloud vendor infrastructure. Your application will be production-ready faster as compared to the Infrastructure-as-a-Service hosting model or the on-premises servers. However, you do not have any control over the underlying hosting environment and the infrastructure that is abstracted to you.

Note   In the case of Platform as a Service, you have no control or minimal control over the underlying hosting environment. However, this cloud hosting approach is cheaper than the Infrastructure-as-a-Service approach.

Software as a Service is another interesting hosting option available. Here, in this case, the vendor creates a software product and hosts it in its cloud environment. You, as a developer, can also build a product and host it in the cloud environment of a vendor and then expose subscription models for your end customers. The customers can purchase the subscription models for your product and get billed either yearly, monthly, daily, or any other options provided by your product subscription model. The customers would configure data and user access for the product. They would not have access to the underlying infrastructure and hosting environment or the application code running on the cloud. Microsoft Office 365 or Netflix are examples of Software as a Service.

Note   In Software as a Service, you have no control over the cloud infrastructure, hosting environment, and application code. You configure the data and access for the application.

Figure 1-1 summarizes the preceding discussion around Infrastructure as a Service, Platform as a Service, and Software as a Service. The figure shows where the responsibilities lie for each of the three architectures.

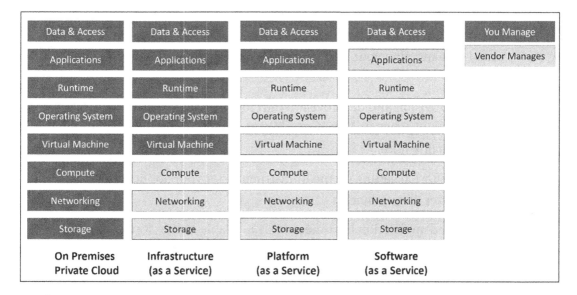

Figure 1-1. *Cloud hosting options*

Cloud Deployment Models

You may choose to host your application on a public cloud vendor like Amazon, Azure, Google, or other cloud providers. Here in the case of the public cloud, cloud infrastructure is managed by the public cloud vendor, and any individual or person can rent our cloud services from the public cloud. However, you do not have control over the cloud infrastructure that is abstracted to you in the case of the public cloud. An organization may choose to create its private cloud, and all the projects in that organization can use the cloud services exposed by the organization's private cloud. Here in the case of private cloud, the organization has greater control over the cloud infrastructure as it owns the infrastructure. However, the organization may incur huge capital expenditure in purchasing and setting up the cloud infrastructure and operational expenditure in maintaining the cloud environment. You may also choose to host your application and its components partly on the public cloud and partly on your organization's private cloud as a hybrid cloud model. For example, your application front end and services run on the public cloud, and the databases run on your organization's private cloud.

The following are the advantages of cloud computing:

- You save the infrastructure ownership and maintenance cost as the cloud vendor manages infrastructure. You can predict the future cloud cost and plan your infrastructure and application budget efficiently.

- You can provision and de-provision the cloud services with a single click and in minutes. You are not locked to the infrastructure if you do not need it anymore.

- You save effort in setting up the infrastructure for your application to ensure faster time to market.

- Your hosted application becomes highly available as the cloud vendor manages the underlying cloud environment and guarantees you high availability for your application based on the Service Level Agreements you have agreed upon with the vendor. You can also host a copy of your application across multiple data centers spread across multiple regions. This strategy would ensure that your application is available even if there is a data center or region-based outage.

- Your application runs on a reliable and fault-tolerant infrastructure managed by the cloud vendor, and you need not worry about these application concerns.

- Your application runs on a highly scalable infrastructure. Whenever the application's incoming requests increase or need more computing power, the underlying cloud environment would create additional infrastructure to manage the load. Also, when additional infrastructure is no more needed, the underlying cloud infrastructure de-provisions them. You may choose to scale manually

by predefining the number of service instances you need, or you
may set up automatic scaling that would help you scale based on
the application performance metrics. For example, if the incoming
load increases, the underlying cloud infrastructure would monitor
the incoming load. When the CPU utilization, memory utilization,
or other performance metrics reach the threshold value set, it would
automatically spin up additional resources.

- Your application runs on an elastic infrastructure, and you can set
  the scaling limits. The underlying infrastructure would not add or
  remove additional service instances beyond that limit, and this action
  would help you control the cost in case of the scaling scenarios. Your
  infrastructure would scale within limits defined by you.

- Hosting your application on the cloud would ensure that your
  application can be available globally. The leading cloud vendors
  have their data centers spread across the globe. You can host your
  application anywhere, provided the cloud vendor has a data center
  available in that region.

- You can manage the customer latency issues for your application.
  You can host a copy of your application in a data center near your
  customers. Cloud-based load balancers are available that operate at
  a global level and can load-balance your applications hosted across
  multiple regions. These load balancers would route the customer
  request to a data center near the customer.

- Your application runs in a highly secured environment managed
  by the cloud vendor. Leading cloud vendors have certified their
  services from leading security agencies and the government. A lot of
  government portals and applications run on the cloud today.

Introduction to Azure

Azure is a cloud offering from Microsoft. It was first announced at Microsoft's Professional Developers Conference in 2008. Microsoft made its cloud platform generally available in February 2010 and launched it as Windows Azure, and in the year 2014, renamed it Microsoft Azure. Today, Microsoft Azure has a wide range of 200 plus cloud-based services that would help you build and host cutting-edge solutions on Azure.

Your application running on Azure can be a simple customer-facing website, a robust data platform, a complex Machine Learning–based intelligent application, or any other new-generation solution. Azure supports a wide range of software languages and frameworks like .NET Core, Java, Python, and many more. Microsoft Azure is a popular cloud choice for leading private organizations and governments across the globe. You can build highly available, reliable, fault-tolerant, and secured solutions on Azure with ease. Your solution on Azure can be based on the Infrastructure-as-a-Service model or Platform-as-a-Service model, or Software-as-a-Service model.

Azure provides a global infrastructure comprising more than 200 physical data centers spread across the globe. These data centers are linked using a highly available and secured interconnected network owned by Microsoft. These data centers are grouped into zones, and a geographic region consists of a group of zones. You can host your Azure solution across data centers in a zone, making the solution locally redundant; or data centers across multiple zones, making the solution zone redundant; or data centers across multiple regions, making the solution geo-redundant.

Azure data centers are spread across the globe, and your solution can be hosted anywhere near your customer base. You can build excellent data backup and recovery strategies for your workloads running on Azure as you can back up your data and solution across data centers in multiple zones or regions. Even if the primary zone or region running your application goes down, your solution running on Azure can be restored and made available in no time from a secondary zone or region where you have a backup for your solution.

Azure provides a wide range of services spread across multiple categories like Compute, Data, Storage, Networking, and many more. Table 1-1 depicts some of the Azure services that are used frequently by cloud practitioners.

Table 1-1. *Few of the popular Azure services*

Category	Services
Compute	Virtual Machine, WebApp, Function App, Kubernetes
Data	SQL, MySQL, Cosmos DB
Storage	Blob Storage, Queue Storage, File Storage, Data Lake
Networking	Virtual Network, Firewall, Load Balancer
Artificial Intelligence	Cognitive Services, Machine Learning Services
Internet of Things (IoT)	IoT Hub

You can provision, delete, or interact with your Azure resources using Azure portal that provides a graphically intuitive user experience or command-line utilities like Azure CLI or Azure PowerShell or REST APIs exposed by these services. You can also build Infrastructure-as-Code solutions using Terraform, Azure ARM templates, Chef, or other popular Infrastructure-as-Code offerings.

Azure resources or services that you create are arranged inside a resource group. A resource group is a logical container for all your resources, and resource groups are grouped inside subscriptions. Subscriptions define the pricing model for the Azure resources you are using. You need to purchase an Azure subscription so that you can start creating your resources. Subscriptions are further grouped into management groups. You can define management and governance strategies for your resources at either the management group level, subscription level, or resource group level. You can have multiple management groups inside a management group. However, you cannot have nested subscriptions or resource groups. Figure 1-2 demonstrates how we can group resources inside the resource groups and subscriptions.

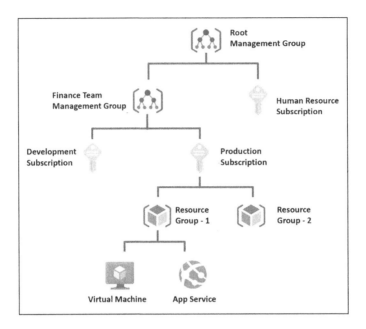

Figure 1-2. *Grouping of Azure resources*

Java Support on Azure

Azure has an excellent support for Java-based applications. You can build a Spring MVC or a Spring Boot or an Open Liberty or any other kind of Java application and can run these applications on Azure seamlessly. However, your Java application should have been developed using Java 8 or above. If you have a legacy Java application, you should modernize your Java application, upgrade it to Java 8 version or above, and run it on Azure.

You may choose to build a Java application and run it on a Linux or Windows Virtual Machine. You may also use a readily available Virtual Machine offering like Oracle WebLogic Server from the Azure Marketplace conveniently. Your hosting environment would be more or less similar to the on-premises server, and you will have complete control over the hosting environment. You may also choose to build your application and host it on Azure WebApp. Azure WebApp is a Platform-as-a-Service offering. Without worrying about the underlying hosting infrastructure and software, you need to build your application and host it on Azure WebApp. You can build modern distributed Java applications using Microservices patterns and host the application as containers in Azure Kubernetes Service. You may also choose to run your application on Azure Spring Cloud. Azure Spring Cloud is a Spring Cloud offering on Azure. You can build robust serverless applications using Java-based Azure Functions, Azure Logic Apps, and other serverless offerings on Azure. In a nutshell, you have a wide range of possibilities available on Azure for your Java applications.

You can integrate your Java applications with other popular Azure services like Azure Active Directory, Azure Redis Cache, Azure SQL, Azure Cosmos DB, Azure Cognitive Services, Azure Logic Apps, and many more. These services would help you build a cloud-native solution without needing any on-premises components for caching, databases, content delivery, authentication, authorization, or other concerns for your application.

All popular Java editors like Eclipse, IntelliJ, and Visual Studio Code support deploying to Azure seamlessly. You can also package and deploy your Java application to Azure using Maven or Gradle. You can leverage popular DevOps tools like Azure DevOps or Jenkins to build Continuous Integration and Continuous Deployment of your application on Azure.

You can monitor your Java application running on Azure using Azure Monitor and Application Insights. You can ingest your application logs to Log Analytics Workspace and query the logs when you need them.

You can integrate your Java application with Azure Active Directory and enable authentication and authorization using OAuth for your Java application. Azure Active Directory is a widely accepted identity management solution on Azure. You can build robust enterprise-grade identity management strategies and enable popular identity features like single sign-on or multifactor authentication for your Java application using Azure Active Directory.

Note   Azure provides native out-of-the-box support for Java applications. Your application should be on Java 8 or above.

Summary

In this chapter, we learned the basics of cloud computing. We explored the different cloud hosting types like Infrastructure as a Service, Platform as a Service, and Software as a Service. We then explored Microsoft Azure and the Java support provided by Microsoft Azure. In the next chapter, we will learn the basics of Azure WebApp and then build a Spring Boot Java application, package it with Maven, and deploy it to Azure WebApp using Maven-based Azure Plugins.

The following are the key takeaways from this chapter:

- Cloud computing is all about renting cloud hosting services from a cloud vendor.

- Microsoft Azure, Amazon Web Services, and Google Cloud Platform are leading cloud vendors today.

- You can host your application on the cloud either using the Infrastructure-as-a-Service (IaaS) model or Platform-as-a-Service (PaaS) model, or Software-as-a-Service (SaaS) model.

- Azure supports hosting Java applications seamlessly.

- Your Java application should be on Java 8 or above to run on Azure.

- You can run your Java application on a Virtual Machine or Azure WebApp or Azure Function or Azure Kubernetes Service, or Azure Spring Cloud.

CHAPTER 2

Java for Azure WebApp

WebApp is a frequently used Azure service. You can build your application and host it inside Azure WebApp without worrying about the hosting infrastructure. The underlying Azure platform takes care of all the infrastructure and the hosting needs. WebApp helps your application go to live in no time as you can provision it in a few minutes and host your application. WebApp supports a wide range of programming languages and frameworks like .NET, Java, PHP, Node.js, and many more. It provides excellent out-of-the-box support for hosting Java applications.

In the previous chapter, we learned the basics of cloud computing and the support of Java on Azure. In this chapter, we will learn the details of Azure WebApp, and then we will host a Java application inside an Azure WebApp.

Structure

In this chapter, we will discuss the following aspects of Java for Azure WebApp:

- Azure WebApp

- App Service Plan

- Deploy Java application on Azure WebApp

- Scaling Java applications hosted on Azure WebApp

Objectives

After studying this chapter, you should be able to get the following learnings:

- Understand the concept of Azure WebApp and App Service Plan

- Deploy Java applications on Azure WebApp

© Abhishek Mishra 2022
A. Mishra, *Microsoft Azure for Java Developers*, https://doi.org/10.1007/978-1-4842-8251-9_2

Azure WebApp

Azure WebApp is a Platform-as-a-Service offering on Azure. You can build HTTP-based applications and services and host them on the Azure WebApp. You need not worry about creating and managing the underlying hosting infrastructure, and the Azure platform will take care of this for you. You need to provision the service and host your application. You can build web applications, REST APIs, and mobile back end using any supported languages like .NET, Java, Node.js, Python, PHP, and Ruby and run it on Azure WebApp. Both the Windows- and Linux-based environments are supported on Azure WebApp. You can also containerize your application using Docker and run it on Azure WebApp.

Azure WebApp is highly available and scalable. You can either configure your WebApp to scale automatically or scale the WebApp manually. It has a rich continuous integration and continuous deployment support and integrates easily with Azure DevOps, Jenkins, Bitbucket, GitHub, and even any local Git repository. It also supports deploying an application using FTP.

You can have multiple deployment slots for the Azure WebApp. Your application would run on a production deployment slot, and you can create a staging deployment slot for an Azure WebApp and host a newly developed version of your application. The majority of the application traffic can be diverted to the production slot, and part of the application traffic can be diverted to the staging slot. Eventually, you can swap the content in the staging slot to the production slot and redirect all the traffic to the production slot once you have enough confidence in the newly developed application. You can automate this process using Infrastructure-as-Code and DevOps solutions.

Note   You can scale the Azure WebApp horizontally by provisional additional identical instances for the WebApp or scale it vertically by changing the App Service Plan. Scaling vertically is referred to as the scale-up process, and scaling horizontally is referred to as the scale-out process.

App Service Plan

Some applications are CPU intensive, and some are memory intensive, and some applications can run on fewer computing resources. Every application has its computing, infrastructure requirement, and other needs like scaling, data storage, and many more, and Azure WebApp caters to this application requirement using App Service Plan. App Service Plan defines the computing resources, scaling, deployment slots, pricing tier, and other necessary features for an Azure WebApp. Based on the application requirement, you can choose an App Service Plan for your WebApp. Every WebApp runs on an App Service Plan. You can share multiple WebApps on an App Service Plan and share the underlying hosting infrastructure across multiple WebApps.

The following pricing tiers are available for Azure WebApp-based App Service Plan:

- Shared Compute

- Dedicated Compute

- Isolated

Shared Compute

Shared Compute offers Free or Shared plans, and the underlying hosting infrastructure would get shared by the WebApp running on App Service Plans for multiple customers. This tier does not offer scaling features, and compute isolation is guaranteed for your application. You can use this tier for development and testing purposes only.

Dedicated Compute

With Dedicated Compute, you have a dedicated underlying hosting infrastructure for all your WebApps running on your App Service Plan. It can be basic, premium, or standard tier. The premium tier offers the maximum number of computing resources and scaling instances followed by the standard and basic tiers. Compute isolation is guaranteed for your application.

Isolated

The Isolated plan provides a dedicated Virtual Network for your Azure. This tier guarantees network isolation along with compute isolation.

Deploy Java Application on Azure WebApp

Let us build a Java Spring Boot application and deploy it on an Azure WebApp. We will use Maven to build and deploy the application to the Azure WebApp. The following are the prerequisites you should be ready with before you start with the deployment steps. You can choose the latest version or any other version that you are comfortable working with for the tools mentioned.

- Visual Studio Code

- Java version 8 or above installed on your system

- A compatible Maven version with your installed Java version installed on your system

- Should have an Azure Subscription with permissions to create a resource group and resources inside the resource group

- Azure CLI installed on your system

Create a Java Spring Boot Application

Let us create a Java Spring Boot application that we will deploy to Azure WebApp. Navigate to the following URL to generate a Java Spring Boot application.

Listing 2-1. Spring Initializr URL

```
https://start.spring.io/
```

Select the *Project* as *Maven Project*, *Language* as *Java*, and *Spring Boot* version. The Spring Boot version keeps getting updated very frequently, and you can use the version based on your preferences or the latest one available. Provide the *Project Metadata* as in Figure 2-1. Select *Packaging* as JAR and *Java* version as *11*.

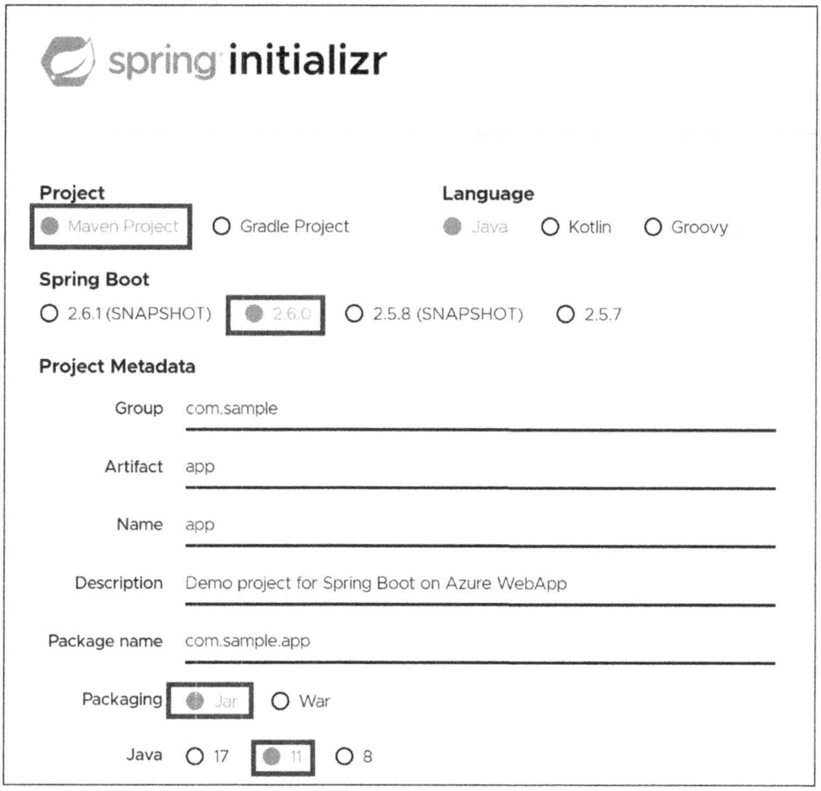

Figure 2-1. *Configure Spring Boot project*

We need to add the Spring Web dependency to our application. Click on the *ADD DEPENDENCIES* button shown in Figure 2-2. We will create a REST API in our sample application, and the Spring Web dependency will help us create it.

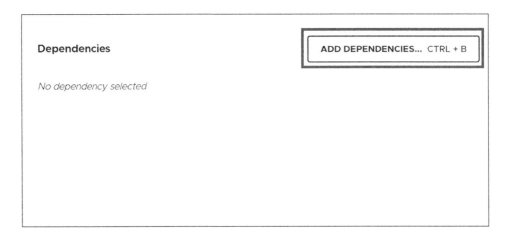

Figure 2-2. *Click ADD DEPENDENCIES*

Select *Spring Web* as in Figure 2-3.

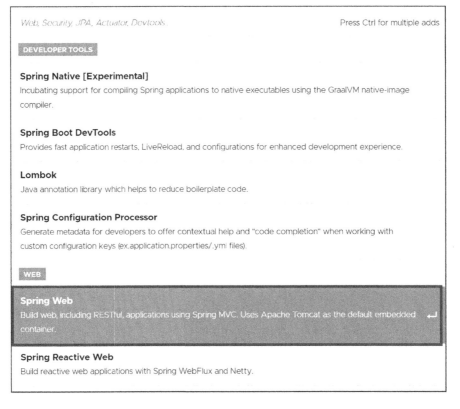

Figure 2-3. *Select Spring Web dependency*

Click on the *GENERATE* button as in Figure 2-4. This action will generate a sample Java Spring Boot application that will get downloaded locally.

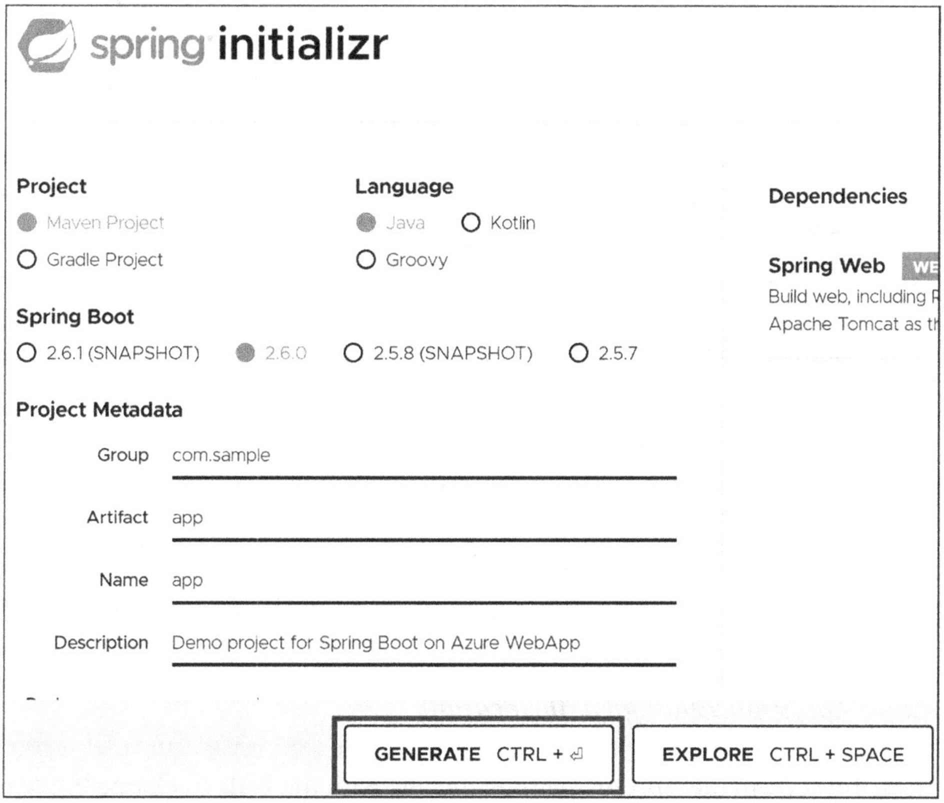

Figure 2-4. *Generate Spring Boot project*

Open the application in Visual Studio Code. Go to the AppApplication.java file. You will find it inside the *java\com\sample\app* folder as in Figure 2-5.

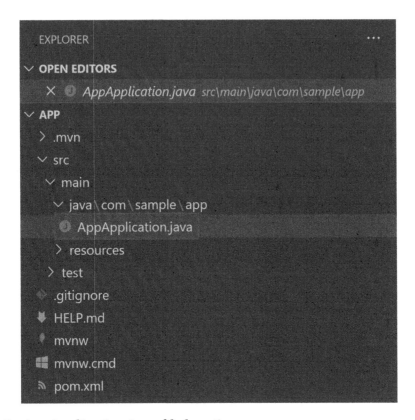

Figure 2-5. *AppApplication.java file location*

Replace the code in the *AppApplication.java* file with the code in Listing 2-2. We are annotating the *AppApplication* class as REST Controller and adding a REST GET API named *hello*. When we invoke this REST API, we will get the *Hello World* string as the response.

Listing 2-2. AppApplication.java

```
package com.sample.app;

import org.springframework.boot.SpringApplication;
import org.springframework.boot.autoconfigure.SpringBootApplication;
import org.springframework.web.bind.annotation.GetMapping;
import org.springframework.web.bind.annotation.RestController;

@SpringBootApplication
@RestController
public class AppApplication {
```

```java
public static void main(String[] args) {
    SpringApplication.run(AppApplication.class, args);
}

@GetMapping("/hello")
public String hello() {
    return String.format("Hello World !!");
}

}
```

Now let us open a new terminal window and build the application using Maven (Figure 2-6).

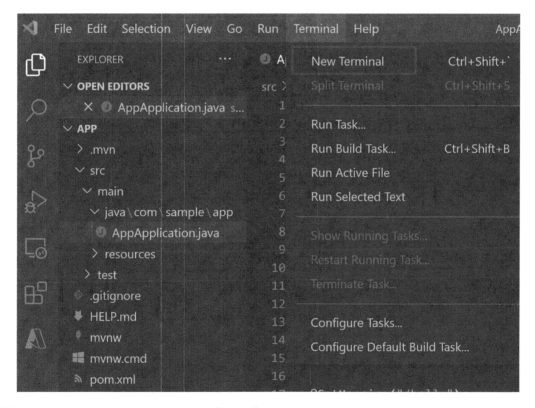

Figure 2-6. *Open a new terminal window*

Let us execute the following command to build the application as in Listing 2-3. Make sure you navigate to the directory in the terminal where the *pom.xml* file is present.

Listing 2-3. Build the application

```
mvn install
```

Once the build is successful, a directory named *target* with the runnable JAR file gets created. Navigate to the *target* directory and execute the following command in the target directory as in Listing 2-4.

Listing 2-4. Run application

```
java -jar app-0.0.1-SNAPSHOT.jar
```

Once the application boots up successfully, browse the following URL in the browser as in Listing 2-5.

Listing 2-5. URL for the running application

```
http://localhost:8080/hello
```

You can see the response from the hello REST API as in Figure 2-7.

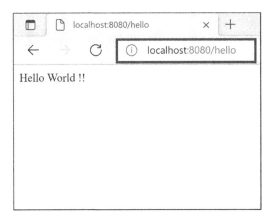

Figure 2-7. *Browse Java Spring Boot REST API*

We can deploy this application to Azure. Now let us provision an Azure WebApp on which we can deploy this application.

Create an Azure WebApp

Now let us spin up an Azure WebApp. We will deploy our Java application here in this WebApp. Go to the Azure portal in the browser using the following link as in Listing 2-6.

Listing 2-6. URL for the Azure portal

```
https://portal.azure.com
```

Click *Create a resource* as in Figure 2-8. This action will navigate you to Azure Marketplace, where you can choose a service to create.

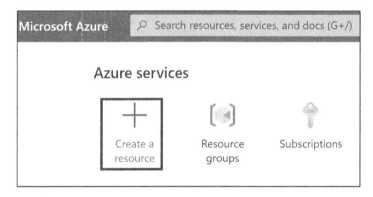

Figure 2-8. *Create a resource*

Select *Web App* as in Figure 2-9. If you do not see the WebApp in the list of the popular products, search for it using the search bar.

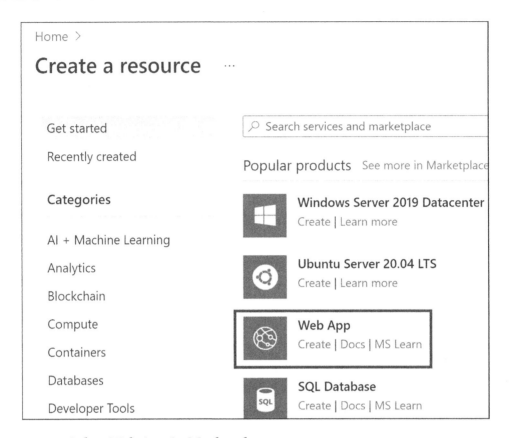

Figure 2-9. *Select Web App in Marketplace*

Provide the subscription, resource group, and name of the WebApp as in Figure 2-10.

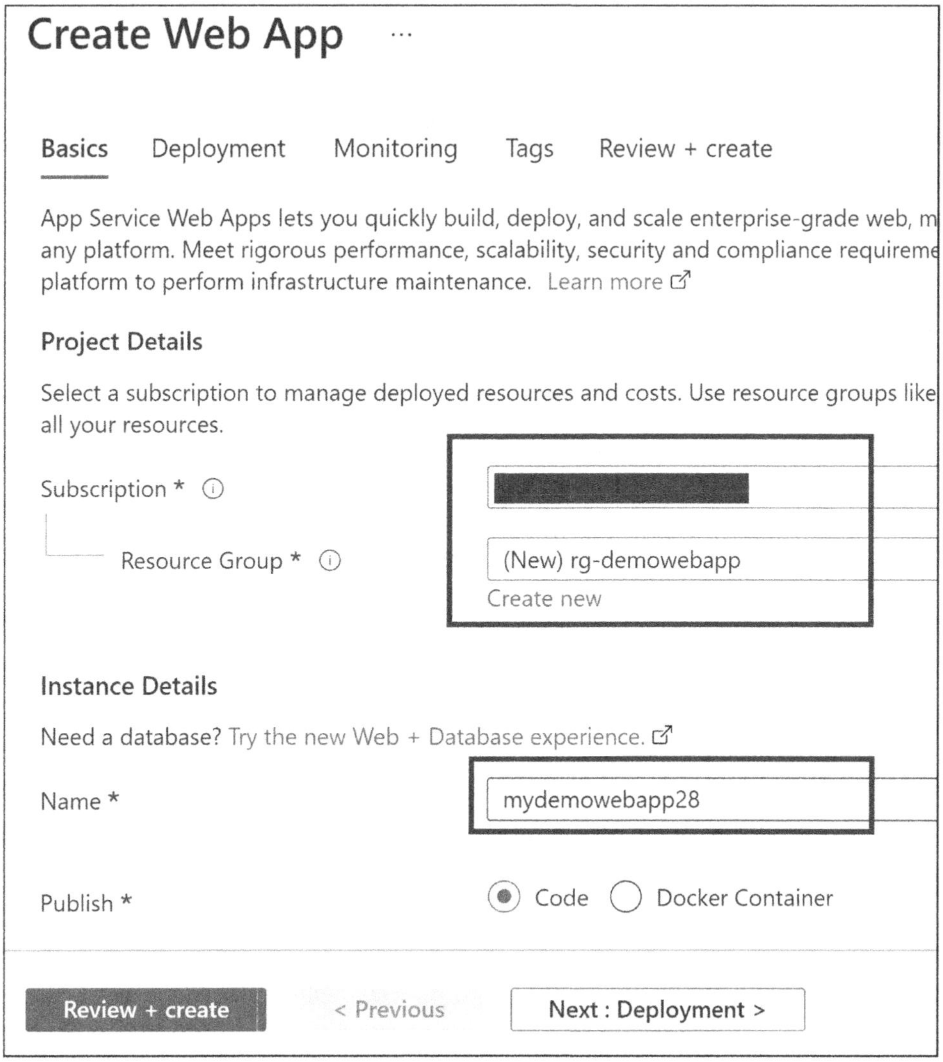

Figure 2-10. *Provide basic details for the WebApp*

Scroll down and provide the code publishing details, region, and the App Service Plan as in Figure 2-11. Click *Review + create*. This action will navigate you to the validation page.

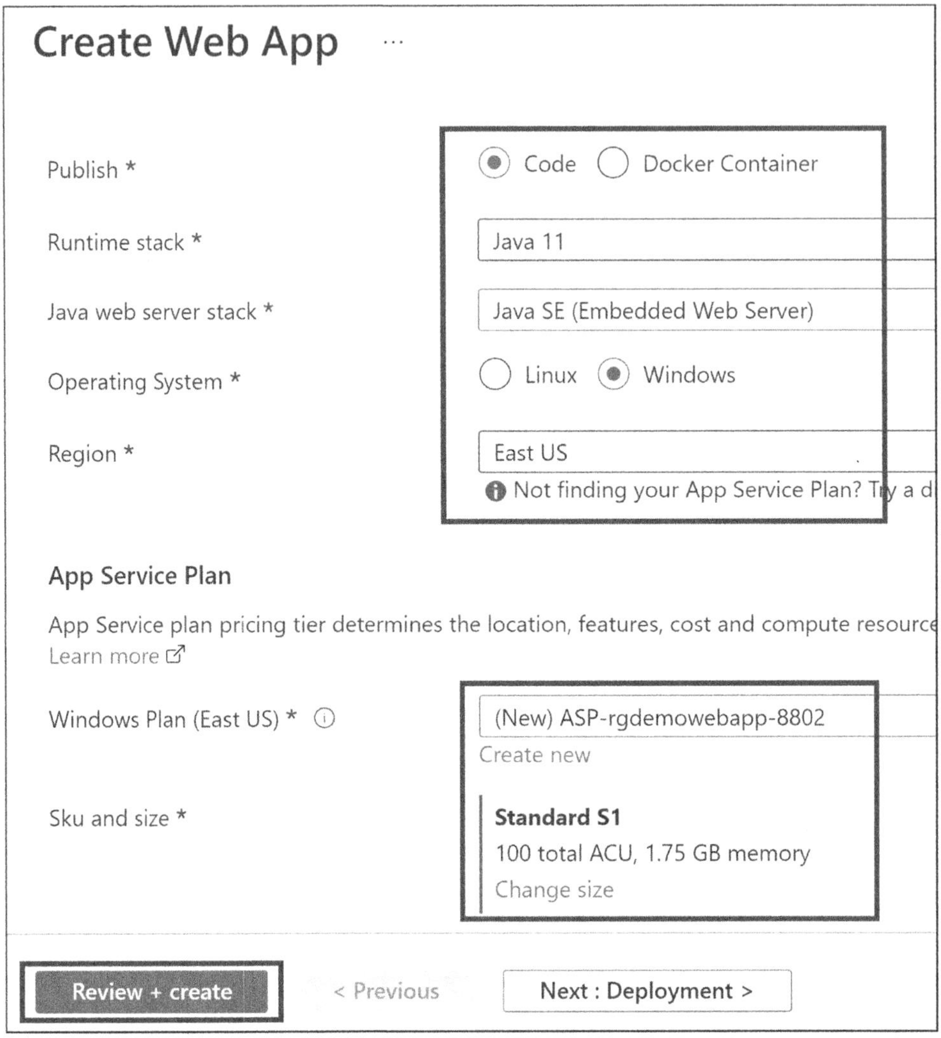

Figure 2-11. *Click Review + create*

Click *Create* as in Figure 2-12. This action will spin up your Azure WebApp.

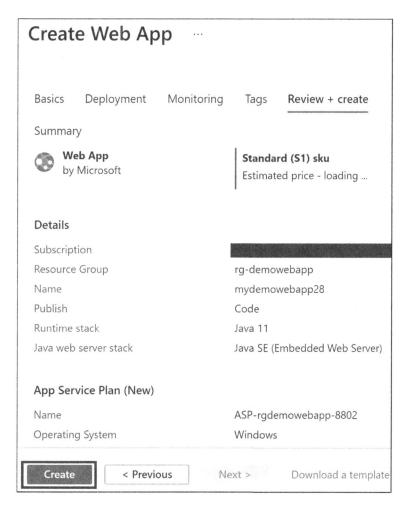

Figure 2-12. *Click Create*

Deploy the Application to Azure WebApp

We have developed our sample application and have also provisioned an Azure WebApp. Now let us use the Maven plug-in and deploy our application to the Azure WebApp. You may have to log in using Azure CLI with `az login` command. Go back to the Visual Studio Code and open a new terminal window. Navigate to the directory in the terminal prompt where the pom.xml file is there. Execute the command from Listing 2-7 in the terminal prompt.

Listing 2-7. Azure Maven plug-in

```
mvn com.microsoft.azure:azure-webapp-maven-plugin:2.2.1:config
```

You will get prompted to enter the choice to select the WebApp we created earlier. You can choose to create a new WebApp as well as in Figure 2-13.

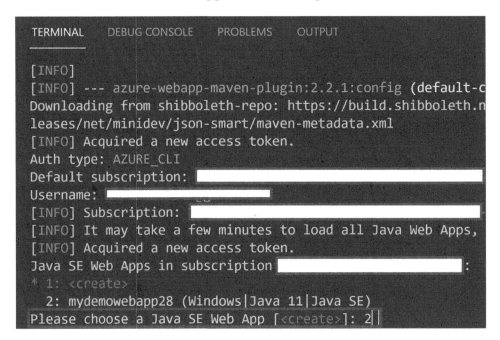

Figure 2-13. *Choose your WebApp*

Validate and confirm your choice as in Figure 2-14.

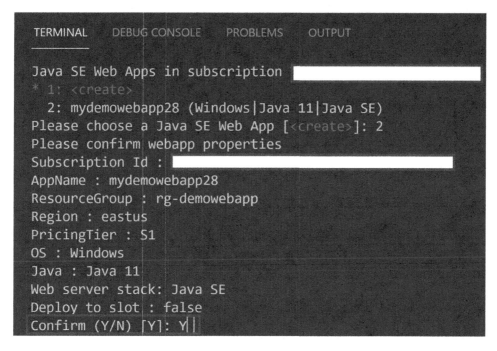

Figure 2-14. *Confirm your selection*

Once this command completes successfully, the *pom.xml* file will get modified, and the WebApp details will get added to it as in Listing 2-8. Use the latest package and plug-in versions available when you are performing this demo.

Listing 2-8. Updated pom.xml

```xml
<?xml version="1.0" encoding="UTF-8"?>
<project xmlns="http://maven.apache.org/POM/4.0.0" xmlns:xsi="http://www.
w3.org/2001/XMLSchema-instance" xsi:schemaLocation="http://maven.apache.
org/POM/4.0.0 https://maven.apache.org/xsd/maven-4.0.0.xsd">
  <modelVersion>4.0.0</modelVersion>
  <parent>
    <groupId>org.springframework.boot</groupId>
    <artifactId>spring-boot-starter-parent</artifactId>
    <version>2.6.0</version>
    <relativePath/>
    <!-- lookup parent from repository -->
  </parent>
```

```
<groupId>com.sample</groupId>
<artifactId>app</artifactId>
<version>0.0.1-SNAPSHOT</version>
<name>app</name>
<description>Demo project for Spring Boot on Azure WebApp</description>
<properties>
  <java.version>11</java.version>
</properties>
<dependencies>
  <dependency>
    <groupId>org.springframework.boot</groupId>
    <artifactId>spring-boot-starter-web</artifactId>
  </dependency>
  <dependency>
    <groupId>org.springframework.boot</groupId>
    <artifactId>spring-boot-starter-test</artifactId>
    <scope>test</scope>
  </dependency>
</dependencies>
<build>
  <plugins>
    <plugin>
      <groupId>org.springframework.boot</groupId>
      <artifactId>spring-boot-maven-plugin</artifactId>
    </plugin>
    <plugin>
      <groupId>com.microsoft.azure</groupId>
      <artifactId>azure-webapp-maven-plugin</artifactId>
      <version>2.2.1</version>
      <configuration>
        <schemaVersion>v2</schemaVersion>
        <subscriptionId>a3759752-01d3-4b0e-ad35-71bd2faa2980</
        subscriptionId>
        <resourceGroup>rg-demowebapp</resourceGroup>
        <appName>mydemowebapp28</appName>
```

```
      <pricingTier>S1</pricingTier>
      <region>eastus</region>
      <appServicePlanName>ASP-rgdemowebapp-8802</appServicePlanName>
      <appServicePlanResourceGroup>rg-demowebapp</
      appServicePlanResourceGroup>
      <runtime>
        <os>Windows</os>
        <javaVersion>Java 11</javaVersion>
        <webContainer>Java SE</webContainer>
      </runtime>
      <deployment>
        <resources>
          <resource>
            <directory>${project.basedir}/target</directory>
            <includes>
              <include>*.jar</include>
            </includes>
          </resource>
        </resources>
      </deployment>
    </configuration>
  </plugin>
 </plugins>
</build>
</project>
```

Now run the following command to deploy your application as in Listing 2-9.

Listing 2-9. Deploy the application to WebApp

```
mvn package azure-webapp:deploy
```

Once the application gets deployed successfully, you can browse the WebApp URL as in Figure 2-15 and see the output. You can go to the Azure portal, open the App Service *Overview* section. You will get the URL to navigate in that section.

Figure 2-15. *Output on browser*

Scaling Java Applications Hosted on Azure WebApp

Scaling is an important aspect of any application. During peak hours, your application should be able to run on additional computing resources, and it should be able to release the additional computing resources once the load decreases. You have the option to scale either vertically or horizontally in the case of Azure WebApp. To scale your WebApp vertically, you need to go to the WebApp in the Azure portal and click *Scale-up (App Service plan)* as in Figure 2-16. You can select the App Service Plan of your choice meeting your need.

Figure 2-16. *Scale-up WebApp*

Then you can switch to another plan and click *Apply* as in Figure 2-17.

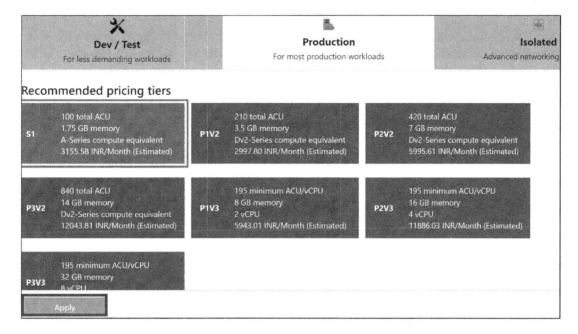

Figure 2-17.   *Click Apply*

You can click *See additional options* to explore more plans as in Figure 2-18.

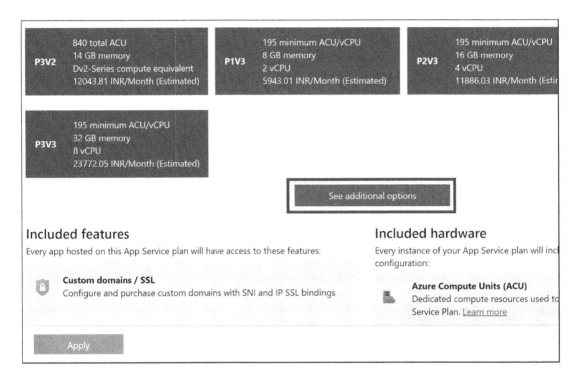

Figure 2-18. *See additional plans*

To scale your WebApp horizontally, you need to go to the WebApp in the Azure portal and click *Scale-out (App Service plan)* as in Figure 2-19. You can scale either manually by specifying the number of instances you need for your application or automatically based on custom metrics and rules like CPU utilization, memory utilization, and other compute resources performance needs.

Figure 2-19. *Scale-out WebApp*

Summary

In this chapter, we learned the details of Azure WebApp and then explored what App Service Plan is and other features of Azure WebApp. We provisioned an Azure WebApp and then deployed a Java Spring Boot application to Azure WebApp using Maven plug-in. We also learned about scaling Azure WebApp at a high level. In the next chapter, we will learn the basics of Azure Functions, and then we will build a Java-based Azure Function.

The following are the key takeaways from this chapter:

- Azure WebApp is a Platform-as-a-Service offering on Azure. You can build HTTP-based applications and services and host them on the Azure WebApp.

- You need not worry about creating and managing the underlying hosting infrastructure, and the Azure platform will take care of this for you.

- App Service Plan defines the computing resources, scaling, deployment slots, pricing tier, and other necessary features for an Azure WebApp.

- The following pricing tiers are available for Azure WebApp-based App Service Plan.

  - Shared Compute

  - Dedicated Compute

  - Isolated

- You can use the Maven plug-in to deploy a Java Spring Boot application to Azure WebApp.

CHAPTER 3

Java-Based Azure Functions

Azure Functions are serverless offerings on Azure. They are best suited to run code that can run for a short duration and perform business logic. Azure Functions can be used as a background worker for your application and perform a background job. They can also perform simple to highly complex business logic and be consumed like an API. Azure Functions are powerful and can deploy modern applications based on complex architecture like microservices. Azure Functions can be used to host the services in the microservices architecture.

In the previous chapter, we learned the basics of Azure WebApp. We then developed a Java Spring Boot application and deployed it on Azure WebApp using the Maven plug-in. In this chapter, we will learn the details of Azure Functions, and then we will build a Java-based Azure Function.

Structure

In this chapter, we will discuss the following aspects of Java for Azure WebApp:

- Introduction to serverless and Azure Functions

- Azure Functions use cases

- Hosting plans

- Triggers and Bindings

- Build a Java-based Azure Function

© Abhishek Mishra 2022
A. Mishra, *Microsoft Azure for Java Developers*, https://doi.org/10.1007/978-1-4842-8251-9_3

Objectives

After studying this chapter, you should be able to get the following learnings:

- Understand the concept of Azure Functions

- Build a Java-based Azure Function

Introduction to Serverless and Azure Functions

Serverless architecture on the cloud is gaining momentum these days. Many modern applications like microservices are adopting serverless-based hosting on the cloud. Serverless hosting is cheaper than Platform-as-a-Service and Infrastructure-as-a-Service hosting models. You get charged only when your service is executing and doing a task, and you do not get any bills if your service is idle and is not performing any activity. You can develop the application and deploy it to the serverless service, and you need not worry about the underlying hosting infrastructure. The Azure platform will provision and manage the infrastructure needed for the serverless service to run. Scaling is an important aspect of any application, whether it runs on the cloud or on-premises. Serverless services can scale out with ease automatically without needing you to make any configuration. You do not have any control over how the serverless services will scale. The serverless services will sense the incoming workload and scale out based on the incoming traffic.

The following are some of the popular serverless services available on Azure:

- Azure Functions

- Durable Functions

- Azure Logic Apps

- Azure Event Grid

- Azure Serverless SQL

- Azure Serverless Kubernetes Service

- Azure Serverless Cosmos DB

Azure Functions are Function-as-a-Service (FaaS) offerings on Azure and are serverless services. You can build your code and host on Azure Functions. You get billed when the Azure Functions execute, and you are not charged when they are idle. The underlying infrastructure on which the Azure Function runs and the scaling aspects are managed by the underlying Azure platform. Azure Functions support running code that executes for a short time interval. However, you can choose an appropriate hosting plan and run your application for a longer duration. Table 3-1 demonstrates the programing language support based on the Function runtime you choose. At present, while authoring this book, there are four runtime versions supported.

***Table 3-1.** Azure Functions runtime and supported programming languages*

Programming Language	Runtime 1.x	Runtime 2.x	Runtime 3.x	Runtime 4.x
C#	.NET 4.8	.NET Core 2.1	.NET Core 3.1, .NET 5	.NET 6
JavaScript	Node.js 6	Node.js 10, 8	Node.js 14, 12, 10	Node.js 14, 16
F#	.NET 4.8	.NET Core 2.1	.NET Core 3.1	.NET 6
Java	No Support	Java 8	Java 11, 8	Java 11, 8
PowerShell	No Support	PowerShell Core 6	PowerShell 7, Core 6	PowerShell 7
Python	No Support	Python 3.7, 3.6	Python 3.9, 3.8, 3.7, 3.6	Python 3.9, 3.8
Typescript	No Support	Supported	Supported	Supported

Azure Functions are based on top of Azure WebJobs. However, Azure WebJobs run as a background worker and always shares the App Service Plan for the Azure WebApp. Azure Functions have a hosting plan of their own. You can also host multiple Azure Functions on an App Service Plan.

Azure Functions execute whenever they get triggered by the supported Triggers. They complete the execution and get into an idle state. Azure Functions again wake up and spring into action only when triggered.

Azure Functions Use Cases

The following are a few scenarios where you can use Azure Functions. However, Azure Functions can fit into a wide range of scenarios and help you build modern cloud-based serverless applications.

- You can build an n-tier application using Azure Functions. You can break the business and data access logic into smaller chunks and host each of these chunks in an Azure Function.

- You can run background processing jobs in the Azure Functions.

- You can use Azure Functions and Durable Functions to build workflow-based applications where you can orchestrate each of the workflow steps using Azure Durable Functions and Azure Functions.

- You can use Azure Functions to build microservices-based applications. Each of the Azure Functions can host a business service.

- You can use Azure Functions to build schedule-based applications that run in a particular time interval or during a particular time of a day or a month or year.

- You can build notification systems to trigger an Azure Function to notify an end user or a system based on conditions and events.

- You can use Azure Functions in the IoT scenarios to perform a business activity or process the ingested data and put it in storage, or send it to the next set of processing.

- You can use Azure Functions and Azure Event Grid in event-driven scenarios where these functions can get triggered and perform a task.

Hosting Plans

Hosting plans decide the underlying infrastructure on which Azure Functions run. They decide the scaling needs, execution interval, virtual network integration, and many other important aspects for your Azure Functions. You can choose your hosting plan for the Azure Function based on your computing requirements like memory usage, CPU usage, and many more. Also, you need to consider the scaling needs, execution time-out, and virtual network integration as other important aspects while deciding the hosting plan you may need. The following are the hosting plans supported by Azure Functions.

Consumption Plan

Consumption Plan is a pure serverless plan. You do not have any control over the hosting and scaling infrastructure. Based on the incoming traffic, it adds additional instances in the runtime, and when the load decreases, it shuts down the extra instances. This plan is cost-effective as you get billed only when the Function is executing, and you do not incur any bill when the Function is idle and is not performing any task. The Functions can execute for five minutes by default, and you can set them to execute for ten minutes at maximum.

The Function gets into sleep or an idle state when it is not executing. Whenever it gets triggered again, it springs into action and starts executing. However, the Function does not start executing as soon as triggered. There is a delay as the Function needs to wake up from the idle state and get ready to serve the request. This delay is called as cold start phenomenon that we get while using this plan.

Premium Plan

Premium Plan makes sure that an instance of an Azure Function is always warmed up and ready to serve the request. This will avoid the cold start phenomenon. Like Consumption Plan, you do not have any control over how the Function scales. However, you have greater control over the infrastructure on which the Azure Function is running. You can choose a SKU for the Plan like EP1, EP2, or EP3 and choose the computing needs for the Function. You can configure the Azure Function to run in a Virtual Network. Using the Premium Plan, Azure Functions can execute for 30 minutes by default, and you can configure it to never time out.

Dedicated Plan

The Dedicated Plan is the same as the WebApp App Service Plan. Azure Functions can run continuously and never get into an idle state when using this plan. This plan would make your Function run just like a WebApp and is not a serverless plan. You can choose an App Service Plan SKU based on your CPU usage, memory, and other computing requirements, and you can either configure auto-scale or scale manually and have full control over how the Function scales.

App Service Environment Plan

This plan provides all features of the Dedicated Plan. It also helps run your Azure Function in an isolated environment inside a virtual network. You get a secured network, high scaling, and computing power.

Kubernetes Plan

This plan runs Azure Functions inside Azure Kubernetes Service and helps run Azure Functions continuously inside the Kubernetes cluster.

Triggers and Bindings

Triggers wake Azure Functions from an idle state and trigger their execution. Azure Functions can be triggered from a wide range of services, and these services trigger Azure Functions and pass the data to process as a payload trigger input. Azure Functions can have a single trigger. You may have scenarios where your Azure Function must interface with external services. For example, it may need to get some data from Azure Blob, process it, and put it back in the Azure Storage Queue. Bindings help you in scenarios where your Function needs to exchange data with other Azure or non-Azure services.

You need not write much code and implement Triggers and Bindings. You can create the Triggers and Bindings for your Azure Function declaratively. This declarative approach saves you from writing complex code and logic needed to interact with other services from your Function code. Triggers are always unidirectional and are an input for the Azure Function. Bindings are bidirectional and can be an input or output for the Azure Function.

Figure 3-1 demonstrates how an Azure Function works with Triggers and Bindings. When an item is added to the Azure Cosmos DB, it triggers the Azure Function. The Azure Function interacts with the Blob Storage using binding and gets the blob data to process. It processes the blob data and sends it to the event hub using an output binding.

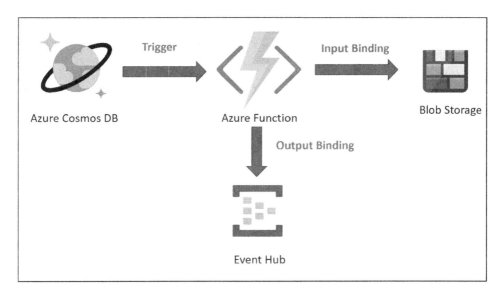

Figure 3-1. *Triggers and Bindings in Azure FunctionsThe following are Triggers supported for Azure Functions Runtime 1.x:*

- Blob storage

- Azure Cosmos DB

- Event Grid

- Event Hubs

- HTTP and webhooks

- IoT Hub

- Queue storage

- Service Bus

- Timer

The following are Triggers supported for Azure Functions Runtime 2.x and more:

- Blob storage

- Azure Cosmos DB

- Dapr

- Event Grid

- Event Hubs

- HTTP and webhooks

- IoT Hub

- Kafka

- Queue storage

- RabbitMQ

- Service Bus

- Timer

The following are the Bindings supported along with Input and Output directions supported for Azure Functions Runtime 1.x:

- Blob storage (Input, Output)

- Azure Cosmos DB (Input, Output)

- Event Grid (Output)

- Event Hubs (Output)

- HTTP and webhooks (Output)

- IoT Hub (Output)

- Mobile Apps (Input, Output)

- Notification Hubs (Output)

- Queue storage (Output)

- SendGrid (Output)

- Service Bus (Output)

- Table storage (Input, Output)

- Twilio (Output)

The following are the Bindings supported along with Input and Output directions supported for Azure Functions Runtime 2.x and above:

- Blob storage (Input, Output)

- Azure Cosmos DB (Input, Output)

- Event Grid (Output)

- Event Hubs (Output)

- HTTP and webhooks (Output)

- IoT Hub (Output)

- Queue storage (Output)

- SendGrid (Output)

- Service Bus (Output)

- Table storage (Input, Output)

- Twilio (Output)

- Dapr (Input, Output)

- Kafka (Output)

- RabbitMQ (Output)

- SignalR (Input, Output)

You cannot create Kafka and RabbitMQ Triggers using Consumption Plan. Dapper Triggers are applicable for Azure Kubernetes Service.

Build a Java-Based Azure Function

Let us create an Azure Function invoked by an HTTP Trigger. HTTP Trigger would help you access Function in the browser. We will pass a person's name as a query string, and then the person's name would get saved to the Storage Queue using an output binding.

Let us create a Storage Account where the Azure Function will create a Queue and put the person's name as a message. Go to the Azure portal and click *Create a resource* as in Figure 3-2.

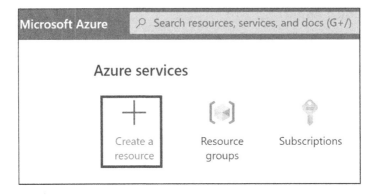

Figure 3-2. *Create a resource*

Search for *Storage Account* as in Figure 3-3 in the Marketplace. You can also find Storage Account in the list of popular services in the Marketplace.

Figure 3-3. *Search for Storage Account*

Click *Create* as in Figure 3-4 to start creating a Storage Account.

Figure 3-4. *Click Create*

Provide subscription details, resource group details, the name for the Storage Account, and location. Click *Review + create* as in Figure 3-5.

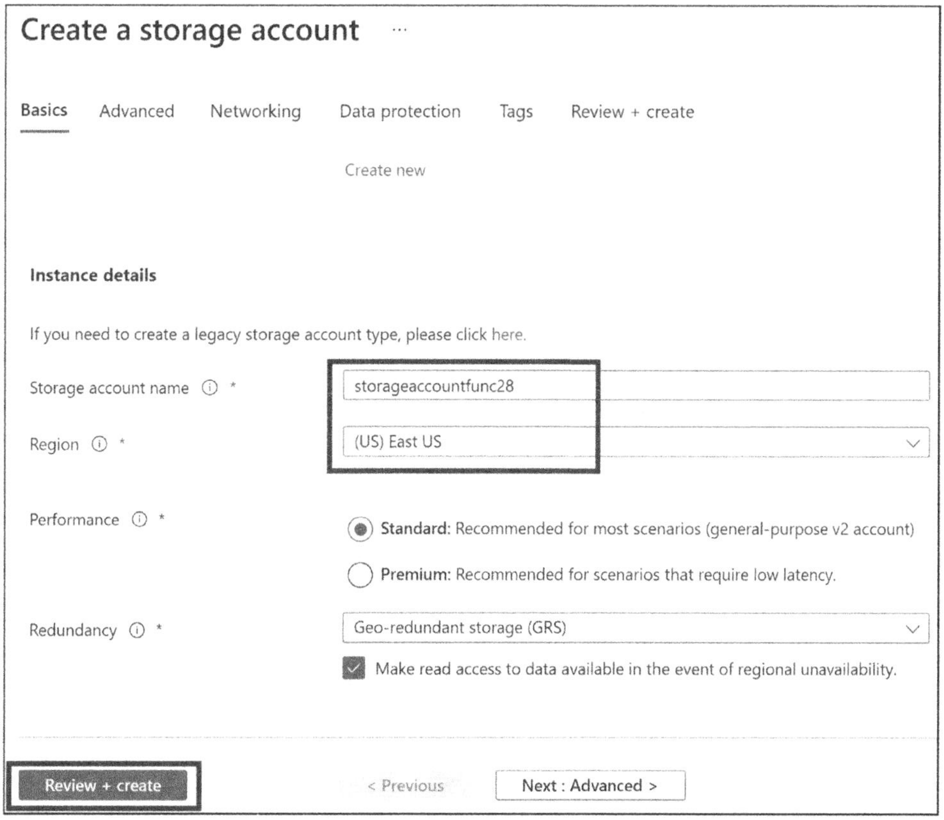

Figure 3-5. *Provide basic details for the Storage Account*

Click *Create* as in Figure 3-6. This will provision a Storage Account for you.

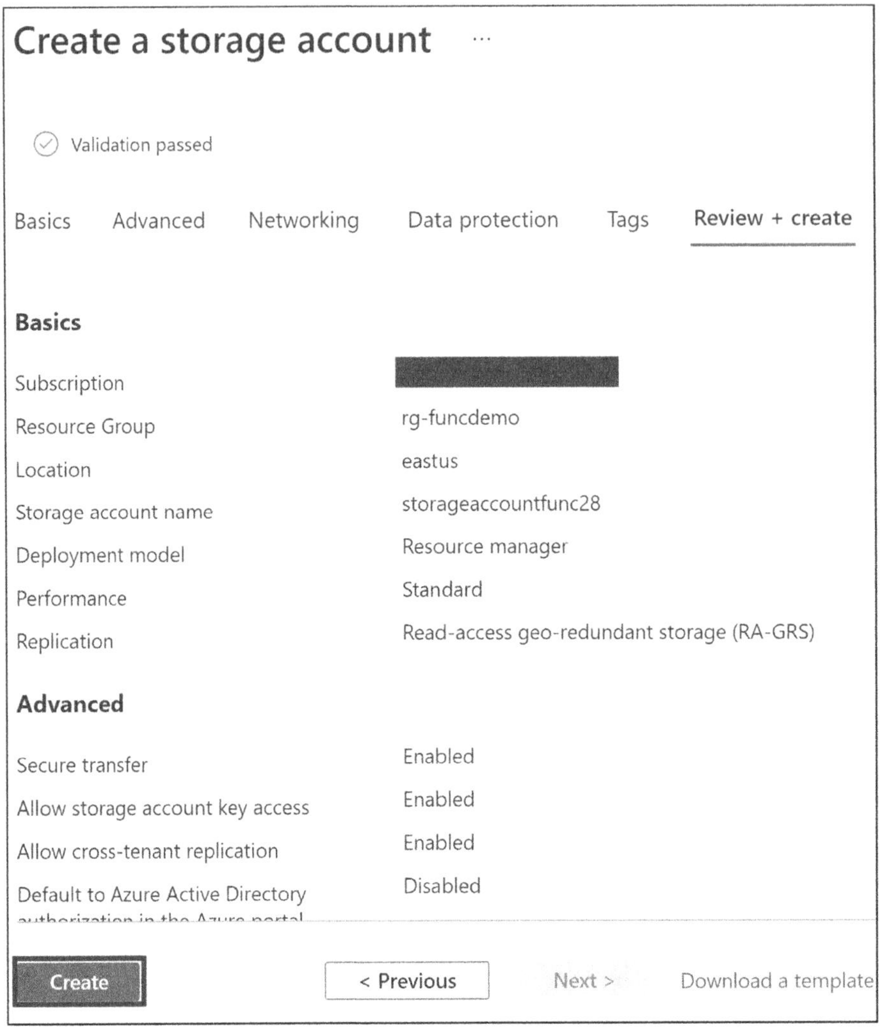

Create a storage account   ...

⊘ Validation passed

Basics   Advanced   Networking   Data protection   Tags   **Review + create**

Basics

Subscription	████████████
Resource Group	rg-funcdemo
Location	eastus
Storage account name	storageaccountfunc28
Deployment model	Resource manager
Performance	Standard
Replication	Read-access geo-redundant storage (RA-GRS)

Advanced

Secure transfer	Enabled
Allow storage account key access	Enabled
Allow cross-tenant replication	Enabled
Default to Azure Active Directory authorization in the Azure portal	Disabled

Create   < Previous   Next >   Download a template

Figure 3-6. *Click Create*

Once the Storage Account gets created, navigate to the Storage Account, go to the *Access Keys* section as in Figure 3-7, and copy the connection string. Later, we will use the connection string to connect to the Storage Account from the Azure Function.

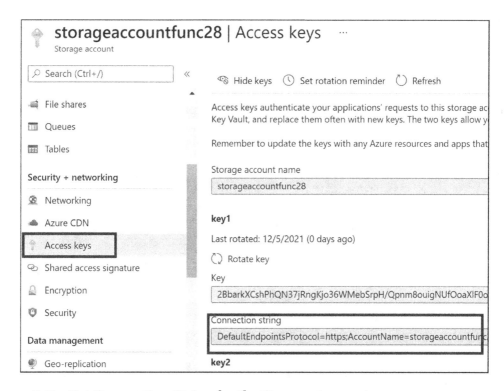

Figure 3-7. *Get Connection String for the Storage Account*

Now let us start creating Azure Function using the Maven plug-in. As a prerequisite, you should have the following utilities already installed:

- Azure Functions Core Tools (latest version)

- Java 11

- Azure CLI

- Visual Studio Code

- Maven (any version compatible with Java 11)

Launch Visual Studio Code, open the folder where you plan to work, and open a new command prompt based on Terminal. Execute the following command as in Listing 3-1 in the Terminal. This will create an Azure Function Code for you locally. We will modify the code further.

Listing 3-1. Generate Azure Function code

```
mvn archetype:generate "-DarchetypeGroupId=com.microsoft.azure"
"-DarchetypeArtifactId=azure-functions-archetype" "-DjavaVersion=11"
```

When prompted, provide the group ID, artifact ID, package name, and version for your Java function and in the end provide your selection confirmation by hitting *Y* as in Figure 3-8.

```
TERMINAL    DEBUG CONSOLE    PROBLEMS    OUTPUT

[INFO] Using property: appServicePlanName = java-functions-app-service-plan
[INFO] Using property: docker = false
[INFO] Using property: javaVersion = 11
[INFO] Using property: resourceGroup = java-functions-group
[INFO] Using property: trigger = HttpTrigger
Confirm properties configuration:
groupId: com.myfunc
groupId: com.myfunc
artifactId: funcdemo
artifactId: funcdemo
version: 1.0-SNAPSHOT
package: com.myfunc
appName: $(artifactId)-$(timestamp)
appRegion: westus
appServicePlanName: java-functions-app-service-plan
docker: false
javaVersion: 11
resourceGroup: java-functions-group
trigger: HttpTrigger
 Y: : Y
```

Figure 3-8. *Maven execution*

The Function gets created with HTTP Trigger Binding that would invoke the Function code from the browser. Let us add an output binding to the Storage Queue. Open the Function.java file as in Figure 3-9.

Figure 3-9. *Function.java file location*

Replace the existing code with the following code as in Listing 3-2. We have added a Queue output binding that integrates with the Storage Account provided with the connection string name *AzureWebJobsStorage*. We will later set the value of *AzureWebJobsStorage* in the Azure Function App *Configuration*. You can see that we are using declarative configuration using the attribute *QueueOutput* to connect to the Storage Queue without needing to write much code. The *queuename* parameter value specifies the Queue name in the Storage Account. The line of code `msg.setValue("Name received : "+name);` adds the message to the Queue.

Listing 3-2. Function.java

```
package com.myfunc;

import com.microsoft.azure.functions.ExecutionContext;
import com.microsoft.azure.functions.HttpMethod;
import com.microsoft.azure.functions.HttpRequestMessage;
import com.microsoft.azure.functions.HttpResponseMessage;
import com.microsoft.azure.functions.HttpStatus;
import com.microsoft.azure.functions.OutputBinding;
import com.microsoft.azure.functions.annotation.AuthorizationLevel;
import com.microsoft.azure.functions.annotation.FunctionName;
import com.microsoft.azure.functions.annotation.HttpTrigger;
import com.microsoft.azure.functions.annotation.QueueOutput;
```

```java
import java.util.Optional;

/**
 * Azure Functions with HTTP Trigger.
 */
public class Function {
    /**
     * This function listens at endpoint "/api/HttpExample". Two ways to
       invoke it using "curl" command in bash:
     * 1. curl -d "HTTP Body" {your host}/api/HttpExample
     * 2. curl "{your host}/api/HttpExample?name=HTTP%20Query"
     */
    @FunctionName("HttpExample")
    public HttpResponseMessage run(
            @HttpTrigger(
                name = "req",
                methods = {HttpMethod.GET, HttpMethod.POST},
                authLevel = AuthorizationLevel.ANONYMOUS)
                HttpRequestMessage<Optional<String>> request,
            @QueueOutput(
                name = "msg",
                queueName = "outqueue",
                connection = "AzureWebJobsStorage")
                OutputBinding<String> msg,
            final ExecutionContext context) {
        context.getLogger().info("Java HTTP trigger processed a request.");

        // Parse query parameter
        final String query = request.getQueryParameters().get("name");
        final String name = request.getBody().orElse(query);

        //Set value to the Queue.
        msg.setValue("Name received : "+name);

        if (name == null) {
            return request.createResponseBuilder(HttpStatus.BAD_REQUEST).
            body("Please pass a name on the query string or in the request
            body").build();
```

```
        } else {
            return request.createResponseBuilder(HttpStatus.OK).body
            ("Hello, " + name).build();
        }
    }
}
```

We have added a QueueOutput binding to our Function. We need to edit the test class as well. Open the *FunctionTest.java* class and replace the following code as in Listing 3-3. We are replacing the *Function().run* method call to include the Output Binding we created in the parameter.

Listing 3-3. FunctionTest.java

```
package com.myfunc;

import com.microsoft.azure.functions.*;
import org.mockito.invocation.InvocationOnMock;
import org.mockito.stubbing.Answer;

import java.util.*;
import java.util.logging.Logger;

import org.junit.jupiter.api.Test;
import static org.junit.jupiter.api.Assertions.*;
import static org.mockito.ArgumentMatchers.*;
import static org.mockito.Mockito.*;

/**
 * Unit test for Function class.
 */
public class FunctionTest {
    /**
     * Unit test for HttpTriggerJava method.
     */
    @Test
    public void testHttpTriggerJava() throws Exception {
        // Setup
        @SuppressWarnings("unchecked")
```

```java
final HttpRequestMessage<Optional<String>> req = mock
(HttpRequestMessage.class);

final Map<String, String> queryParams = new HashMap<>();
queryParams.put("name", "Azure");
doReturn(queryParams).when(req).getQueryParameters();

final Optional<String> queryBody = Optional.empty();
doReturn(queryBody).when(req).getBody();

doAnswer(new Answer<HttpResponseMessage.Builder>() {
    @Override
    public HttpResponseMessage.Builder answer(InvocationOnMock
    invocation) {
        HttpStatus status = (HttpStatus) invocation.
        getArguments()[0];
        return new HttpResponseMessageMock.HttpResponse
        MessageBuilderMock().status(status);
    }
}).when(req).createResponseBuilder(any(HttpStatus.class));

final ExecutionContext context = mock(ExecutionContext.class);
doReturn(Logger.getGlobal()).when(context).getLogger();

// Invoke
final OutputBinding<String> msg = (OutputBinding<String>)
mock(OutputBinding.class);
final HttpResponseMessage ret = new Function().run(req, msg,
context);

// Verify
assertEquals(ret.getStatus(), HttpStatus.OK);
    }
}
```

Now let us modify the *pom.xml* file. You may choose to replace the resource group name, Function App name, and Function location with a value of your choice as in Listing 3-4. We need to make sure that the Function App name is unique and no other

Azure Function exists with this name. For example, you can use *myfunc-demo-28*. If this name is not taken up by anyone in the Azure infrastructure, then you will not get any error, and you can use it.

Listing 3-4. pom.xml

```
<?xml version="1.0" encoding="UTF-8" ?>
<project xmlns="http://maven.apache.org/POM/4.0.0" xmlns:xsi="http://www.
w3.org/2001/XMLSchema-instance" xsi:schemaLocation="http://maven.apache.
org/POM/4.0.0 http://maven.apache.org/xsd/maven-4.0.0.xsd">
    <modelVersion>4.0.0</modelVersion>

    <groupId>com.myfunc</groupId>
    <artifactId>funcdemo</artifactId>
    <version>1.0-SNAPSHOT</version>
    <packaging>jar</packaging>

    <name>Azure Java Functions</name>

    <properties>
        <project.build.sourceEncoding>UTF-8</project.build.sourceEncoding>
        <java.version>11</java.version>
        <azure.functions.maven.plugin.version>1.14.1</azure.functions.
        maven.plugin.version>
        <azure.functions.java.library.version>1.4.2</azure.functions.java.
        library.version>
        <functionAppName>myfunc-demo-28</functionAppName>
    </properties>

    <dependencies>
        <dependency>
            <groupId>com.microsoft.azure.functions</groupId>
            <artifactId>azure-functions-java-library</artifactId>
            <version>${azure.functions.java.library.version}</version>
        </dependency>

        <!-- Test -->
        <dependency>
```

```xml
            <groupId>org.junit.jupiter</groupId>
            <artifactId>junit-jupiter</artifactId>
            <version>5.4.2</version>
            <scope>test</scope>
        </dependency>

        <dependency>
            <groupId>org.mockito</groupId>
            <artifactId>mockito-core</artifactId>
            <version>2.23.4</version>
            <scope>test</scope>
        </dependency>
    </dependencies>

    <build>
        <plugins>
            <plugin>
                <groupId>org.apache.maven.plugins</groupId>
                <artifactId>maven-compiler-plugin</artifactId>
                <version>3.8.1</version>
                <configuration>
                    <source>${java.version}</source>
                    <target>${java.version}</target>
                    <encoding>${project.build.sourceEncoding}</encoding>
                </configuration>
            </plugin>
            <plugin>
                <groupId>com.microsoft.azure</groupId>
                <artifactId>azure-functions-maven-plugin</artifactId>
                <version>${azure.functions.maven.plugin.version}</version>
                <configuration>
                    <!-- function app name -->
                    <appName>${functionAppName}</appName>
                    <!-- function app resource group -->
                    <resourceGroup>rg-myjavafunc-demo</resourceGroup>
                    <!-- function app service plan name -->
```

```
<appServicePlanName>java-functions-app-service-plan
</appServicePlanName>
<!-- function app region-->
<!-- refers https://github.com/microsoft/azure-
maven-plugins/wiki/Azure-Functions:-Configuration-
Details#supported-regions for all valid values -->
<region>westus</region>
<!-- function pricingTier, default to be consumption if
not specified -->
<!-- refers https://github.com/microsoft/azure-
maven-plugins/wiki/Azure-Functions:-Configuration-
Details#supported-pricing-tiers for all valid
values -->
<!-- <pricingTier></pricingTier> -->
<!-- Whether to disable application insights, default
is false -->
<!-- refers https://github.com/microsoft/azure-maven-
plugins/wiki/Azure-Functions:-Configuration-Details for
all valid configurations for application insights-->
<!-- <disableAppInsights></disableAppInsights> -->
<runtime>
    <!-- runtime os, could be windows, linux or docker-->
    <os>windows</os>
    <javaVersion>11</javaVersion>
</runtime>
<appSettings>
    <property>
        <name>FUNCTIONS_EXTENSION_VERSION</name>
        <value>~3</value>
    </property>
</appSettings>
</configuration>
<executions>
    <execution>
        <id>package-functions</id>
```

```
                    <goals>
                        <goal>package</goal>
                    </goals>
                </execution>
            </executions>
        </plugin>
        <!--Remove obj folder generated by .NET SDK in maven clean-->
        <plugin>
            <artifactId>maven-clean-plugin</artifactId>
            <version>3.1.0</version>
            <configuration>
                <filesets>
                    <fileset>
                        <directory>obj</directory>
                    </fileset>
                </filesets>
            </configuration>
        </plugin>
    </plugins>
  </build>
</project>
```

Let us build and package the Azure Function code using the following Maven command as in Listing 3-5.

Listing 3-5. Build and package the Function application

```
mvn clean package
```

Log in to Azure using the following Azure CLI command as in Listing 3-6

Listing 3-6. Log in to Azure

```
az login
```

Select your subscription as in Listing 3-7.

Listing 3-7. Select the subscription

```
az account set -s "Your Subscription"
```

Execute the following command as in Listing 3-8.

Listing 3-8. Deploy Function to Azure

```
mvn azure-functions:deploy
```

Note   With WSL, the default authentication type is DEVICE_CODE for Azure login. We need to open a browser, input the device code, and log in. The default authentication type for CMD is Azure CLI. No extra login is needed if you are already logged in.

If you run into a name conflict error, you must change *functionAppName* in *pom.xml* with a unique name and run mvn clean package and mvn azure-functions:deploy again.

Once the build completes, copy the Function URL as in Figure 3-10. We will use this to invoke the Azure Function from the browser later.

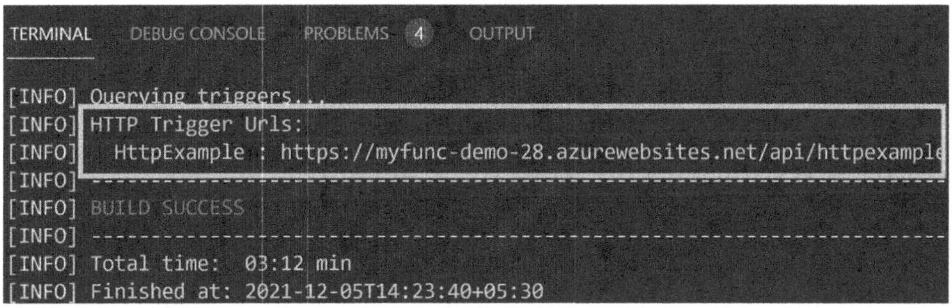

Figure 3-10. *Function URL*

Navigate to the Azure Function that we created. You can find it inside the resource group provided in the POM file. Go to the *Configuration* section. You will find the *Edit* button. Replace the value with the Storage Account connection string that we created earlier. Hit the *OK* button to save the value. Click *Save* as in Figure 3-11 to save the application settings.

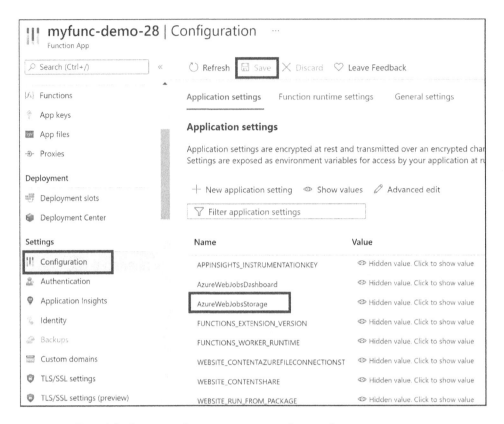

Figure 3-11. *Provide Storage Account connection string*

Now invoke the Function URL with a query string parameter name in the browser as in Listing 3-9.

Listing 3-9. Browse the Function URL

```
https://myfunc-demo-28.azurewebsites.net/api/httpexample?name=Abhishek
```

Go to the Storage Account and see the queue item added as in Figure 3-12.

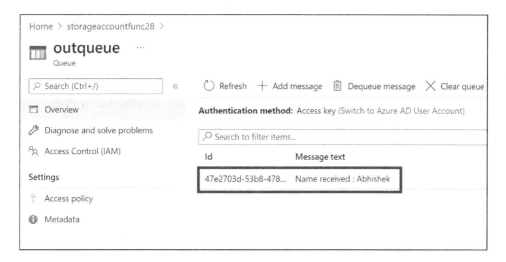

Figure 3-12. *Storage Account Queue output*

Summary

In this chapter, we learned the details of Azure Functions, explored the hosting plans available for Azure Functions, and then learned the concept of Triggers and Bindings. We then developed an Azure Function that gets triggered using an HTTP Trigger and puts a message in the Storage Queue using Output Queue Binding. We then deployed the Function to Azure using the Maven plug-in. In the next chapter, we will learn how to containerize a Java application and run it on Azure Kubernetes Service.

The following are the key takeaways from this chapter:

- You can build your application and host on serverless services without creating and managing hosting infrastructure. These services scale automatically without needing to make any scaling configuration, and you get charged only when the service is executing.

- Azure Functions are Function-as-a-Service (FaaS) offerings on Azure and are serverless services.

- Hosting plans decide the underlying infrastructure on which Azure Functions run. They decide the scaling needs, execution interval, virtual network integration, and many other important aspects for your Azure Functions. Hosting plans available are Consumption Plan, Premium Plan, Dedicated Plan, App Service Environment Plan, and Kubernetes Plan.

- Triggers wake Azure Functions from an idle state and start their execution. Bindings help the Azure Function exchange data with other Azure or non-Azure services. You create Triggers and Bindings declaratively without needing to write much code.

CHAPTER 4

Containerizing Java Applications with Azure Kubernetes Service

Containers are modern application hosting options today. You can build your application, containerize your application along with the hosting environment and application dependencies, and then keep the containerized image in a centralized registry. You can pull the containerized image in the target environments and run it as containers with ease. You can build the image once and run it in many environments without setting up any hosting or application dependencies. An application may consist of multiple containers. For example, you can have a container for the user interface, a container for the business layer, and another container for data access. All these containers in the application need to communicate with each other securely. The containers should be always up and running to serve the client request. You should manage all these containers with ease and address architectural concerns like availability, reliability, scalability, and many more. Kubernetes is a container orchestration platform that would help you orchestrate and manage these containers. It would address all cross-cutting concerns that we discussed.

In the previous chapter, we learned the basics of Azure Functions. We then created a Java-based Azure Function and deployed it on Azure. In this chapter, we will learn the details of Azure Kubernetes Service, and then we will containerize a Java application and run it on Azure Kubernetes Service.

© Abhishek Mishra 2022
A. Mishra, *Microsoft Azure for Java Developers*, https://doi.org/10.1007/978-1-4842-8251-9_4

Structure

In this chapter, we will discuss the following aspects of containerizing Java applications with Azure Kubernetes Service:

- Introduction to containers
- Understanding Azure Kubernetes Service
- Containerize a Java application and run it on Azure Kubernetes Service

Objectives

After studying this chapter, you should be able to get the following learnings:

- Understand the concept of Azure Kubernetes Service
- Build and run Java applications on Azure Kubernetes Service

Introduction to Containers

We build an application and make it ready for production use. To host the application, we purchase a hosting server and an operating system and install the hosting software and all necessary dependencies to run. Once the hosting environment is ready, along with the application dependencies, we host the application on the server. We end up spending a lot of time and effort in procuring a hosting server and making it ready for the application to run on it. We sometimes get into the complexities of configuring the hosting environment and the dependencies that further add to the delay. Suppose you have multiple environments in your enterprise. In that case, you will have to spend the same amount of effort to get the application up and running across multiple environments like test, acceptance, or production.

You may choose to host your application on Virtual Machines. You can purchase a powerful server and run multiple Virtual Machines on the server. In the case of Virtual Machines, you purchase a server, install an operating system on the server referred to as the host operating system, and then install a virtualization software like Hyper-V. The virtualization software virtualizes the underlying server hardware like the CPU, RAM, disks, and other infrastructure and runs multiple Virtual Machines on the server. These Virtual Machines run in isolation and have their share of the virtualized hardware infrastructure. Each virtual machine has an operating system referred to as the guest operating system. You need to install the hosting software like Tomcat or IIS, or node.js and application dependencies on these Virtual Machines and then host your applications on these Virtual Machines. Here in the case of the virtual machine, you need to spend effort in preparing the hosting environment and making the virtual machine ready to host the application. This application hosting approach is almost the same as hosting your application on a physical server. However, the advantage you get here is that you share the underlying hardware infrastructure and run multiple applications in isolation in the Virtual Machines. This approach saves you cost.

Containers are a smarter way of hosting your application. You can build your application, containerize it, and keep it in a container registry along with all necessary application dependencies. The container registry stores the container images. Azure Container Registry and Docker Hub are examples of container registry. You may choose to allow everyone to use your images without needing any authentication. You will have to store your container images in a public container registry like the Docker Hub for such scenarios. You may use a private container registry like Azure Container Registry and provide your container images to authenticated users who have access to the container registry.

Once you have the container image in the container registry, you can get a server with an operating system and install the container runtime software like containerd or Docker. And then pull the container image and run it on the server. You need not configure the hosting environment or the application dependencies. The container image has the application dependencies and the hosting software along with the application. Once you pull the container image and run it as a container, your application is up and running. The container runtime virtualizes the underlying operating system and runs the containers as operating system threads. Figure 4-1 demonstrates the difference between Virtual Machines and containers.

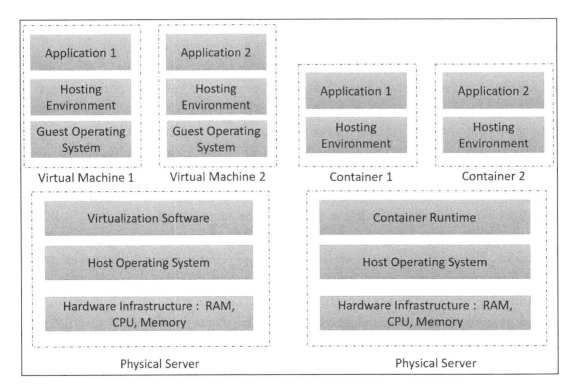

Figure 4-1. *Virtual Machines and containers*

Note   Containers are lightweight as compared to Virtual Machines. In the case of Virtual Machines, you virtualize the underlying hardware infrastructure, and the virtual machine has an operating system in it. In the case of containers, the server's operating system is virtualized, and the containers run as operating system threads without needing an operating system for itself.

Understanding Azure Kubernetes Service

Applications may need multiple containers to host each of their modules. Let us take an example of a three-tier loosely coupled application that has a user interface tier, a business logic tier, and a data access tier. We need to create a container image for the user interface tier, a container image for the business logic tier, and a container image for the data access tier. Then we can run each of these images as containers in the production environment. Think of a scenario when the data access container goes down. In that case, the entire application will go down as the business layer container will not connect with the database without the data access layer. Also, what will happen if there is a sudden surge in the incoming request for the application. We may have to add more containers to handle the incoming requests dynamically. These containers should be able to communicate securely. The container and application health should be monitored for performance degradation and failures. You must take care of all these concerns.

There can be thousands of containers in an application to manage. To make your life easy, we have container orchestrators like Kubernetes, Docker Swarm, and many more. These orchestrators manage these containers and ensure that the containers are highly available, reliable, scalable, fault-tolerant, and secured. They address all the concerns we discussed for the containers in an application. For example, if a container dies, the orchestrator will spin up another container in no time to replace the container that died.

Kubernetes is an open-source container orchestrator offering from Google. It consists of a master node or the control plane and multiple worker nodes. Your containers run inside the pods in the worker nodes. Virtual Machines are worker nodes in most cases. If you are planning to scale at a very high rate, then you can use serverless nodes that are Azure Container Instances. Serverless nodes can scale automatically based on incoming traffic and spin out much faster as compared to Virtual Machines. The control plane controls and manages the worker nodes. It decides which worker node to run the pods and closely monitors the pods and the worker nodes. You can run identical containers called replicas as a replica set. For example, you can have multiple pods for the data access tier in a replica set. If one of the replicas in a replica set goes down, other replicas are still available to serve the request until another replica spins up. You can configure your Kubernetes cluster to scale the pods or the worker nodes automatically when the incoming load increases.

Setting up the Kubernetes cluster is cumbersome. You may have to spend a lot of effort and time to get your Kubernetes cluster up and running. The control plane is the most complex part of the Kubernetes cluster. Cloud providers like Amazon, Microsoft, and Google help you spin out the Kubernetes cluster in minutes. They provide Kubernetes as a service on their cloud and abstract all necessary complexities while spinning up the Kubernetes cluster and managing the control plane for you. You have no control over the control plane. The underlying cloud platform manages the control plane for you, and you can manage the worker nodes and the application container deployment. Such Kubernetes offering on cloud is referred to as managed Kubernetes service. Azure Kubernetes Service is an example of managed Kubernetes service on Azure.

Note   Load balancer service exposes your application on HTTP port, while node port exposes your application on a nonstandard port from 30000 to 32767.

The application containers running inside pods should be exposed to the end users to access the application. Even you may have scenarios where a pod should be exposed only inside the cluster for another pod to consume. Such scenarios are handled using the Kubernetes services running inside the cluster. A cluster IP service allows pods to communicate internally. The load balancer service and the node port service allow the pods to be exposed to the end users. Let us go back to the three-tier application example that we discussed earlier. We need to expose the user interface tier to the end user. The user interface tier should communicate with the business logic tier, and the business logic tier should communicate with the data access tier. The business logic tier and the data access tier should not be exposed to the external users, and its access should be limited inside the cluster. To address this scenario, we can have a load balancer service in front of the user interface tier so that the user interface tier gets exposed to the end user. You can have a cluster IP service in front of the business logic tier and the data access tier to limit its communication within the cluster.

As a developer, you containerize the application and push it to the container registry. You then spin up the Kubernetes cluster and build a deployment YAML file for the Kubernetes cluster. The deployment YAML file will have all necessary details like the number of replicas, services, containers to run on the cluster, and many more details needed for the application containers to run on Kubernetes worker nodes. You then pass on this deployment file to the control plane. The control plane then schedules the pods on the worker nodes based on the information you have provided in the YAML file. The pods will pull the container images from the container registry specified in the deployment file and then start them as containers.

Containerize a Java Application and Run It on Azure Kubernetes Service

Let us build a Java Spring Boot application, containerize it, push it to Azure Container Registry, and run it in the Azure Kubernetes Service cluster. We will use Spring Initializr to generate the Spring Boot application and create a Docker file manually.

You should have Docker Desktop installed on your local system to containerize your application as a prerequisite. Docker provides a community edition for Docker Desktop to experiment with Docker offerings and try out the Docker containers. You can use the Docker Desktop community edition.

We will create the Azure Kubernetes Service and the Azure Container Registry first. Then we will build the application, containerize it, push it to the Azure Container Registry, and then run the application container on Azure Kubernetes Service.

Create Azure Container Registry

Azure Container Registry is a private Docker registry and can store container images on Azure platform. The images stored will be accessible to only those who have access to the registry. It can also store artifacts like Helm Charts and other artifacts pertaining to Open Container Initiative (OCI) specifications. Let us create an Azure Container Registry. Go to the Azure portal and click *Create a resource,* as shown in Figure 4-2.

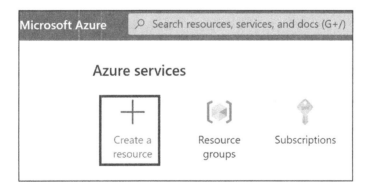

Figure 4-2. *Create a resource*

Click on the *Containers* tab. You will get all Container-related offerings here, and you can see them in Figure 4-3. Click *Container Registry*.

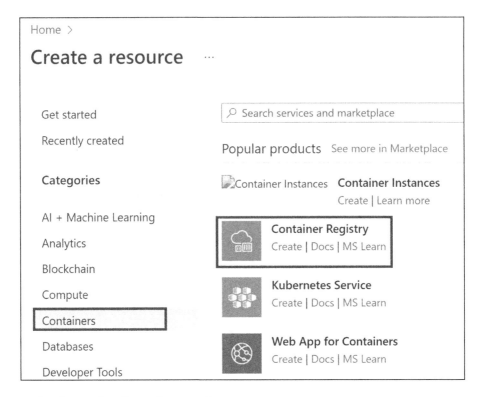

Figure 4-3. *Go to the Containers tab*

Provide subscription, resource group, name, SKU, and location for the container registry. Click *Review + create* as shown in Figure 4-4.

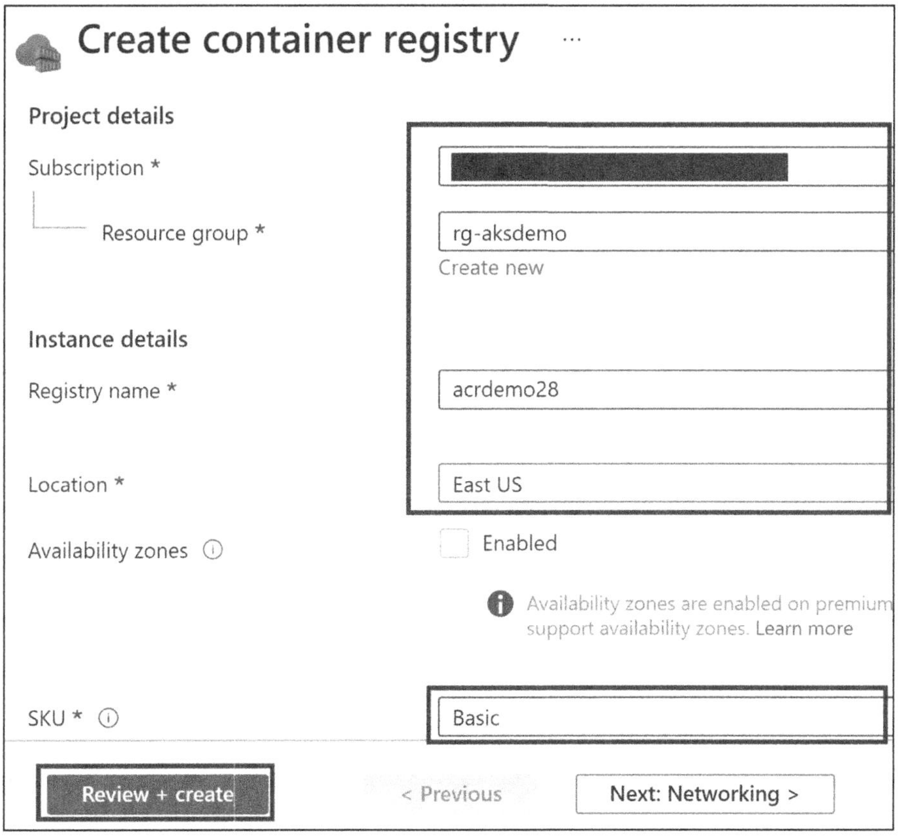

Figure 4-4. *Provide basic details*

Click *Create* as shown in Figure 4-5. This will spin up an Azure Container Registry for you.

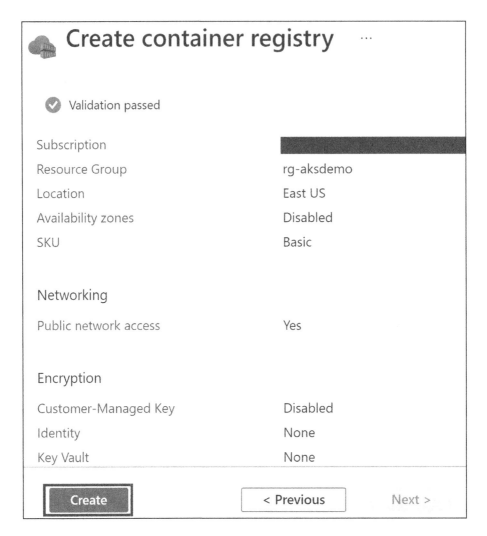

Figure 4-5. *Click Create*

Once the container registry gets created, go to the Azure portal and navigate to the container registry. Click *Access keys* as shown in Figure 4-6. Enable Admin user. Copy the login server, username, and password. We will use these credentials to push the container images to the container registry later.

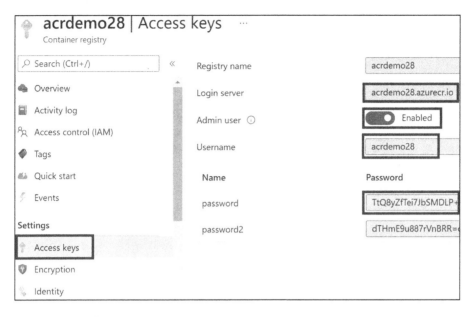

Figure 4-6. Access keys

Create an Azure Kubernetes Service

Now let us create an Azure Kubernetes Service. We will run our application container on this Kubernetes cluster. Go to the Azure portal and click *Create a resource* as shown in Figure 4-7.

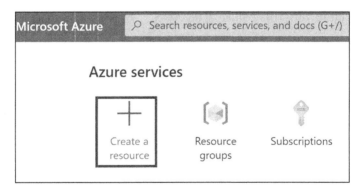

Figure 4-7. Create a resource

Go to the *Containers* tab and click *Kubernetes Service* as shown in Figure 4-8.

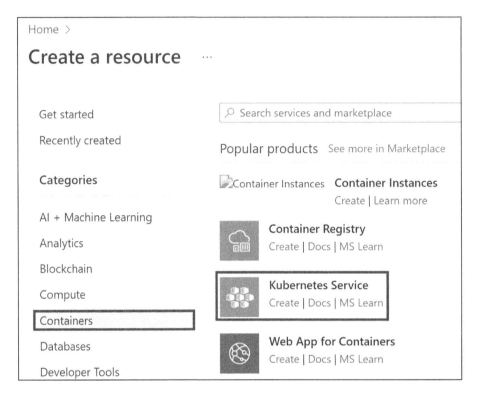

Figure 4-8. *Create a Kubernetes service*

Provide subscription, resource group, and cluster configuration. Let us select *Dev/Test ($)* as the cluster configuration as shown in Figure 4-9. This is the basic configuration available, and this will save us costs.

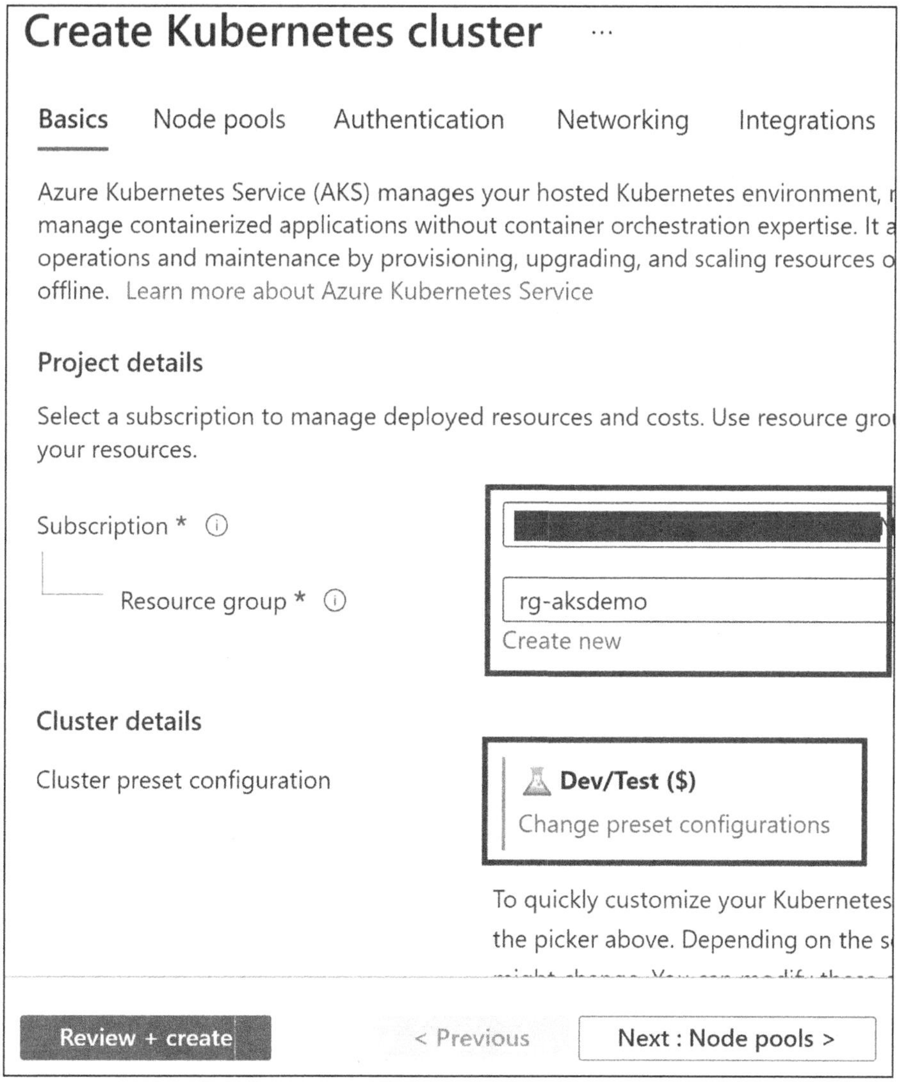

Create Kubernetes cluster   ···

Basics   Node pools   Authentication   Networking   Integrations

Azure Kubernetes Service (AKS) manages your hosted Kubernetes environment, manage containerized applications without container orchestration expertise. It a operations and maintenance by provisioning, upgrading, and scaling resources o offline. Learn more about Azure Kubernetes Service

Project details

Select a subscription to manage deployed resources and costs. Use resource gro your resources.

Subscription * ⓘ

Resource group * ⓘ

rg-aksdemo

Create new

Cluster details

Cluster preset configuration

🧪 **Dev/Test ($)**

Change preset configurations

To quickly customize your Kubernetes
the picker above. Depending on the s

| Review + create | < Previous | Next : Node pools > |

Figure 4-9. Provide basic details

Scroll down and provide cluster name, region, and other necessary details as shown in Figure 4-10.

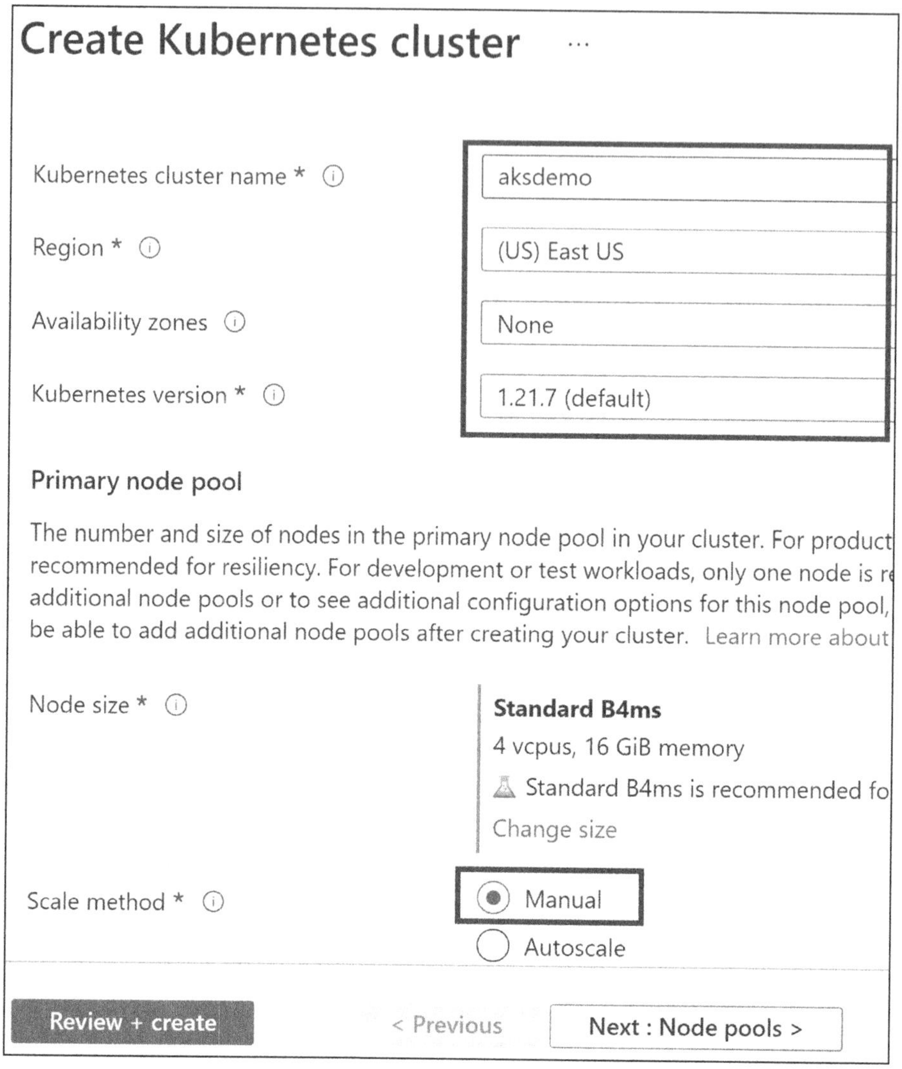

Create Kubernetes cluster   ...

Kubernetes cluster name * ⓘ   aksdemo

Region * ⓘ   (US) East US

Availability zones ⓘ   None

Kubernetes version * ⓘ   1.21.7 (default)

Primary node pool

The number and size of nodes in the primary node pool in your cluster. For product
recommended for resiliency. For development or test workloads, only one node is re
additional node pools or to see additional configuration options for this node pool,
be able to add additional node pools after creating your cluster. Learn more about

Node size * ⓘ   **Standard B4ms**
                                      4 vcpus, 16 GiB memory
                                      ⚠ Standard B4ms is recommended fo
                                      Change size

Scale method * ⓘ   ⦿ Manual
                                      ◯ Autoscale

    Review + create   < Previous   Next : Node pools >

Figure 4-10. *Provide cluster details*

Scroll down and provide the number of nodes in the cluster as 1 as shown in
Figure 4-11. The higher the number of nodes, the higher the cost for the cluster.

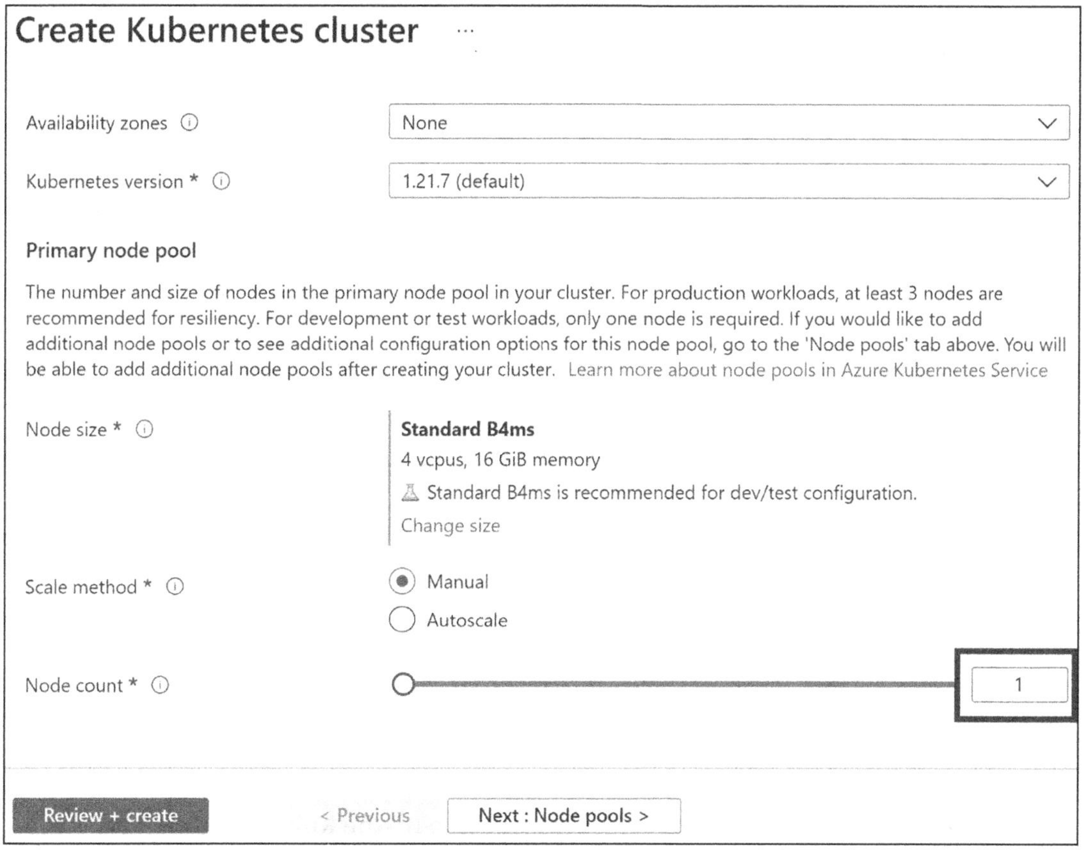

Create Kubernetes cluster   ⋯

Availability zones ⓘ

| None | ⌄ |

Kubernetes version * ⓘ

| 1.21.7 (default) | ⌄ |

Primary node pool

The number and size of nodes in the primary node pool in your cluster. For production workloads, at least 3 nodes are recommended for resiliency. For development or test workloads, only one node is required. If you would like to add additional node pools or to see additional configuration options for this node pool, go to the 'Node pools' tab above. You will be able to add additional node pools after creating your cluster. Learn more about node pools in Azure Kubernetes Service

Node size * ⓘ

Standard B4ms
4 vcpus, 16 GiB memory
⚗ Standard B4ms is recommended for dev/test configuration.
Change size

Scale method * ⓘ

⦿ Manual
◯ Autoscale

Node count * ⓘ

| ◯────────────────────────── | 1 |

Review + create   < Previous   Next : Node pools >

Figure 4-11. *Provide the number of nodes*

Go to the *Integrations* tab. Select the Azure Container Registry that we created earlier. This step would help us integrate Azure Container Registry with the Kubernetes cluster, and the pods running inside the nodes can pull the container images from the container registry seamlessly. You can enable container monitoring that will help you get the performance metrics and logs for the cluster. Click *Review + create* as shown in Figure 4-12.

Figure 4-12. *Provide container registry integration details*

Click *Create* as shown in Figure 4-13. This will spin up the Kubernetes cluster.

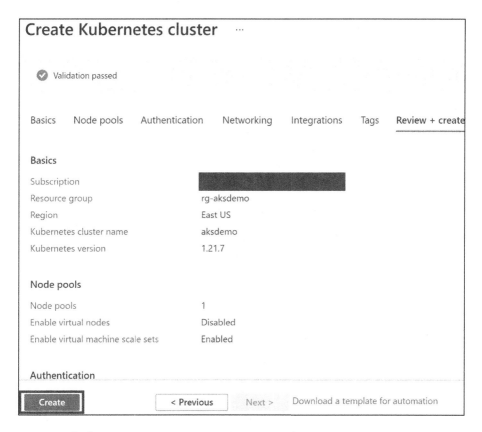

Figure 4-13. *Click Create*

Containerize a Java Application

Let us create an application using Spring Initializr and containerize it using Docker. Go to the URL shown in Listing 4-1 for Spring Initializr.

Listing 4-1. Spring Initializr URL

```
https://start.spring.io/
```

Let us provide the group name, artifact ID, and other necessary details for your Java application as shown in Figure 4-14.

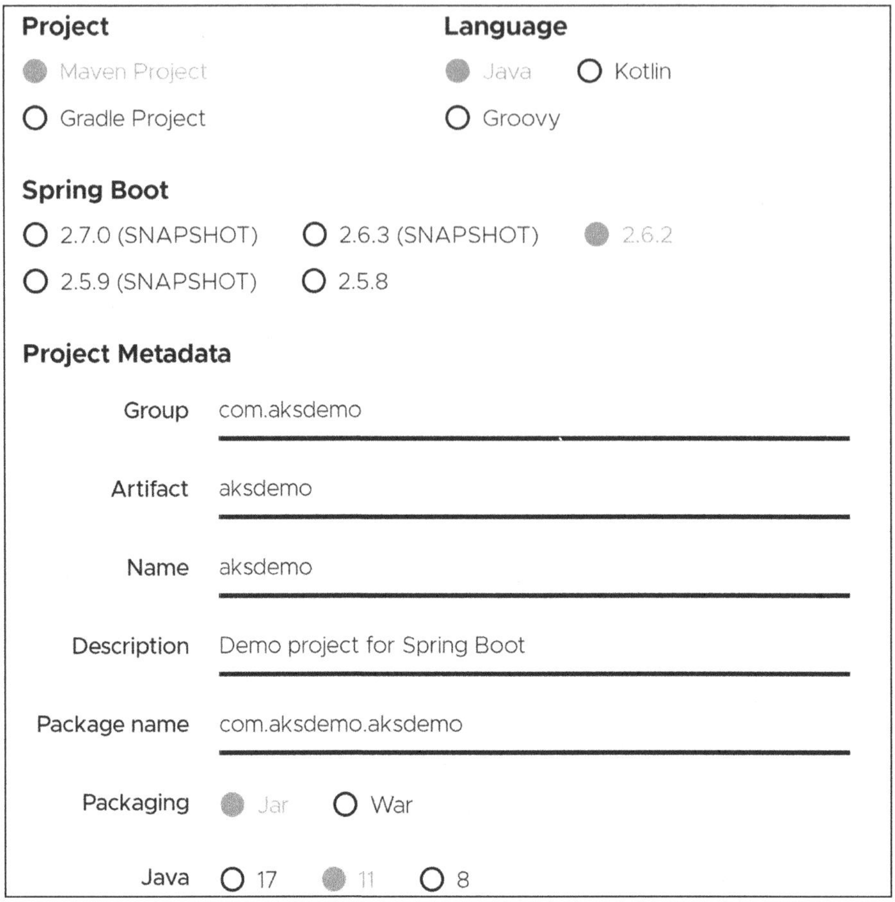

Project   **Language**

● Maven Project   ● Java   ○ Kotlin

○ Gradle Project   ○ Groovy

Spring Boot

○ 2.7.0 (SNAPSHOT)   ○ 2.6.3 (SNAPSHOT)   ● 2.6.2

○ 2.5.9 (SNAPSHOT)   ○ 2.5.8

Project Metadata

Group   com.aksdemo

Artifact   aksdemo

Name   aksdemo

Description   Demo project for Spring Boot

Package name   com.aksdemo.aksdemo

Packaging   ● Jar   ○ War

Java   ○ 17   ● 11   ○ 8

Figure 4-14. *Generate a Spring Boot Java application*

Add the Spring Web dependencies as shown in Figure 4-15. Generate the Java application project and download it.

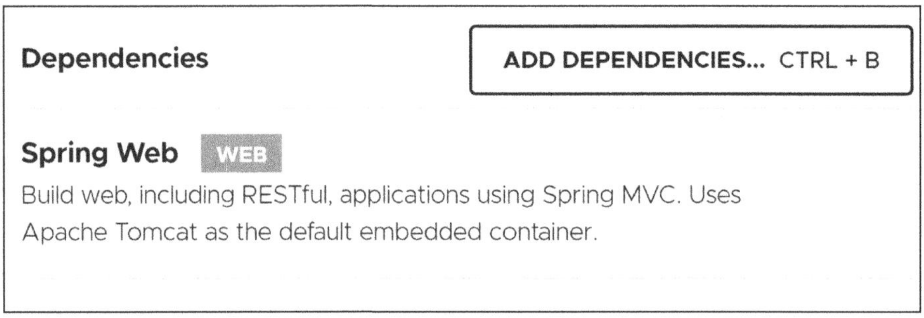

Dependencies   **ADD DEPENDENCIES...** CTRL + B

Spring Web `WEB`

Build web, including RESTful, applications using Spring MVC. Uses
Apache Tomcat as the default embedded container.

Figure 4-15. *Add the Spring Web dependencies*

In the Java application, modify the Java file with the main method shown in Listing 4-2. We need to add a service accessible using the *hello* route. The service returns the value *Hello World !!.*

Listing 4-2. Java application code

```
package com.aksdemo.aksdemo;

import org.springframework.boot.SpringApplication;
import org.springframework.boot.autoconfigure.SpringBootApplication;
import org.springframework.web.bind.annotation.GetMapping;
import org.springframework.web.bind.annotation.RequestParam;
import org.springframework.web.bind.annotation.RestController;

@SpringBootApplication
@RestController
public class AksdemoApplication {

    public static void main(String[] args) {
        SpringApplication.run(AksdemoApplication.class, args);
    }

    @GetMapping("/hello")
    public String hello() {
        return String.format("Hello World !!");
    }

}
```

Now let us build the application using the command shown in Listing 4-3.

Listing 4-3. Build the Java application

```
mvn clean install
```

Once the Maven build is successful, we can containerize the application. The JAR file will get generated inside the target folder. The target folder gets created once the build is successful. Let us create the Docker file using the following code listing. The file should be named *Dockerfile* without any extension. Make sure you create the Docker file as shown in Listing 4-4 in the directory where the application pom.xml file is there.

The Docker file uses the base image as *openjdk:11*. It will copy the application JAR file to the /usr/app folder. Make sure that you replace the JAR name in the Docker file listed as follows with the name of the JAR file that gets generated for you in the target folder. It will then expose port 8080 and define the application JAR file as the entry point so that the JAR will start up whenever the container boots up.

Listing 4-4. Dockerfile

```
FROM openjdk:11
COPY target/aksdemo-0.0.1-SNAPSHOT.jar /usr/app/
WORKDIR /usr/app
EXPOSE 8080
ENTRYPOINT ["java","-jar","aksdemo-0.0.1-SNAPSHOT.jar"]
```

Now let us run the command shown in Listing 4-5 to containerize the application. You should run this command where the Docker file is present.

Listing 4-5. Build the Docker image

```
docker build -t aksdemo:demo .
```

Now let us verify if the container image gets created as shown in Figure 4-16 by running the command shown in Listing 4-6.

Listing 4-6. List Docker images

```
docker image ls
```

Figure 4-16. *Containerized image*

Let us start the container and check if we can access the application. You can start the application using the command shown in Listing 4-7. We are mapping the system port 8080 on your laptop to port 8080 of the container where the application is running.

Listing 4-7. Run the docker container

```
docker run --publish 8080:8080 --detach --name aksdemo aksdemo:demo
```

Once the Docker container gets started, browse the URL shown in Listing 4-8 as in Figure 4-17.

Listing 4-8. URL for the container running locally

```
http://localhost:8080/hello
```

Figure 4-17. *Container executing locally*

Now let us push the container image to the Azure Container Registry that we created earlier. Run the command shown in Listing 4-9 to log in to the Azure Container Registry. You will be prompted for credentials that you will get in the Access keys section of the Azure Container Registry.

Note   Instead of using Docker command to push images to the Azure Container Registry, you may use the Azure CLI command `az acr build --registry [ACRName] --image [ImageName]` . to build and push the container image to the Azure Container Registry. This is a neater way to push the image as compared to using traditional Docker commands. Replace *[ACRName]* with the name of the Azure Container Registry and *[ImageName]* with the name of the Docker image that you need to create. You must log in to the Azure subscription using the `az login` command before you try the `az acr` command.

Replace *[ACRName]* with the name of your Azure Container Registry.

Listing 4-9. Log in to the Azure Container Registry

```
docker login [ACRName].azurecr.io
```

Run the command shown in Listing 4-10 to tag the container image with the Azure Container Registry name. Replace *[ACRName]* with the name of your Azure Container Registry.

Listing 4-10. Tag the Docker image with the Azure Container Registry

```
docker tag aksdemo:demo [ACRName].azurecr.io/aksdemo:demo
```

Push the container image to the container registry shown in Listing 4-11. Replace *[ACRName]* with the name of your Azure Container Registry.

Listing 4-11. Push the Docker image to the Azure Container Registry

```
docker push [ACRName].azurecr.io/aksdemo:demo
```

Once the image gets pushed, you can see the image in the Azure Container Registry in the *Repositories* section as shown in Figure 4-18.

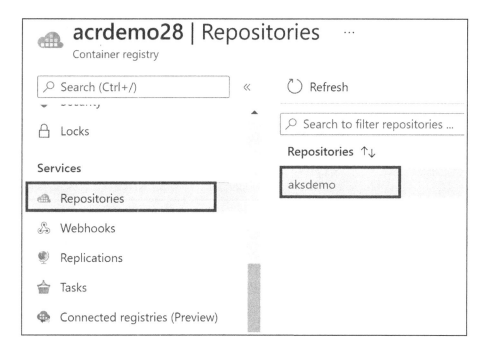

Figure 4-18. *Container image in the Azure Container Registry*

Run the Container on Azure Kubernetes Service

Now we have containerized the Java application and have pushed it to the Azure Container Registry. Let us run the container image on Azure Kubernetes Service. We will use the *Azure Cloud Shell* to execute the *Azure CLI* and *kubectl* commands to deploy the container image on Azure Kubernetes Service. If you are planning to try this locally on your system, then you need to install Azure CLI and kubectl locally. You must also log in to the Azure environment locally before you try out the illustrated steps. With *Azure Cloud Shell,* you need not do any installations or log in to the Azure environment and you can get started directly with the commands illustrated here. Go to the Azure portal and click Azure Cloud Shell. Select the *Bash* prompt when the cloud shell opens up as shown in Figure 4-19.

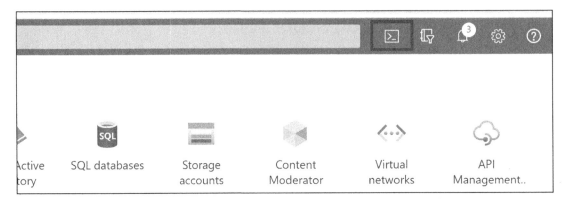

Figure 4-19. *Open Azure Cloud Shell*

We need to fetch the credentials locally on the cloud shell and authenticate with the Azure Kubernetes Service. Run the command shown in Listing 4-12 to get authenticated.

Listing 4-12. Get the cluster credentials

```
az aks get-credentials -n aksdemo -g rg-aksdemo –admin
```

Now let us open the *nano* editor and create the *deploy.yaml* file. In this YAML, we specify the container image repository details, the number of replicas, the load balancer service for exposing the pod to the Internet, and the port details where the image would run on the pod and the load balancer service. In a nutshell, we are defining the Kubernetes deployment configuration with three replicas and a load balancer service that will expose the application to the Internet. Run the command shown in Listing 4-13 to open the nano editor.

Listing 4-13. Open the nano editor

```
nano deploy.yaml
```

Paste the YAML shown in Listing 4-14 in the deploy.yaml. Save the YAML and close the nano editor.

Note   You need to provide the image path in Listing 4-14 based on the Azure Container Registry you are using and the name of the container image that you created.

Listing 4-14. Deploy.yaml

```yaml
apiVersion: apps/v1
kind: Deployment
metadata:
 name: mydemoapp
 labels:
   app: mydemoapp
spec:
 selector:
   matchLabels:
     app: mydemoapp
 replicas: 3
 template:
   metadata:
     labels:
       app: mydemoapp
   spec:
     containers:
     - name: mydemoapp
       image: acrdemo28.azurecr.io/aksdemo:demo
       resources:
         requests:
           cpu: 100m
           memory: 100Mi
         limits:
           cpu: 200m
           memory: 200Mi
       ports:
       - containerPort: 8080
---
apiVersion: v1
kind: Service
metadata:
 name: mydemoappservice
spec:
```

```
type: LoadBalancer
ports:
- port: 8080
selector:
  app: mydemoapp
```

Run the command shown in Listing 4-15 to deploy the application container image in the Azure Kubernetes Service.

Listing 4-15. Deploy to Azure Kubernetes Service

```
kubectl apply -f deploy.yaml
```

We have specified three replicas, so we should have three pods running in the cluster. Run the command shown in Listing 4-16 to list the running pods as shown in Figure 4-20.

Listing 4-16. Get the pods running in the cluster

```
kubectl get pods
```

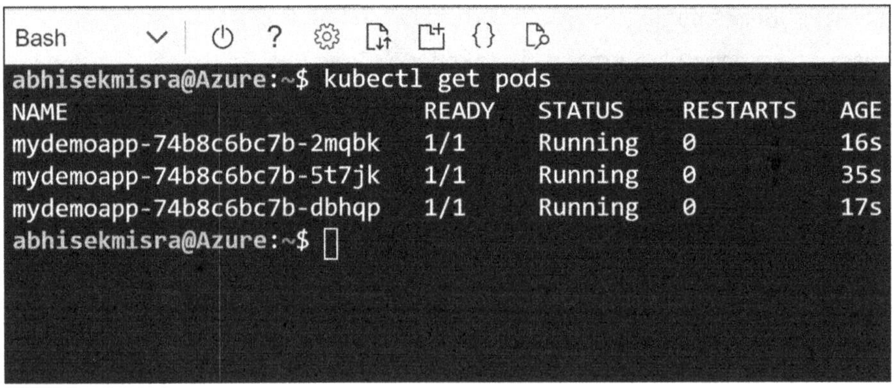

Figure 4-20. *Pods running in the cluster*

Run the command shown in Listing 4-17 to inspect the load balancer service. Copy the external IP address as shown in Figure 4-21 for the load balancer service. We need this IP address to browse the application running on the cluster.

Listing 4-17. Get the load balancer service details

```
kubectl get services
```

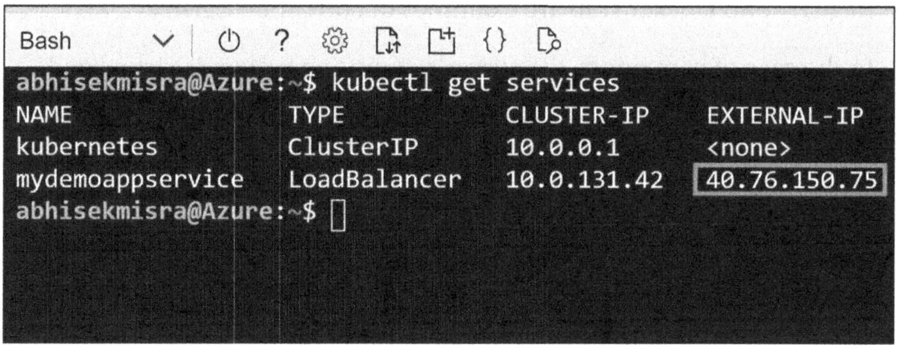

Figure 4-21. *Load balancer service*

Browse the external IP address and you can see the application output as shown in Figure 4-22.

```
←   →   C   ⚠ Not secure   http://40.76.150.75:8080/hello

Hello World !!
```

Figure 4-22. *Browse the application running in the cluster*

Summary

In this chapter, we learned the details of containers and Kubernetes. We then learned what Azure Kubernetes Service is. We then developed a Java Spring Boot application, containerized it in a Docker image, and pushed it to the Azure Container Registry. We pulled the container image and ran it on the Azure Kubernetes Service cluster. We explored basic Docker and kubectl commands that will help us interact with the Docker engine and the Kubernetes cluster. In the next chapter, we will build a Java application and run it on Azure Spring Cloud.

The following are the key takeaways from this chapter:

- You can build your application, containerize it, and keep it in a container registry along with all necessary application dependencies.

- The container registry stores the container images. Azure Container Registry and Docker Hub are examples of container registry.

- In the case of containers, the server's operating system is virtualized, and the containers run as operating system threads without needing an operating system for themselves.

- Kubernetes is an open source container orchestrator offering from Google. It consists of a master node or the control plane and multiple worker nodes.

- Your containers run inside the pods in the worker nodes.

- Azure Kubernetes Service is a managed Kubernetes offering on Azure.

## CHAPTER 5

Running Java Applications on Azure Spring Cloud

You are building a Spring Boot–based microservices application that you will host on Azure using the Platform-as-a-Service model. You need to take care of concerns like keeping application configurations for different environments, integrating with Platform-as-a-Service (PaaS) databases on Azure, and leveraging Azure Redis for caching needs. You may have to integrate application insights for logging and monitoring and configure automatic scaling for your services and many more. You also need to integrate your application hosting environment with a Git repository, Azure DevOps pipelines, or Jenkins. And you need to achieve all these requirements without making any code changes and use configurations as much as possible. Azure Spring Cloud will help you here with ease.

In the previous chapter, we learned the basics of Azure Kubernetes Service. We then created a Java-based application, containerized it, and deployed it on Azure Kubernetes Service. In this chapter, we will learn the details of Azure Spring Cloud, and then we will provision an Azure Spring Cloud service and deploy the application in the service.

Structure

In this chapter, we will discuss the following aspects of deploying Java applications on Azure Spring Cloud:

- Introduction to Azure Spring Cloud
- Create an Azure Spring Cloud service

© Abhishek Mishra 2022
A. Mishra, *Microsoft Azure for Java Developers*, https://doi.org/10.1007/978-1-4842-8251-9_5

- Deploy a Java application on Azure Spring Cloud

Objectives

After studying this chapter, you should be able to get the following learnings:

- Understand the concept of Azure Spring Cloud
- Build and run Java applications on Azure Spring Cloud

Introduction to Azure Spring Cloud

Spring Cloud is a Java Virtual Machine–based open source framework that helps developers to build robust cloud-based Java solution. You can incorporate a variety of cross-cutting concerns like distributed messaging, service discovery, load balancing, service registrations, routing, and many more with ease.

Azure Spring Cloud is a Platform-as-a-Service-based offering. Spring Cloud is not just for Java application, so it can also host .NET Core applications using Steeltoe. You need to focus on building the application. The underlying platform will take care of the hosting requirements. You need to provision the service and deploy your application to it.

You can build microservices-based applications using Spring Cloud. It provides excellent built-in support for managing application configuration and service discovery. It integrates well with Azure services like Azure Active Directory, Application Insights, Azure Redis Cache, Storage Account, Cosmos DB, and other PaaS databases and services without writing any code. You can define service bindings for the application instances on Azure Spring Cloud and easily integrate with other Azure services.

Application instances running on Azure Spring Cloud can scale using automatic configuration based on scaling criteria and conditions. It also supports manual scaling, where you need to specify the number of instances you need to run manually.

Azure Spring Cloud works well for Continuous Integration and Continuous Deployment scenarios using Azure DevOps, Jenkins, Maven, Gradle, Terraform, and many more. You can integrate source control repositories like Azure Repos, GitHub, and Git repository and embrace the DevOps way of building your application with ease.

You can build enterprise-grade applications using Azure Spring Cloud. Azure Spring Cloud runs on top of VMware Infrastructure on Azure. It provides excellent support for end-to-end application life cycle management. You can address enterprise-level concerns like monitoring, auditing, security, scalability, availability, and many more with ease.

Create an Azure Spring Cloud Service

Let us create an Azure Spring Cloud service using the Azure portal. Go to the Azure portal and search for *azure spring apps*, as shown in Figure 5-1, and then click *Azure Spring Apps* in the result.

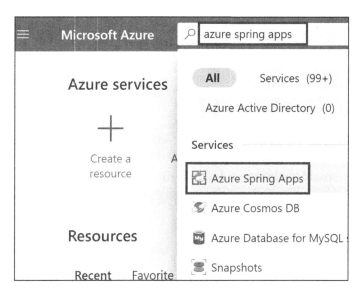

Figure 5-1. *Search for Azure Spring Apps*

Click *Create* as in Figure 5-2. You will get navigated to screen where you can create Azure Spring Cloud.

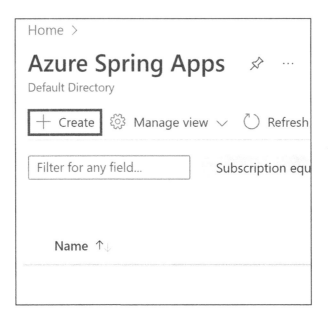

Figure 5-2. *Click Create*

Provide resource group name, subscription name, spring cloud name, location, and tier. Click *Review + create* as shown in Figure 5-3.

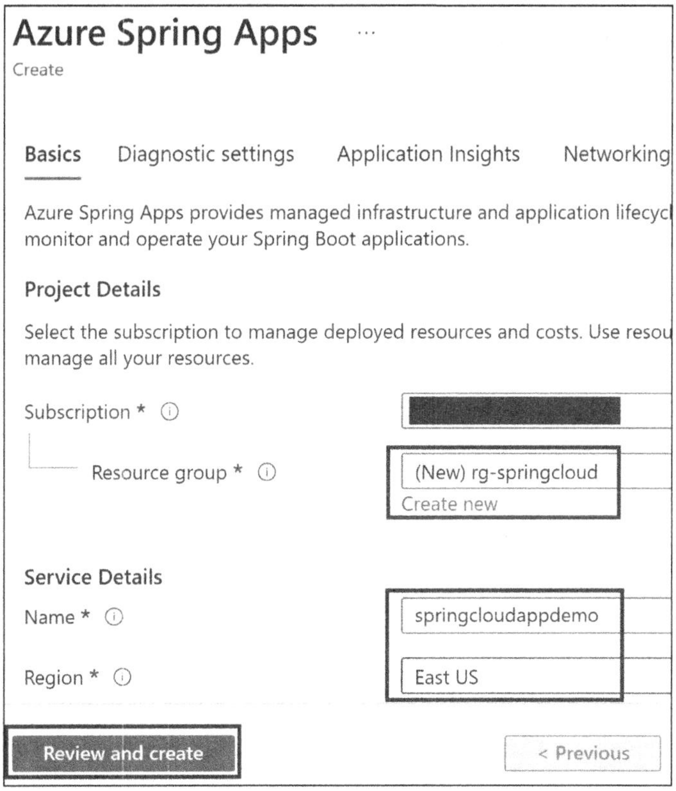

Azure Spring Apps ⋯
Create

Basics   Diagnostic settings   Application Insights   Networking

Azure Spring Apps provides managed infrastructure and application lifecycl
monitor and operate your Spring Boot applications.

Project Details

Select the subscription to manage deployed resources and costs. Use resou
manage all your resources.

Subscription * ⓘ   [_____]

   └──── Resource group * ⓘ   (New) rg-springcloud
                            Create new

Service Details

Name * ⓘ   springcloudappdemo

Region * ⓘ   East US

Review and create   < Previous

Figure 5-3. *Click Review + create*

Click *Create* as shown in Figure 5-4. This action will provision Azure Spring Cloud.

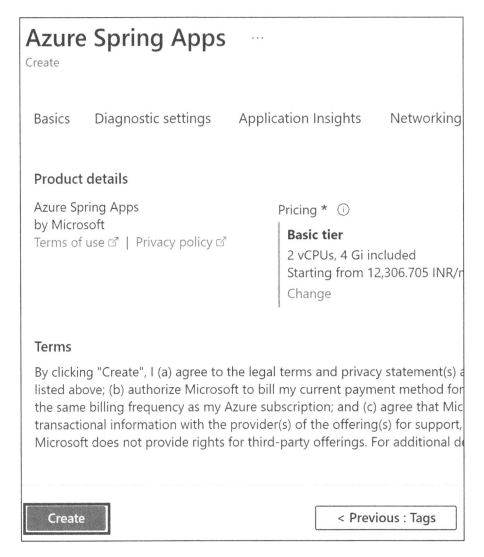

Figure 5-4. *Click Create*

Once the Azure Spring Cloud service gets created, navigate to the service in the portal. We need to create an App instance to deploy the Spring Boot application. Go to the *Apps* section and click *Create App* as shown in Figure 5-5.

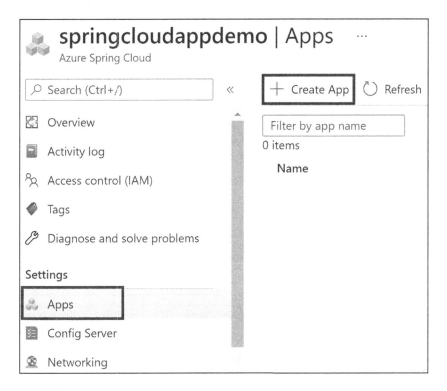

Figure 5-5. *Click Apps*

Provide the instance name, runtime version as Java 11, instance count as 1, and other compute details. Click *Create* as shown in Figure 5-6. The app instance will get created.

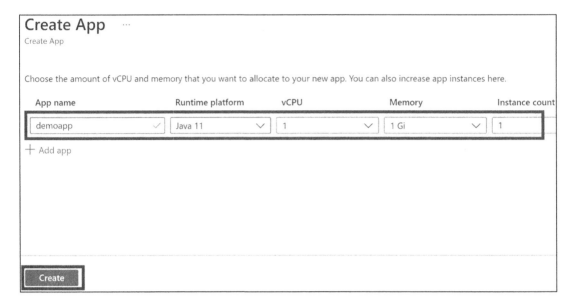

Figure 5-6. *Create App*

Click on the App we created as shown in Figure 5-7. You will get navigated inside the App we created.

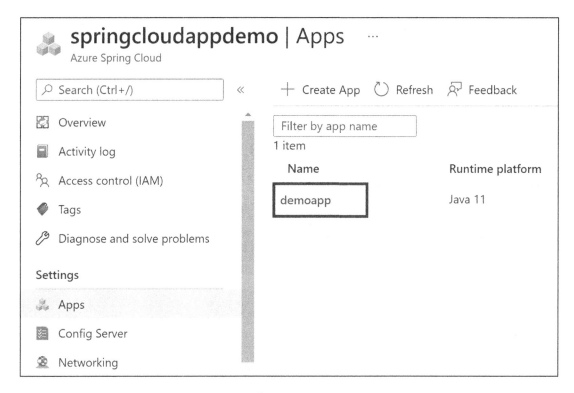

Figure 5-7. *Click on the App created*

We need to access the app using a public URL. Click *Assign endpoint* as shown in Figure 5-8.

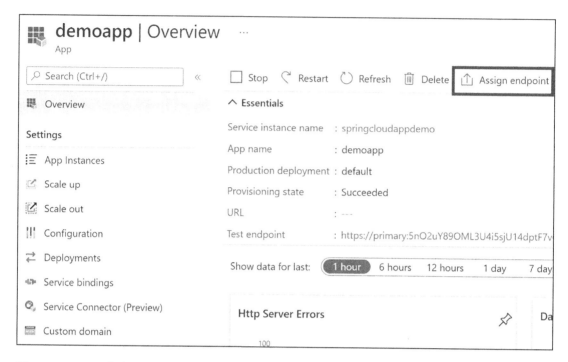

Figure 5-8. *Click Assign endpoint*

Once the URL gets assigned, click on the URL as shown in Figure 5-9.

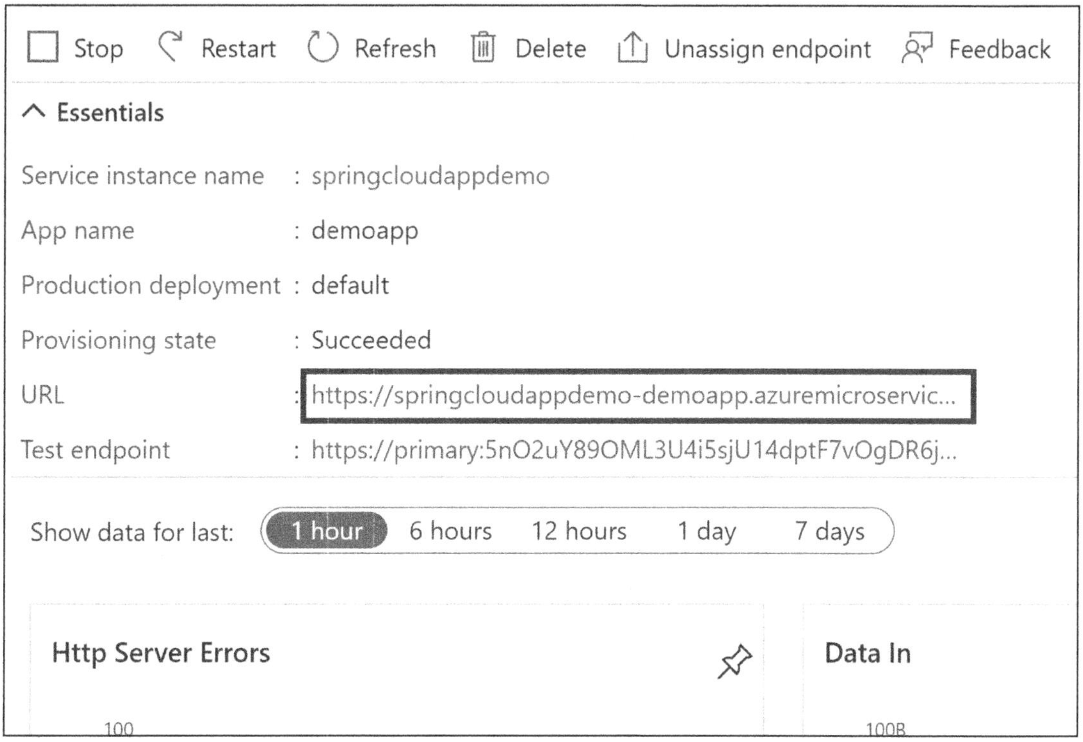

☐ Stop   ↻ Restart   ⟳ Refresh   🗑 Delete   ⬆ Unassign endpoint   👥 Feedback

∧ **Essentials**

Service instance name   : springcloudappdemo

App name   : demoapp

Production deployment : default

Provisioning state   : Succeeded

URL   : https://springcloudappdemo-demoapp.azuremicroservic...

Test endpoint   : https://primary:5nO2uY89OML3U4i5sjU14dptF7vOgDR6j...

Show data for last: (**1 hour**   6 hours   12 hours   1 day   7 days)

Http Server Errors   📌   **Data In**

100   100B

Figure 5-9.   *Click on the Azure Spring Cloud public URL*

The URL will serve you the default app running on the Spring Cloud service as shown in Figure 5-10.

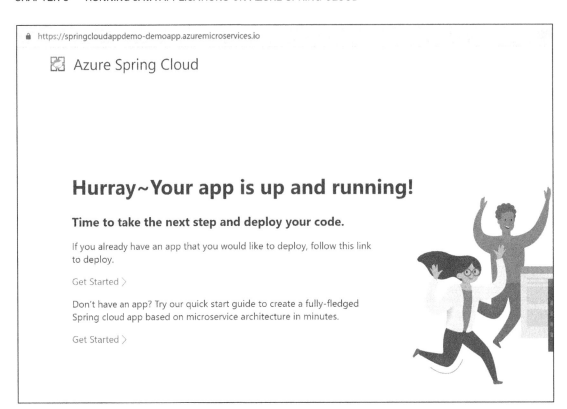

Figure 5-10. *Default page for App*

Deploy a Java Application on Azure Spring Cloud

Now let us build a Java Spring Boot application that we will deploy to the Azure Spring Cloud service we created earlier. We will integrate the Azure Spring Cloud service with Azure Redis Cache using service binding and then write to the Azure Redis Cache from the Java Spring Boot application. We need not write any code or configuration in the application code for the Azure Redis Cache integration.

As a prerequisite, you should have an Azure Redis Cache. We will explore how to provision Azure Redis Cache in Chapter 9.

Let us go to the Spring Initializr using the URL shown in Listing 5-1.

Listing 5-1. Spring Initializr URL

```
https://start.spring.io/
```

Provide group, artifact, name, and other basic details for the project. Select 11 as Java version and JAR as packaging as shown in Figure 5-11.

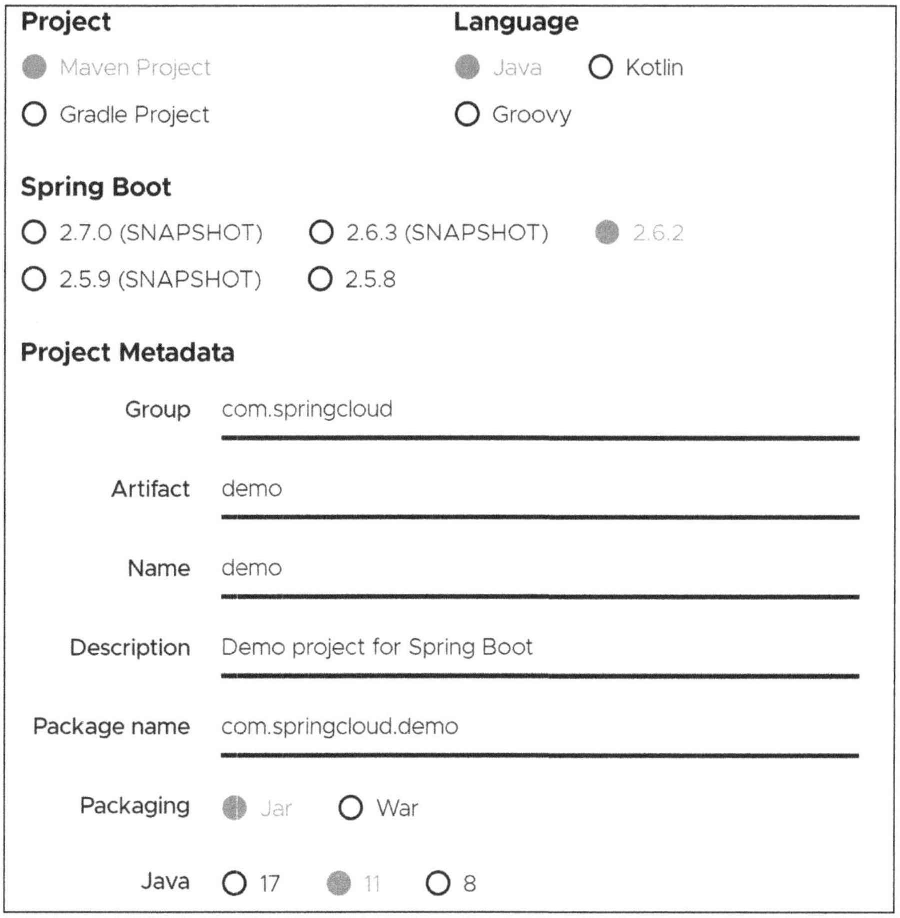

Project   **Language**

⬤ Maven Project   ⬤ Java   ◯ Kotlin

◯ Gradle Project   ◯ Groovy

Spring Boot

◯ 2.7.0 (SNAPSHOT)   ◯ 2.6.3 (SNAPSHOT)   ⬤ 2.6.2

◯ 2.5.9 (SNAPSHOT)   ◯ 2.5.8

Project Metadata

Group   com.springcloud

Artifact   demo

Name   demo

Description   Demo project for Spring Boot

Package name   com.springcloud.demo

Packaging   ⬤ Jar   ◯ War

Java   ◯ 17   ⬤ 11   ◯ 8

Figure 5-11. *Provide project details*

Add the *Spring Web* and *Spring Data Reactive Redis* dependencies and generate the project as shown in Figure 5-12.

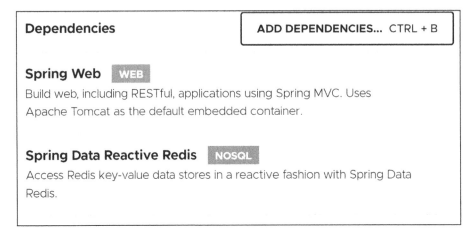

Figure 5-12. *Add project dependencies*

We need to integrate Azure Redis Cache with the Azure Spring Cloud application instance we created. Go to the application instance and then navigate to the *Service bindings* section. Click *Create service binding* as shown in Figure 5-13.

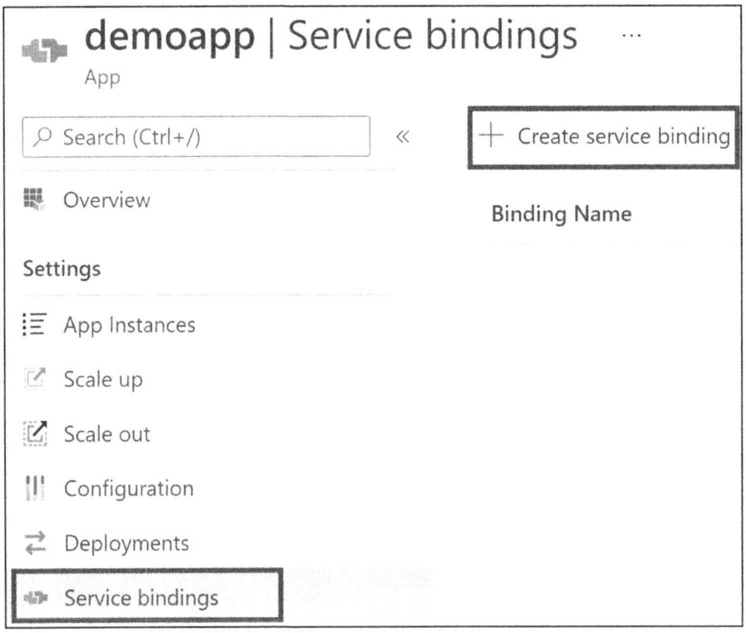

Figure 5-13. *Go to the Service bindings section*

Provide necessary details for the service binding. We need to give a name for the service binding, select the Azure Redis Cache that we need to bind, and provide the access key. You can create a Redis Cache by following the steps mentioned in Chapter 9. Make sure that you select *Use SSL* as *False* as shown in Figure 5-14. The dependency we are using in the application code to work with Azure Redis Cache does not support SSL. To keep things simple, we are using this dependency. However, other dependencies are available for Redis Cache that will work with SSL.

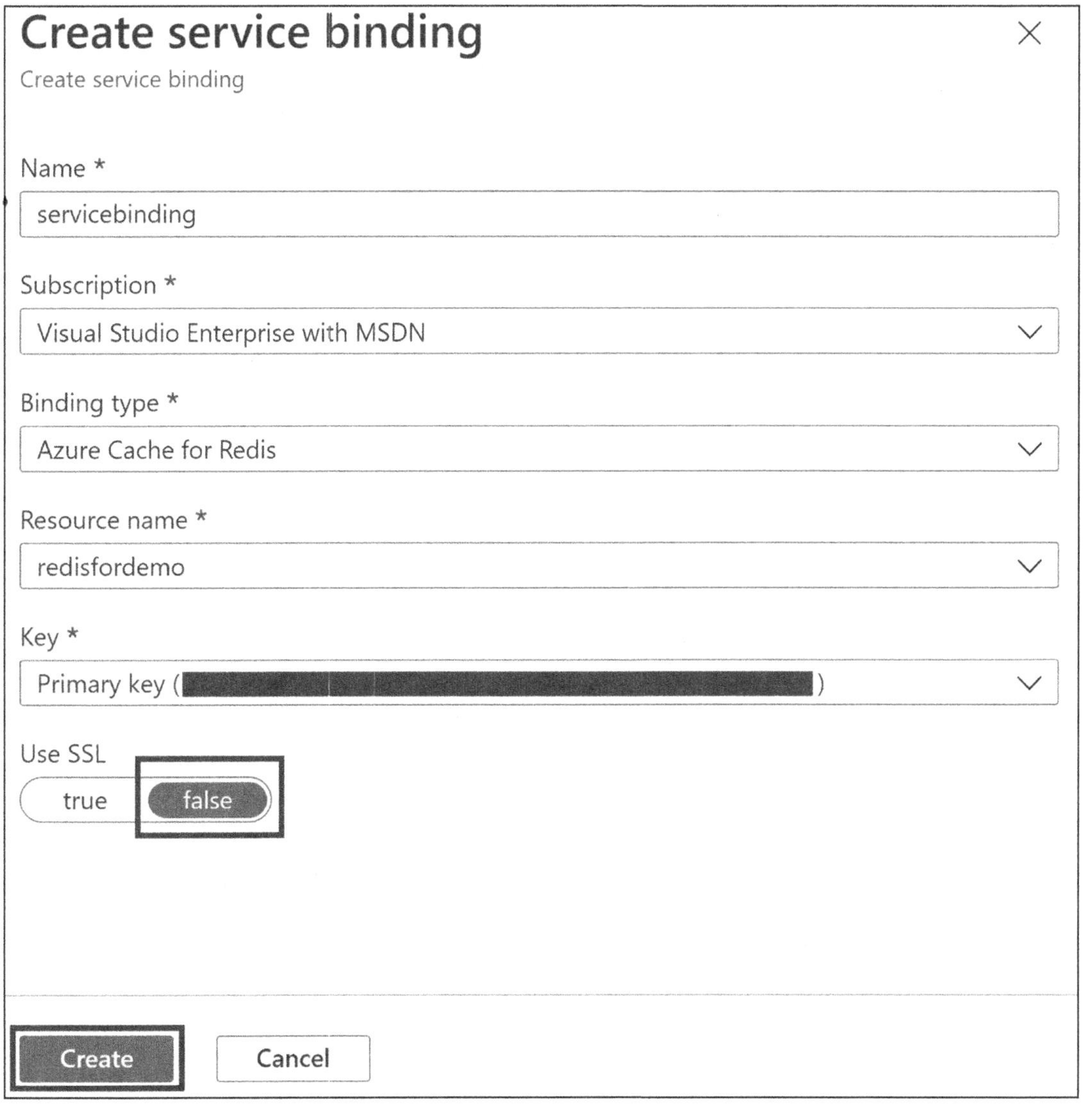

Figure 5-14. *Create service binding*

Modify the Java file having the main function as in Listing 5-2. We have added the *hello* method where we are writing the value *Hello World !!!!* to the Azure Redis Cache using the key *helloworld*. And we are rereading the value and returning from the API call.

Listing 5-2. Write to Azure Redis Cache

```
package com.springcloud.demo;

import org.springframework.web.bind.annotation.RequestMapping;
import org.springframework.web.bind.annotation.RestController;
import org.springframework.beans.factory.annotation.Autowired;
import org.springframework.boot.SpringApplication;
import org.springframework.boot.autoconfigure.SpringBootApplication;
import org.springframework.data.redis.core.StringRedisTemplate;
import org.springframework.data.redis.core.ValueOperations;

@SpringBootApplication
@RestController
public class DemoApplication {

    @Autowired
    private StringRedisTemplate template;

    public static void main(String[] args) {
        SpringApplication.run(DemoApplication.class, args);
    }

    @RequestMapping("/hello")
    public String hello() {
        ValueOperations<String, String> ops = this.template.opsForValue();

        // Add a Hello World string to your cache.
        String key = "helloworld";
        if (!this.template.hasKey(key)) {
        ops.set(key, "Hello World !!!!");
        }
        return ops.get(key);
    }

}
```

Execute the Maven command shown in Listing 5-3 to build and package the JAR file.

Listing 5-3. Package application using Maven

```
mvn clean install
```

Execute the Maven command shown in Listing 5-4 to configure the POM file with Azure Spring Cloud configuration. We will generate Java 8 version POM file that we can change later to Java 11.

Listing 5-4. Configure pom with azure-spring-cloud-maven-plugin

```
mvn com.microsoft.azure:azure-spring-cloud-maven-plugin:1.7.0:config
```

Select your subscription when prompted. Provide the name of the app as the one we created earlier. Ensure that you provide the necessary input to make it a public app when prompted as shown in Figure 5-15.

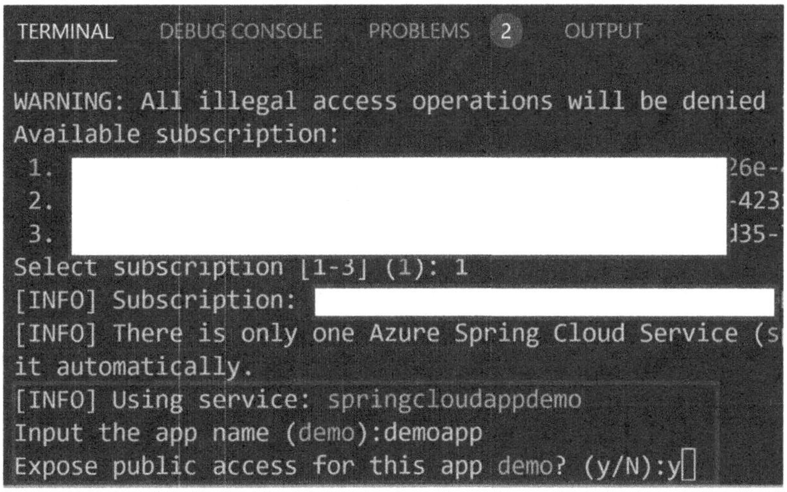

Figure 5-15. *Update the POM file to include Azure Spring Cloud Plugin*

The POM file will get updated with azure-spring-cloud-maven-plugin along with its dependencies. Make sure that you have Java 11 in the plug-in configuration.

Execute the Maven command shown in Listing 5-5 to deploy the JAR file to the Azure Spring Cloud. Browser will prompt you authenticate and sign in to Azure.

Listing 5-5. Deploy the application to Azure Spring Cloud

```
mvn azure-spring-cloud:deploy
```

Make sure that you have enabled non-SSL access for the Azure Redis Cache as shown in Figure 5-16.

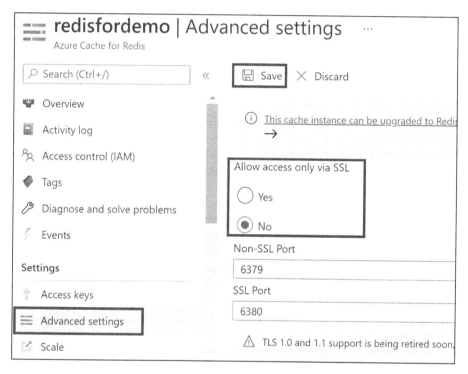

Figure 5-16. *Allow non-SSL access for Azure Redis Cache*

Once the deployment is complete, browse the app URL for the `hello` API, and you can see the value stored in Azure Redis Cache in response as shown in Figure 5-17.

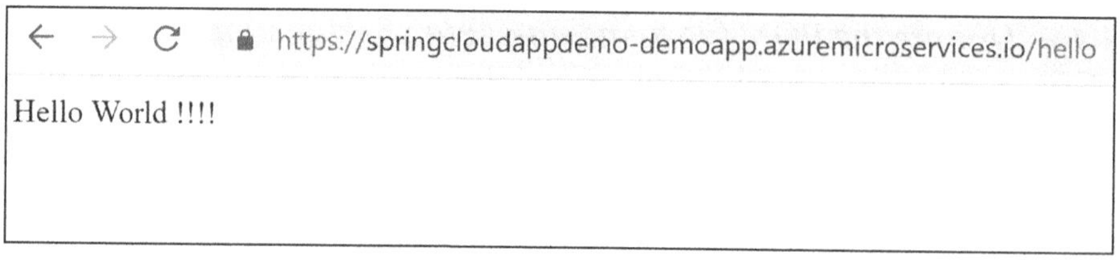

Figure 5-17. *Browse the application running on Azure Spring Cloud*

Summary

In this chapter, we learned the details of Azure Spring Cloud. We learned how to integrate other Azure services with application running on Azure Spring Cloud using service bindings and also explored how to use Maven commands to deploy application jars to Azure Spring Cloud. We then developed a Java Spring Boot application and deployed it on Azure Spring Cloud. In the next chapter, we will learn how to work with Azure Storage programmatically from Java applications.

The following are the key takeaways from this chapter:

- Azure Spring Cloud helps you host Spring Boot applications on Azure without making code changes.

- It can host both Java and .NET Core applications.

- It is best suited for running microservices-based applications.

- You need to focus on building the application. The underlying platform will take care of the hosting requirements. You need to provision the Azure Spring Cloud service and deploy your application on it.

- Using service bindings, you can integrate with other Azure services without making code changes.

PART II

Integrating Java Applications with Popular Azure Services

CHAPTER 6

Integrating with an Azure Storage Account

You may have a requirement to store images, files, and other binary large object data in Azure for your application. You may also need to implement a queue-based data structure for your application or semi-structured table data in Azure. You can use Azure Storage for all such requirements. Microsoft provides packages that can be used in your Java application code to interact with your Storage account.

In the previous chapter, we learned the basics of Azure Spring Cloud. We then created a Java-based application and hosted it on Azure Spring Cloud. In this chapter, we will learn the details of the Azure Storage service, and then we will provision Azure Storage and work with Azure Storage from the Java application code.

Structure

In this chapter, we will discuss the following aspects of the Azure Storage service:

- Introduction to Azure Storage

- Creating an Azure Storage Account

- Working with Azure Storage Blob

- Working with Azure Storage Queue

- Working with Azure Storage Table

© Abhishek Mishra 2022
A. Mishra, *Microsoft Azure for Java Developers*, https://doi.org/10.1007/978-1-4842-8251-9_6

Objectives

After studying this chapter, you should be able to do the following:

- Understand the concept of Azure Storage service

- Work with Azure Storage service from Java applications

Introduction to Azure Storage

Azure Storage is a Platform-as-a-Service offering that stores images, files, and other data objects as blobs. It provides an SMB-based file system to store files and has also support for NFS, offers you a queue-based messaging data store, and helps you store NoSQL table data in the Azure environment. It is highly scalable, available, and secured. The following are offerings for Azure Storage:

- *Azure Containers (Blobs)* help you store images, videos, files, and other binary large object data. You can keep big unstructured data like Virtual Machine disks.

- *Azure Files* provide a managed file share to keep your files and access using SMB, NFS, or HTTP protocol.

- *Azure Queues* provide a queue-based messaging store for your application.

- *Azure Tables* help you store semi-structured NoSQL data.

Data replication is an important design aspect for data stores on the cloud. This mechanism helps you recover data during a disaster or an outage and keeps your business running. Azure Storage supports the following data replications or redundancy mechanisms:

- *Locally Redundant Storage (LRS)* helps you store three copies of your data in the same data center. If the data center goes down, you will not be able to access the data.

- *Zone-Redundant Storage (ZRS)* stores three copies of data in different data centers or storage clusters separated physically in a region. If a data center goes down, you can still access data stored in other data centers. However, if there is a region-wide outage, you will not be able to access the data.

- *Geo-Redundant Storage (GRS)* duplicates your data three times in a primary region, and then all the duplicated set of data is replicated to a secondary region. If the primary region goes down, you can access the data from the secondary region.

- *Read Access Geo-Redundant Storage (RA-GRS)* is the same as Geo-Redundant Storage. However, the data in the secondary region is read-only.

You can choose either a standard tier or a premium tier to store the data on Azure Storage. The Standard tier stores your data in a standard hard disk, and the premium tier stores your data in an SSD disk. The premium tier is more performant than the standard tier. The following are the types of Storage Accounts available on Azure:

- *General Purpose V1* accounts are legacy storage service accounts and support blob, file, queue, and table service. It supports only the standard tier and all replication options except ZRS.

- *General Purpose V2* accounts support blob, file, queue, and table service. It supports the standard and premium tier and all replication options.

- *Blob Storage* helps you store block blobs and append blobs. It supports only the standard tier and all replication options except ZRS.

- *File Storage* provides you with file service. It supports the premium tier and LRS and ZRS replication options.

- *Block Blob* helps you store block blobs and append blobs. It supports the premium tier and LRS and ZRS replication options.

> **Note**   Block Blobs store binary and text data. Page Blobs help you store large files like virtual hard disks. Append Blobs are the same as Block Blobs but highly performant append operations.

Create an Azure Storage Account

Let us create an Azure Storage account. Go to the Azure portal shown in Figure 6-1 and click *Create a resource*. You will be taken to the Marketplace, as shown in Figure 6-2.

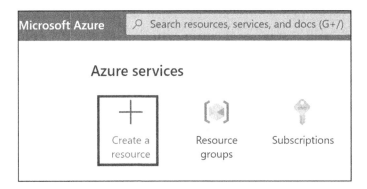

Figure 6-1. *Create a resource*

Search for *Storage Account* in the Marketplace as shown in Figure 6-2. Then click *Create*.

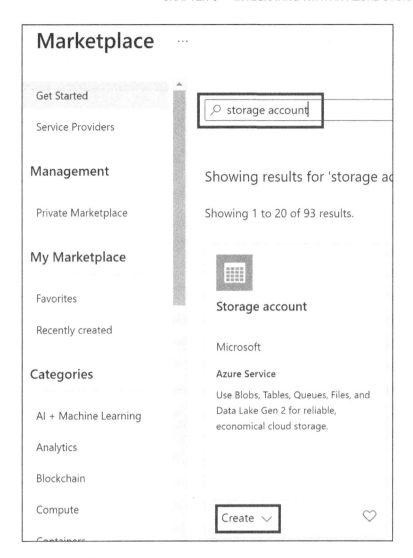

Figure 6-2. *Search for Storage Account*

You will now be on the Create a storage account dialog shown in Figure 6-3. Provide subscription details, resource group name, storage account name, region, and performance tier and click *Review + create.*

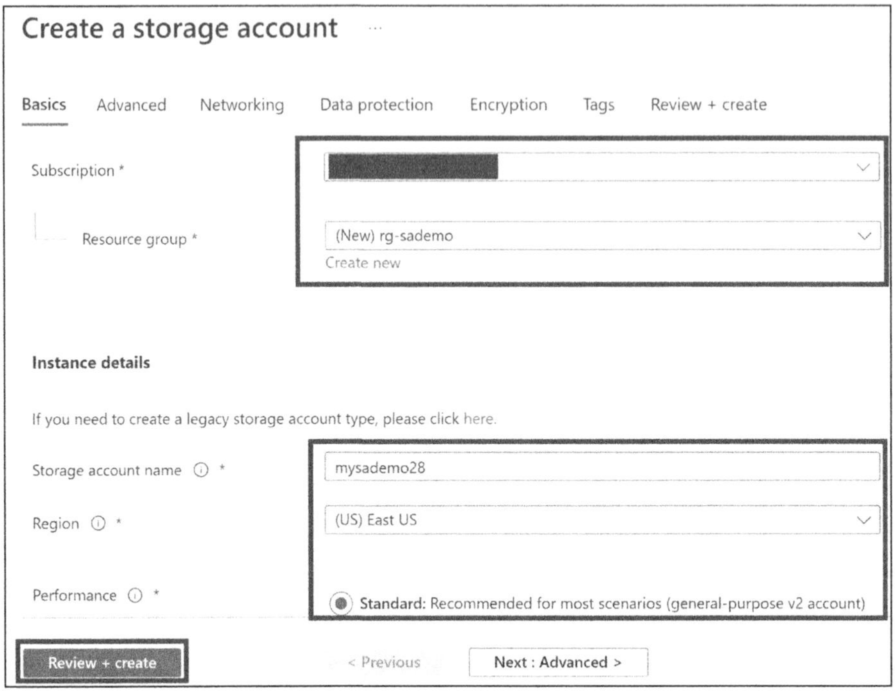

Figure 6-3. *Provide Storage Account basic details*

Click *Create* as shown in Figure 6-4. This would spin up the Storage Account.

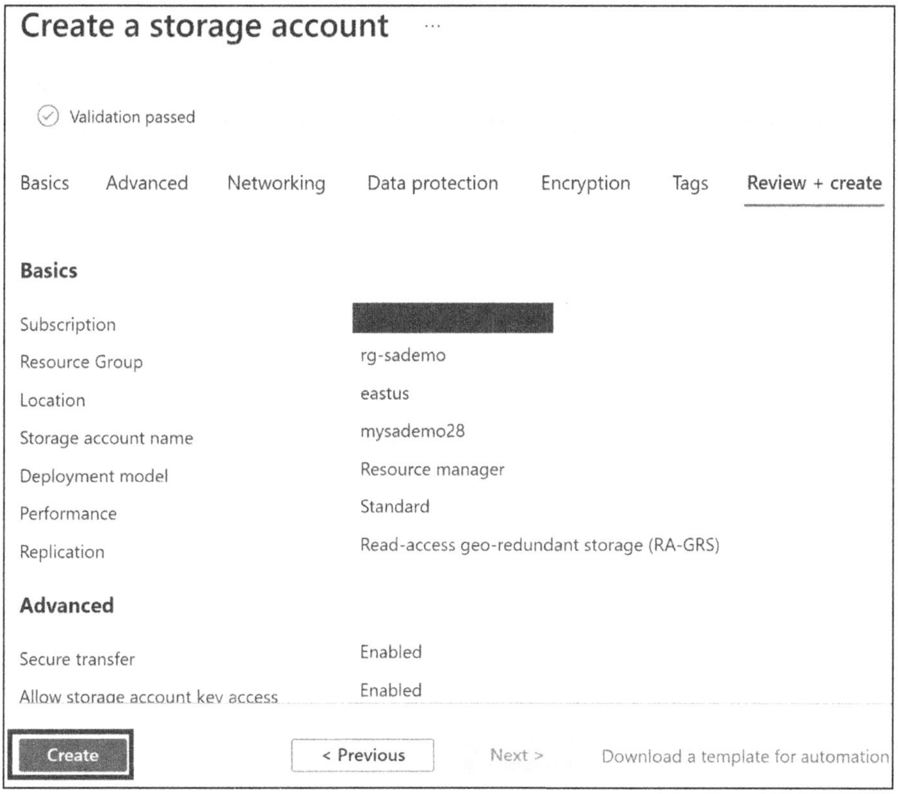

Figure 6-4. *Create Storage Account*

Working with Azure Storage Blob

Let us create a Maven-based Java console application using your favorite Java editors and implement logic to create a blob container, create a blob inside the container, and then read the blob we created inside the container.

Add the package dependency shown in Listing 6-1 to the POM file of your Java application.

Listing 6-1. Storage account package dependency

```
<dependency>
    <groupId>com.azure</groupId>
    <artifactId>azure-storage-blob</artifactId>
    <version>12.13.0</version>
```

```
</dependency>
```

Go to the Storage Account in the Azure portal and get the connection string for the Storage Account in the Access keys section as shown in Figure 6-5.

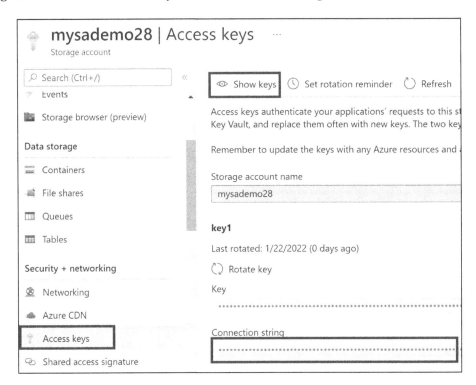

Figure 6-5. *Get access keys*

Now go to the main method of the Java class and add the following code to create a blob container. You need to create a *BlobServiceClient* object to help you work with the blob containers inside the Storage Account. You need to list all available containers using the *listBlobContainers* function and check if your container exists. Create the container using function *createBlobContainer* if it does not exist, else get the reference to the existing container using function *getBlobContainerClient*.

Listing 6-2. Create a container

```
String connectionString = "{Provide your Connection String}";
String containerName = "sample";

// Build the BlobServiceClient from connection string
```

```
BlobServiceClient blobClient = new BlobServiceClientBuilder().connectionStr
ing(connectionString).buildClient();

// Check if Container exists
// List all containers and then check if the container already exists
var existingContainers = blobClient.listBlobContainers();
Boolean containerExists = false;
for(BlobContainerItem containerItem : existingContainers)
{
    if(containerItem.getName().equalsIgnoreCase(containerName)) {
        containerExists = true;
    }
}

//If the container does not exist then create the container
// If the container exists then get reference for the existing container
BlobContainerClient container;
if(!containerExists) {
    // Create container
     container = blobClient.createBlobContainer(containerName);
}
else {
    // Get reference to the existing container
     container = blobClient.getBlobContainerClient(containerName);
}
```

Now let us create a blob with some data inside the container. Use the *getBlobClient* function to create a reference for the blob you are planning to upload, and then use the upload method to *upload* the blob with content *Hello Blob !!!!*. The code is demonstrated in Listing 6-3.

Listing 6-3. Create a blob inside the container

```
//Create a blob inside the container
String blobName = "sample.txt";
BlobClient blob = container.getBlobClient(blobName);
String data = "Hello Blob !!!!";
```

```
InputStream dataStream = new ByteArrayInputStream(data.getBytes(StandardCha
rsets.UTF_8));
blob.upload(dataStream,data.length(),true);
```

Now let us iterate all the blobs in our container and get the data in each blob. Use the *listBlobs* function to get all the blobs inside the container. Iterate through all the blobs and use the *getBlobClient* function to reference the blob. Use the *download* function to get the blob in an output stream as in Listing 6-4.

Listing 6-4. List all blobs and read the blobs

```
// Read all blobs in the container
var blobs = container.listBlobs();
// Iterate through each of the blobs in the container
for(BlobItem blobItem : blobs){
    // Get blob name
    System.out.println("Blob Name : "+blobItem.getName());
    // Read blob data
    BlobClient blobRead = container.getBlobClient(blobItem.getName());
    int blobSize = (int) blobRead.getProperties().getBlobSize();
    ByteArrayOutputStream outputStream = new ByteArrayOutputStream(
    blobSize);
    blobRead.download(outputStream);
    System.out.println("Blob Data : "+outputStream.toString());
}
```

Listing 6-5 is the complete code performing operations on the blob container.

Listing 6-5. Working with the blob container

```
import com.azure.storage.blob.*;
import com.azure.storage.blob.models.*;
import java.io.*;
import java.nio.charset.StandardCharsets;

public class BlobDemo {
    public static void main(String args[])
    {
```

```java
String connectionString = "{Provide Connection String}";

// Build the BlobServiceClient from connection string
BlobServiceClient blobClient = new BlobServiceClientBuilder().conne
ctionString(connectionString).buildClient();

// Check if Container exists
// List all containers and then check if the container
already exists
var existingContainers = blobClient.listBlobContainers();
Boolean containerExists = false;
for(BlobContainerItem containerItem : existingContainers)
{
    if(containerItem.getName().equalsIgnoreCase(containerName)) {
        containerExists = true;
    }
}

//If the container does not exist then create the container
// If the container exists then get reference for the existing
container
BlobContainerClient container;
if(!containerExists) {
    // Create container
     container = blobClient.createBlobContainer(containerName);
}
else {
    // Get reference to the existing container
     container = blobClient.getBlobContainerClient(containerName);
}

//Create a blob inside the container
String blobName = "sample.txt";
BlobClient blob = container.getBlobClient(blobName);
String data = "Hello Blob !!!!";
InputStream dataStream = new ByteArrayInputStream(data.
getBytes(StandardCharsets.UTF_8));
```

```
        blob.upload(dataStream,data.length(),true);

        // Read all blobs in the container
        var blobs = container.listBlobs();
        // Iterate through each of the blobs in the container
        for(BlobItem blobItem : blobs){
            // Get blob name
            System.out.println("Blob Name : "+blobItem.getName());
            // Read blob data
            BlobClient blobRead = container.getBlobClient(blobItem.
            getName());
            int blobSize = (int) blobRead.getProperties().getBlobSize();
            ByteArrayOutputStream outputStream = new ByteArrayOutputStream(
            blobSize);
            blobRead.download(outputStream);
            System.out.println("Blob Data : "+outputStream.toString());
        }
    }
}
```

You can also see the container created and the blob in the Azure portal as shown in Figure 6-6 once you execute the project.

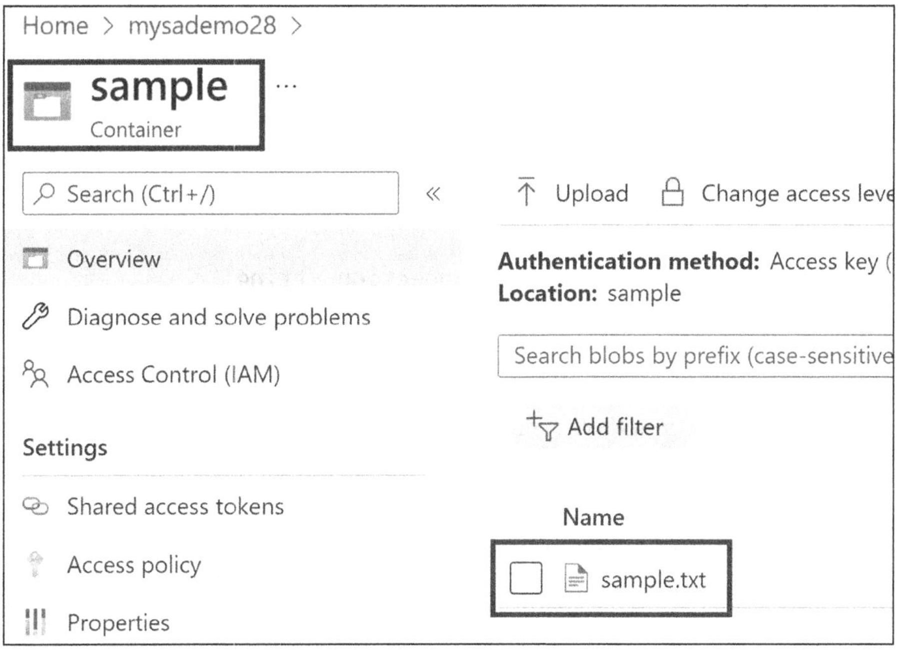

Figure 6-6. *Container and blob created*

Working with Azure Storage Queue

Let us create a Maven-based Java console application using your favorite Java editors and implement logic to create a storage queue, send messages to the queue, and then read the messages from the queue.

Listing 6-6 shows a package dependency. Add that dependency to the POM file of your Java application.

Listing 6-6. Add package dependency to the POM file

```
<dependency>
    <groupId>com.azure</groupId>
    <artifactId>azure-storage-queue</artifactId>
    <version>12.0.1</version>
</dependency>
```

We have already copied the connection string from the Azure portal. Let us go to the main method and add the following code to create the queue. We are getting the *QueueCient* object and creating a queue using the *create* function as in Listing 6-7.

Listing 6-7. Create a queue

```
String queueName = "sample-queue";
String connectionString = "{Provide connection string}";

// Get reference to QueueClient
QueueClient queueClient = new QueueClientBuilder().connectionString(connect
ionString).queueName(queueName).buildClient();

//Create Queue
queueClient.create();
```

We are adding messages to the queue using *sendMessage* function as in Listing 6-8.

Listing 6-8. Add messages to the queue

```
//Add message to the Queue
queueClient.sendMessage("My Message Added");
queueClient.sendMessage("My Message Added 01");
queueClient.sendMessage("My Message Added 02");
queueClient.sendMessage("My Message Added 04");
```

We are reading the first message from the queue using the *peekMessage* function as in Listing 6-9.

Listing 6-9. Peek message from queue

```
//Peek message from the Queue
var message = queueClient.peekMessage();
System.out.println("Peek first message in queue : "+message.
getMessageText());
```

We are reading all the messages from the queue and deleting the read messages using the *receiveMessages* function as in Listing 6-10.

Listing 6-10. Read all messages from queue

```
//Get all messages from the queue and remove them from the queue
var messages = queueClient.receiveMessages(queueClient.getProperties().
getApproximateMessagesCount());

for(QueueMessageItem msg:messages){
    System.out.println("Added Message : "+msg.getMessageText());
}
```

Listing 6-11 shows the complete code to perform queue operations. You can check the item that got added in the Storage Queue. Go to the storage account in the Azure portal and click *Storage browser* and then click *Queue*.

Listing 6-11. Working with storage queue

```
import com.azure.storage.queue.*;
import com.azure.storage.queue.models.*;
import java.io.*;
import java.nio.charset.StandardCharsets;

public class QueueDemo {
    public static void main(String args[])
    {
        String queueName = "sample-queue";
        String connectionString = "{Provide connection string}";

        // Get reference to QueueClient
        QueueClient queueClient = new QueueClientBuilder().connectionString
        (connectionString).queueName(queueName).buildClient();

        //Create Queue
        queueClient.create();

        //Add message to the Queue
        queueClient.sendMessage("My Message Added");
        queueClient.sendMessage("My Message Added 01");
        queueClient.sendMessage("My Message Added 02");
        queueClient.sendMessage("My Message Added 04");
```

```
        //Peek message from the Queue
        var message = queueClient.peekMessage();
        System.out.println("Peek first message in queue : "+message.
        getMessageText());

        //Get all messages from the queue and remove them from the queue
        var messages = queueClient.receiveMessages(queueClient.
        getProperties().getApproximateMessagesCount());

        for(QueueMessageItem msg:messages){
            System.out.println("Added Message : "+msg.getMessageText());
        }
    }
}
```

Working with Table Storage

Now let us work with Table Storage. We will create a table, add a record to it, and then retrieve the record from the table. Table Storage stores data using partition key and row key. Partition key helps you spread the data across multiple partitions. For example, you are storing geographic data; you can use country names as partition keys. You can store the country-specific data in the partition represented by the country name as the partition key. Row key is the primary key for the data you are storing in the partition.

Let us add the following package dependency in the POM file as in Listing 6-12.

Listing 6-12. Add dependency

```
<dependency>
    <groupId>com.azure</groupId>
    <artifactId>azure-data-tables</artifactId>
    <version>12.1.5</version>
</dependency>
```

We have already copied the connection string from the Azure portal. Let us go to the main method and add the following code to create the table. We are getting the *TableServiceClient* object and creating a queue using the *createTableIfNotExists* function as in Listing 6-13. The table will only be created if it does not exist.

Listing 6-13. Create the table

```
String tableName="students";
String connectionString="{Provide Connection String}";

// Create table
TableServiceClient tableServiceClient = new TableServiceClientBuilder()
        .connectionString(connectionString)
        .buildClient();
TableClient tableClient = tableServiceClient.createTableIfNotExists(t
ableName);
```

We created the *TableEntity* object using the row key and the partition key for the
data. We then populated the properties for the *TableEntity* object with the data we need
to insert into the table as in Listing 6-14.

Listing 6-14. Add record to table

```
// Add record to the table
String partitionKey="Electronics Department";
String rowKey="Sam";
TableEntity entity = new TableEntity(partitionKey, rowKey)
        .addProperty("Age", 22)
        .addProperty("Grade", "A")
        .addProperty("Marks", 88);

tableClient.createEntity(entity);

// Add another record to the table
tableClient = tableServiceClient.getTableClient(tableName);
rowKey = "Rob";
entity = new TableEntity(partitionKey, rowKey)
        .addProperty("Age", 24)
        .addProperty("Grade", "B")
        .addProperty("Marks", 60);

tableClient.createEntity(entity);
```

We can form a filter query and fetch the data stored in the table as in Listing 6-15. The *listEntities* function fetches the data from the table.

Listing 6-15. Retrieve records from the table

```
//Retrieve the records in the table
tableClient = tableServiceClient.getTableClient(tableName);
String filterQuery = "PartitionKey eq 'Electronics Department'";
ListEntitiesOptions options = new ListEntitiesOptions().
setFilter(filterQuery);

// Loop through the result set and display.
tableClient.listEntities(options, null, null).forEach(tableEntity -> {
    System.out.println(tableEntity.getPartitionKey() +
            " " + tableEntity.getRowKey() +
            "\t" + tableEntity.getProperty("Age") +
            "\t" + tableEntity.getProperty("Grade") +
            "\t" + tableEntity.getProperty("Marks"));
});
```

Listing 6-16 shows the complete code for the table operation.

Listing 6-16. Table operation

```
import com.azure.data.tables.*;
import com.azure.data.tables.models.*;

import java.io.*;
import java.nio.charset.StandardCharsets;

public class TableDemo {
    public static void main(String args[])
    {
        String tableName="students";
        String connectionString="{Provide Connection String}";

        // Create table
        TableServiceClient tableServiceClient =
        new   TableServiceClientBuilder()
```

```
        .connectionString(connectionString)
        .buildClient();
TableClient tableClient = tableServiceClient.createTableIfNotExists
(tableName);

// Add record to the table
String partitionKey="Electronics Department";
String rowKey="Sam";
TableEntity entity = new TableEntity(partitionKey, rowKey)
        .addProperty("Age", 22)
        .addProperty("Grade", "A")
        .addProperty("Marks", 88);

tableClient.createEntity(entity);

// Add another record to the table
tableClient = tableServiceClient.getTableClient(tableName);
rowKey = "Rob";
entity = new TableEntity(partitionKey, rowKey)
        .addProperty("Age", 24)
        .addProperty("Grade", "B")
        .addProperty("Marks", 60);

tableClient.createEntity(entity);

//Retrieve the records in the table
tableClient = tableServiceClient.getTableClient(tableName);
String filterQuery = "PartitionKey eq 'Electronics Department'";
ListEntitiesOptions options = new ListEntitiesOptions().
setFilter(filterQuery);

// Loop through the result set and display.
tableClient.listEntities(options, null, null).
forEach(tableEntity -> {
    System.out.println(tableEntity.getPartitionKey() +
            " " + tableEntity.getRowKey() +
            "\t" + tableEntity.getProperty("Age") +
            "\t" + tableEntity.getProperty("Grade") +
```

```
                    "\t" + tableEntity.getProperty("Marks"));
    });

  }
}
```

Let us check the table that got added in the Storage Account. Go to the storage account in the Azure portal and click *Storage browser* and then click *Tables* as shown in Figure 6-7.

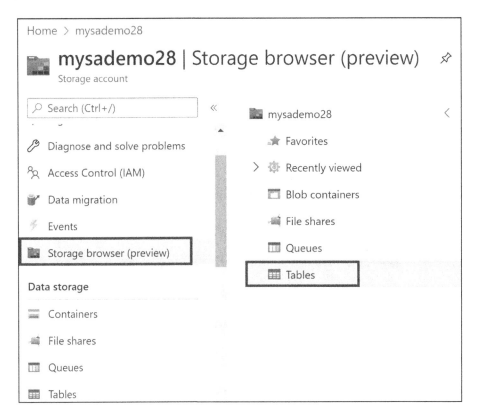

Figure 6-7. *Go to Storage browser*

You can see the table that we created as shown in Figure 6-8.

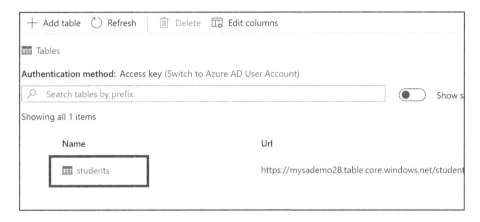

Figure 6-8. *Click on the table we created*

Click on the table we created. You can see the data we added in the table as shown in Figure 6-9.

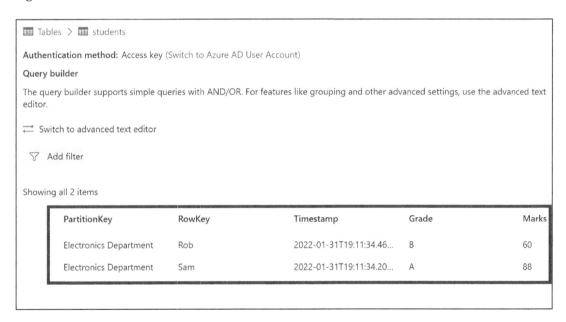

Figure 6-9. *Data added to the table*

Summary

In this chapter, we learned the details of Azure Storage and explored the concept of Blob, Queue, Table, and File. We learned how to create an Azure Storage using the Azure portal. We then developed a Java code and then performed operations on Queue, Table, and Blob. In the next chapter, we will learn how to work with Azure SQL database programmatically from Java applications.

The following are the key takeaways from this chapter:

- Azure Containers (Blobs) help you store images, videos, files, and other binary large object data.

- Azure Files provide a managed file share to keep your files and access using SMB, NFS, or HTTP protocol.

- Azure Queues provide a queue-based messaging store for your application.

- Azure Tables help you store semi-structured NoSQL data.

- Azure Storage is a Platform-as-a-Service offering that stores images, files, and other data objects as blobs. It provides an SMB-based file system to store files, offers you a queue-based messaging data store, and helps you store NoSQL table data in the Azure environment.

## CHAPTER 7

Azure SQL from Java Applications

Applications use a relational database to store data. We need to set up a relational database server and host the application database on the server. Azure provides an SQL database that is a Platform-as-a-Service offering. You need not purchase any server infrastructure or create a virtual machine on the cloud to install the SQL server. Instead, you need to provision the SQL database service on Azure and start using the database. And when you do not need the database anymore, you can decommission the service.

In the previous chapter, we learned the Azure Storage service concepts. We then created a Java-based application and worked with Azure Storage services. In this chapter, we will learn the details of the Azure SQL database service, and then we will provision the Azure SQL database and work with the Azure SQL database from the Java application code.

Structure

In this chapter, we will discuss the following aspects of the Azure Storage service:

- Introduction to Azure SQL database
- Create an Azure SQL database
- Work with Azure SQL database
- Securing Azure databases

Objectives

After studying this chapter, you should be able to get the following learnings:

© Abhishek Mishra 2022
A. Mishra, *Microsoft Azure for Java Developers*, https://doi.org/10.1007/978-1-4842-8251-9_7

- Understand the concept of the Azure SQL database

- Work with Azure SQL database from Java application

Introduction to Azure SQL Database

Azure provides relational databases like Microsoft SQL, MySQL, PostgreSQL, and MariaDB as Platform-as-a-Service offerings. The Azure platform manages the underlying server infrastructure for these databases. You can spin out these databases in a few minutes and start using them. The data stored in these databases are highly scalable, secured, and available. You can provision the database matching your compute needs and desired performance level.

The underlying Azure platform manages all database activities like backup, patching, and upgrades. Azure SQL database always runs on the latest stable version for the Microsoft SQL Server engine. The underlying platform automatically updates the SQL database engine without manual intervention whenever a new stable version is available. It is highly available and provides 99.99% availability.

You may choose to deploy a single database that is fully managed by the underlying Azure platform and guarantees you isolation from other databases or choose to run multiple single databases on an elastic pool sharing the compute resources like CPU and memory. You can provision the SQL database using the vCore-based purchasing model, where you can reserve the amount of memory, number of vCores, and storage speed based on your requirements. You may also choose the DTU-based purchasing model for the SQL database, where you can choose the number of DTUs based on your requirement. Azure SQL also provides a serverless purchase model. You will get billed only when the SQL database is used, and there are database transactions for serverless databases. When there are no transactions, then the database goes to the idle state and wakes up whenever there is a database transaction.

Note   DTU stands for Database Transaction Unit and is a number based on the combination of CPU, Memory, and Data I/O performance specification.

Azure SQL database does not support Microsoft SQL Server features like linked server, SQL agent, SQL data sync, SQL Auditing, Service Broker, and many more. You may face challenges in migrating an on-premises SQL Server database as is to Azure if you are using such features. However, you can use Azure SQL Managed Instance in such cases that supports almost all the on-premises SQL Server Enterprise Edition capabilities on Azure. Azure SQL Managed Instance is also a Platform-as-a-Service relational database offering on Azure. You can get native Virtual Network Integration with Azure SQL Managed Instance that is not supported by Azure SQL Database. However, features like SQL Server Analysis Services (SSAS) and SQL Server Reporting Services (SSRS) are not supported by Azure SQL Managed Instance and Azure SQL Database.

Create an Azure SQL Database

Let us create an Azure SQL database using the Azure portal as in Figure 7-1. Go to the Azure portal and click *Create a resource*. We will create a table in the database and connect to the table from the Java Spring Boot application.

Figure 7-1. *Create a resource*

You will get navigated to Azure Marketplace. Click *Databases* and then click *SQL Database* as in Figure 7-2.

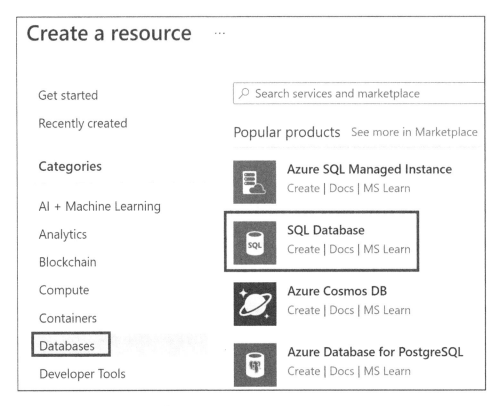

Figure 7-2. *Click SQL Database*

Let us provide the subscription details, resource group name, and name of the database. We need to create a database server on which the database will reside. You may choose to reuse an existing database or create a new database. Let us create a new one. Click *Create new* as in Figure 7-3.

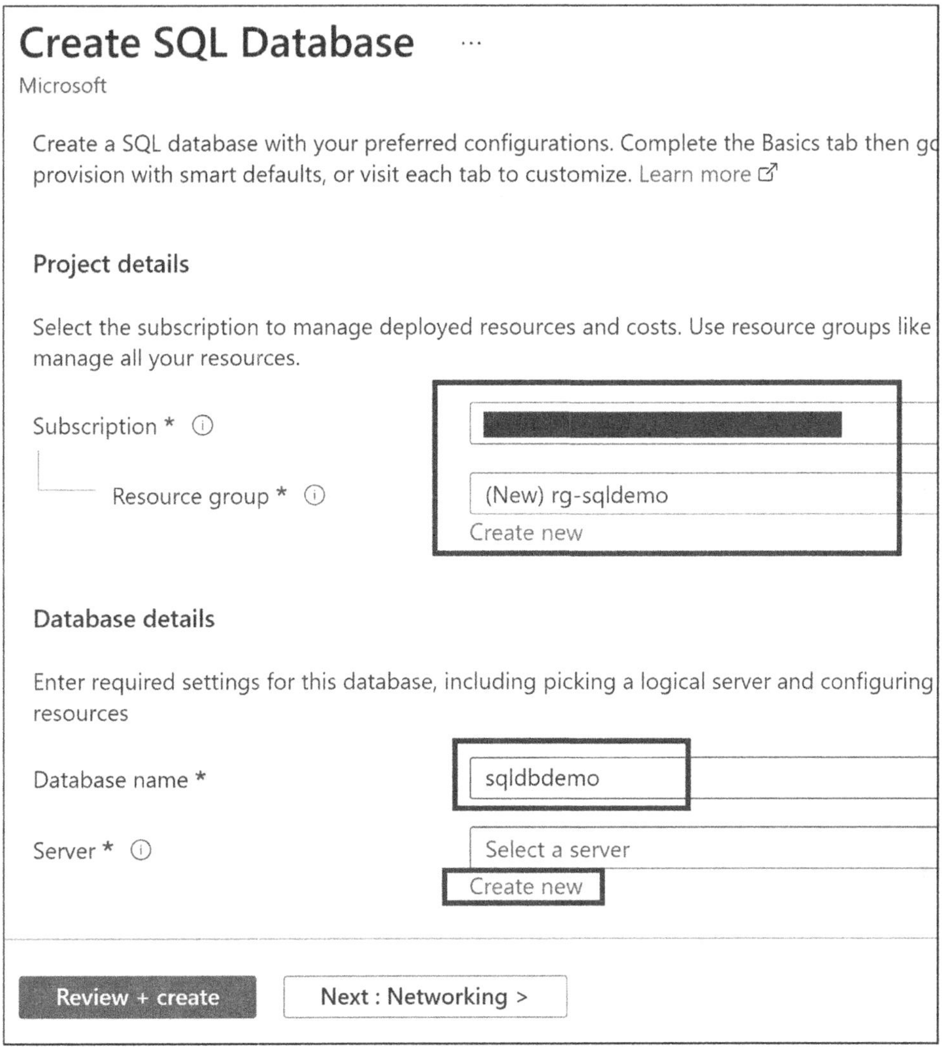

Create SQL Database ⋯

Microsoft

Create a SQL database with your preferred configurations. Complete the Basics tab then g̣
provision with smart defaults, or visit each tab to customize. Learn more ☐

Project details

Select the subscription to manage deployed resources and costs. Use resource groups like
manage all your resources.

Subscription * ⓘ

        Resource group * ⓘ

(New) rg-sqldemo

Create new

Database details

Enter required settings for this database, including picking a logical server and configuring
resources

Database name *

sqldbdemo

Server * ⓘ

Select a server

Create new

Review + create   Next : Networking >

Figure 7-3. *Provide basic details*

Provide the name of the SQL server and the authentication details, and then click *OK*
as in Figure 7-4. You will get navigated back to the *basic* tab.

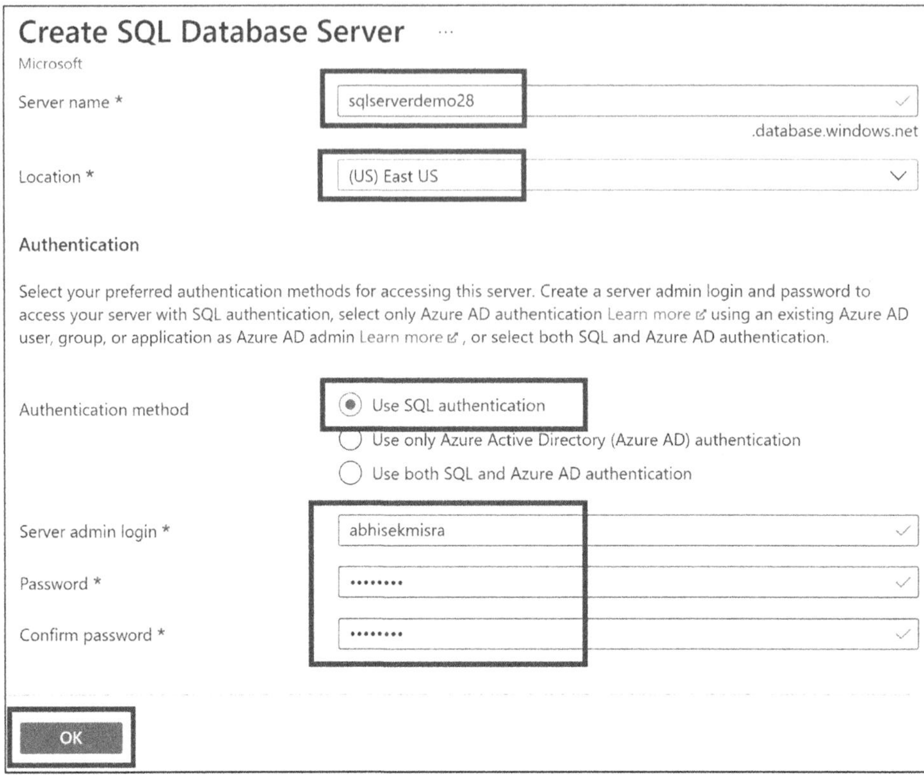

Figure 7-4. *Provide database credentials*

Scroll down and select the right compute and storage requirement based on your need. You will get billed accordingly. Click *Next : Networking* to navigate to the networking tab as in Figure 7-5.

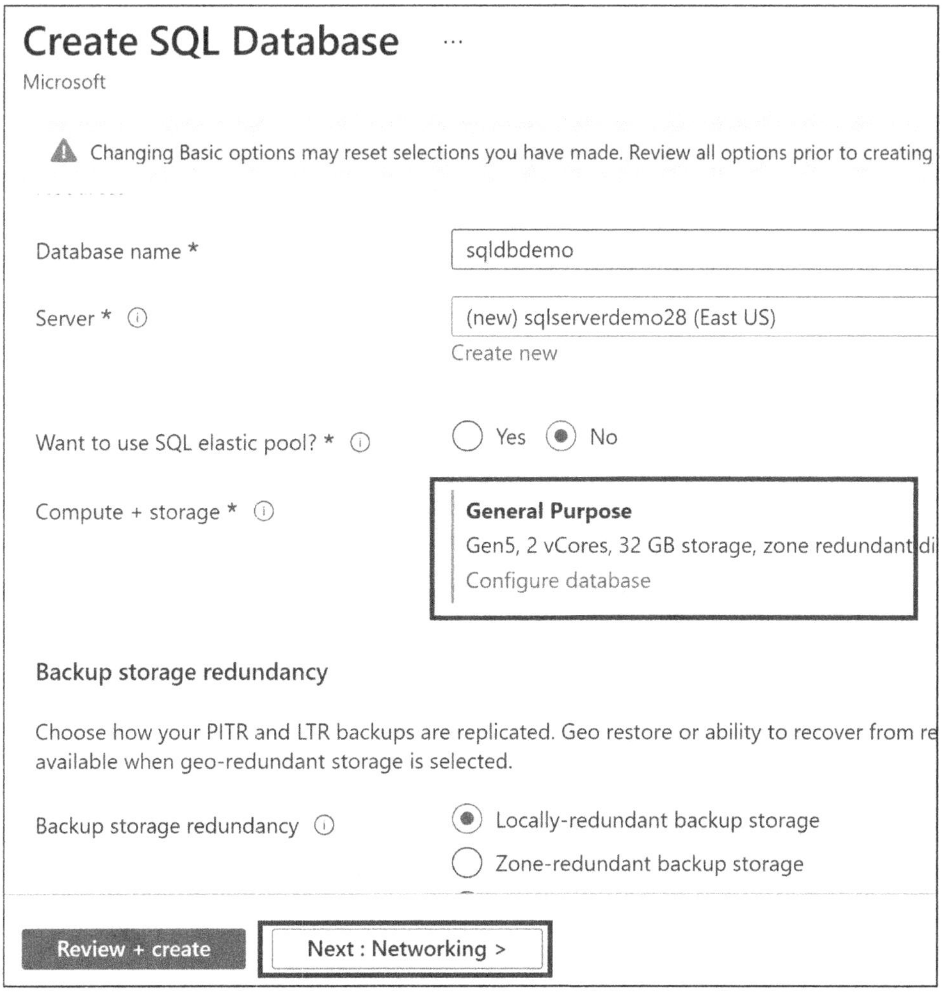

Create SQL Database ...

Microsoft

⚠ Changing Basic options may reset selections you have made. Review all options prior to creating

Database name *	sqldbdemo
Server * ⓘ	(new) sqlserverdemo28 (East US)
	Create new

Want to use SQL elastic pool? * ⓘ   ◯ Yes ⦿ No

Compute + storage * ⓘ

General Purpose
Gen5, 2 vCores, 32 GB storage, zone redundant di
Configure database

Backup storage redundancy

Choose how your PITR and LTR backups are replicated. Geo restore or ability to recover from re available when geo-redundant storage is selected.

Backup storage redundancy ⓘ   ⦿ Locally-redundant backup storage
                                 ◯ Zone-redundant backup storage

[Review + create] [Next : Networking >]

Figure 7-5. *Provide basic details*

In the demo, we will access it over the public Internet. Select *Public endpoint.* Add the IP address of your laptop to the firewall settings so that you can access the database from the code running on your laptop. Click *Review + create* as in Figure 7-6.

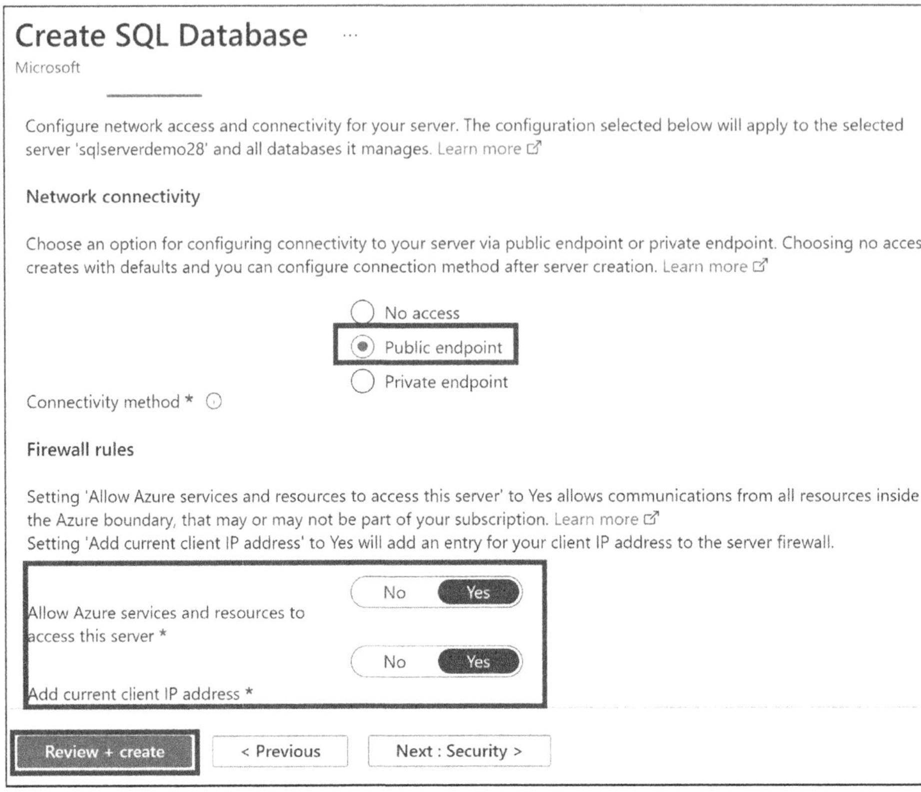

Create SQL Database ...
Microsoft

Configure network access and connectivity for your server. The configuration selected below will apply to the selected server 'sqlserverdemo28' and all databases it manages. Learn more ⬈

Network connectivity

Choose an option for configuring connectivity to your server via public endpoint or private endpoint. Choosing no access creates with defaults and you can configure connection method after server creation. Learn more ⬈

    ○ No access
    ◉ Public endpoint
    ○ Private endpoint

Connectivity method * ⓘ

Firewall rules

Setting 'Allow Azure services and resources to access this server' to Yes allows communications from all resources inside the Azure boundary, that may or may not be part of your subscription. Learn more ⬈
Setting 'Add current client IP address' to Yes will add an entry for your client IP address to the server firewall.

Allow Azure services and resources to access this server * | No   **Yes** |

Add current client IP address * | No   **Yes** |

| **Review + create** | | < Previous | | Next : Security > |

Figure 7-6. *Click Review + create*

Review the configuration and click *Create* as in Figure 7-7. The Azure SQL database will get created.

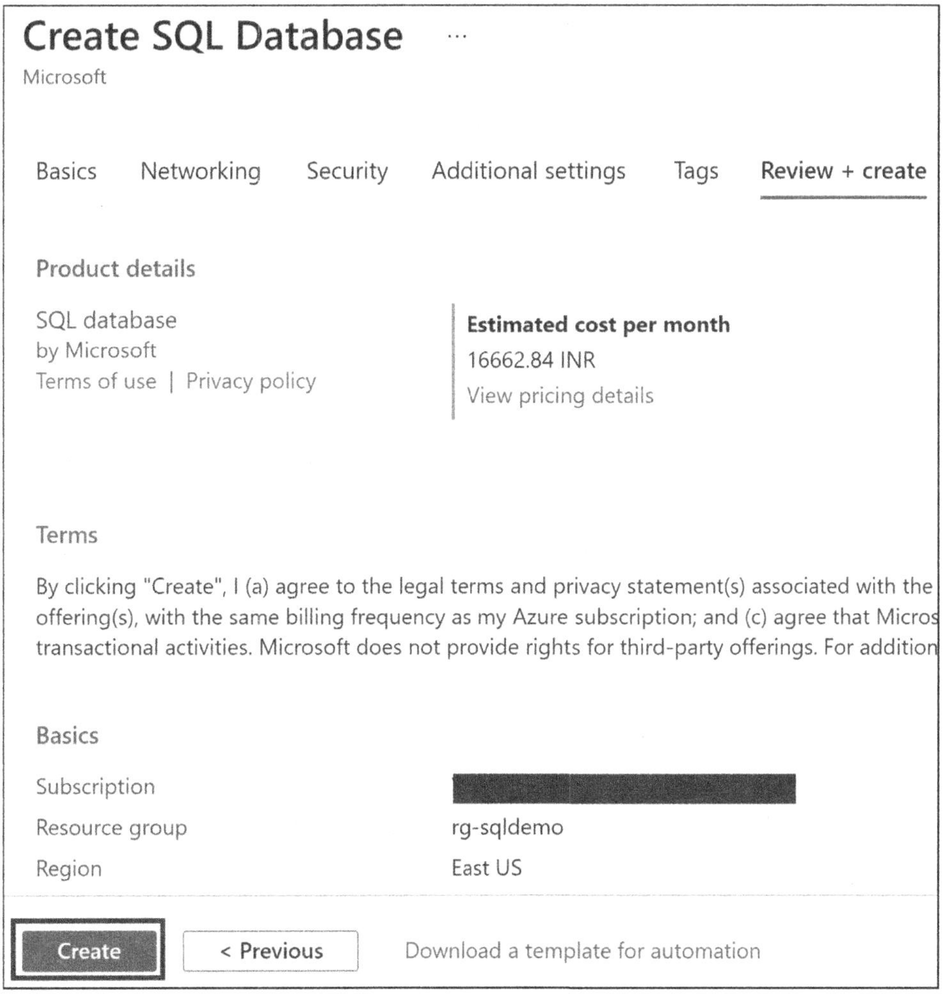

Create SQL Database ...

Microsoft

Basics   Networking   Security   Additional settings   Tags   **Review + create**

Product details

SQL database
by Microsoft
Terms of use | Privacy policy

Estimated cost per month

16662.84 INR

View pricing details

Terms

By clicking "Create", I (a) agree to the legal terms and privacy statement(s) associated with the
offering(s), with the same billing frequency as my Azure subscription; and (c) agree that Micros
transactional activities. Microsoft does not provide rights for third-party offerings. For addition

Basics

Subscription

Resource group   rg-sqldemo

Region   East US

[Create]   [< Previous]   Download a template for automation

Figure 7-7. *Click Create*

Once the SQL database gets created, go to the SQL database in the Azure portal and
click *Connection strings* as in Figure 7-8. Copy the Connection string for *JDBC*. We will
need this in our code to connect to the database.

Figure 7-8. *Go to Connection strings*

Azure portal provides query editor. Click *Query editor* as in Figure 7-9, and provide the database credentials. Now let us create a table named *student*.

Figure 7-9. *SQL query editor*

Execute the script from Listing 7-1 in the query editor to create a student table.

Listing 7-1. Create a student table

```
create table student
(
    roll int identity primary key,
    name varchar(100),
    age int,
    marks int
)
```

Work with Azure SQL Database

Let us develop a Java Spring Boot code that will insert records into the student table and get the data inserted from the student table. Go to the Spring Initializr portal using the URL shown in Listing 7-2.

Listing 7-2. Spring Initializr URL

```
https://start.spring.io/
```

Provide the Maven project details. Make sure that you select Java 11 as the runtime version as in Figure 7-10.

Figure 7-10. *Provide project details*

Add the Spring Web, Spring Data JDBC, and MS SQL Server Driver dependencies as in Figure 7-11 and generate the Java Spring Boot project.

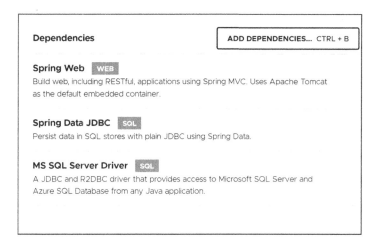

Figure 7-11. *Add dependencies*

Let us create a *Student* class as in Listing 7-3 in the folder where the *DemoApplication* class is present. The *Student* class works as a domain model for the *student* database table.

Listing 7-3. Student class

```
package com.database.demo;

import org.springframework.data.annotation.Id;

public class Student {

    public Student(){

    }

    public Student(String name, int age, int marks){
        this.name = name;
        this.age = age;
        this.marks = marks;
    }

    @Id
    private int roll;
```

```java
    private String name;

    private int age;

    private int marks;

    private int getRoll()
    {
        return roll;
    }

    private void setRoll(int roll)
    {
        this.roll = roll;
    }

    public String getName() {
        return name;
    }

    public void setName(String name) {
        this.name = name;
    }

    public int getAge() {
        return age;
    }

    public void setAge(int age) {
        this.age = age;
    }

    public int getMarks() {
        return marks;
    }

    public void setMarks(int marks) {
        this.marks = marks;
    }
}
```

Now let us add a *StudentRepository* interface as in Listing 7-4 in the same folder where we have the *Student* class and the *DemoApplication* class. The *StudentRepository* interface works as the repository class for the database and the domain model. The Spring Data JDBC manages this repository class.

Listing 7-4. StudentRepository class

```
package com.database.demo;

import org.springframework.data.repository.CrudRepository;
public interface StudentRepository extends CrudRepository<Student,
Integer> {
}
```

Go to the *application.properties* file in the *src/main/resources* folder and add the database connection details as in Listing 7-5. You can get the connection details from the connection string we copied earlier for the database. Make sure that you replace *[database name]* with the name of the database, *[database server name]* with the name of the database server, *[username]* with your database username, and *[password]* with the database password.

Listing 7-5. Application.properties file

```
logging.level.org.springframework.jdbc.core=DEBUG

spring.datasource.url=jdbc:sqlserver://[database server
name].database.windows.net:1433;database=[database
name];encrypt=true;trustServerCertificate=false;hostNameInCertificate=*.
database.windows.net;loginTimeout=30;
spring.datasource.username=[username]@[database server name]
spring.datasource.password=[password]

spring.sql.init.mode=always
```

Go to the *DemoApplication* Java class and convert it into a REST Controller using the *RestController* attribute. Add the *createStudents* POST method to insert a Student record to the student table and add a *getStudents* GET method to fetch all the records in the *student* table. See Listing 7-6 for the code.

Listing 7-6. DemoApplication class

```java
package com.database.demo;

import org.springframework.boot.SpringApplication;
import org.springframework.boot.autoconfigure.SpringBootApplication;
import org.springframework.http.HttpStatus;
import org.springframework.web.bind.annotation.*;

@SpringBootApplication
@RestController
@RequestMapping("/")
public class DemoApplication {

    public static void main(String[] args) {
        SpringApplication.run(DemoApplication.class, args);
    }

    private final StudentRepository studentRepository;

    public DemoApplication(StudentRepository studentRepository) {
        this.studentRepository = studentRepository;
    }

    @PostMapping("/")
    @ResponseStatus(HttpStatus.CREATED)
    public Student createStudents(@RequestBody Student student) {
        return studentRepository.save(student);
    }

    @GetMapping("/")
    public Iterable<Student> getStudents() {
        return studentRepository.findAll();
    }

}
```

Run the application. Once the application is started, go to the Postman tool and fire a POST call to insert a record. Make sure that you have added the Content-Type header as in Figure 7-12.

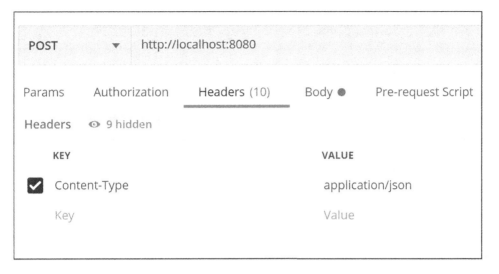

Figure 7-12. *Add the Content-Type header*

Note   To build and run your application, navigate to the application folder where the POM file is there. Run the command `mvn clean install` to build the JAR. Navigate to the folder where the JAR file got generated and run the command `java -jar [jar name]` to start the application.

Fire the POST call in the Postman tool as in Figure 7-13.

Figure 7-13. *Fire the POST call*

Go to the Query Editor in the SQL Server service in the Azure portal and execute a select query, and you can see the inserted record as in Figure 7-14.

Figure 7-14. *Verify the inserted record in the Query Editor*

Go to the Postman tool and fire a GET call to get all the inserted records as in Figure 7-15.

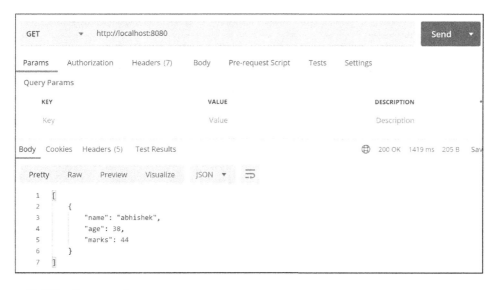

Figure 7-15. *Get result*

Securing Azure Databases

Let us secure the Azure database we created. We can set the firewall on the Azure SQL server and specify who can access the database. If needed, we can integrate the database with Virtual Network to make sure that the database is accessible privately from within the virtual network. We can also selectively allow a range of IP addresses to access the database. You can manage the data in transit by enabling TLS for the database to make sure that the data gets transported over a secured channel. To enable the firewall, go to the *Overview* section for the SQL database in the Azure portal and click *Set server firewall* as in Figure 7-16.

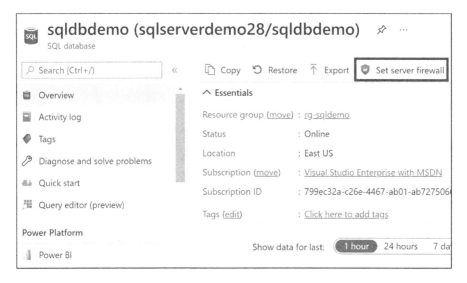

Figure 7-16. *Click Set server firewall*

You can manage the firewall settings like setting TLS, whitelisting IP addresses to access the database, and many more as in Figure 7-17.

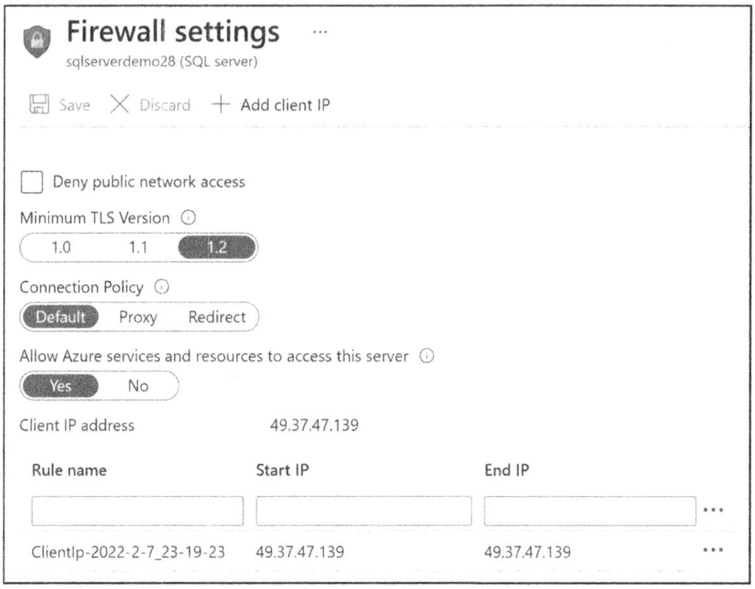

Figure 7-17. *Server firewall*

Data at rest is encrypted using Transparent data encryption default as in Figure 7-18. It is not advisable to turn this encryption off.

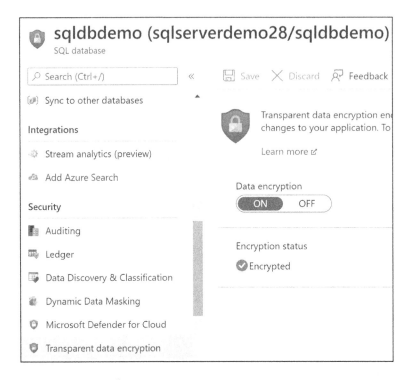

Figure 7-18. *Transparent data encryption*

Summary

In this chapter, we learned Azure SQL's details and how to create an Azure SQL database using the Azure portal. We then developed a Java Spring Boot code and performed an insert and read operation on the Azure SQL database. In the next chapter, we will learn how to work with Azure Cosmos DB programmatically from Java applications.

The following are the key takeaways from this chapter:

- Azure provides relational databases like Microsoft SQL, MySQL, PostgreSQL, and MariaDB as Platform-as-a-Service offerings.

- You may choose to deploy a single database for Azure SQL that is fully managed by the underlying Azure platform and guarantees you isolation from other databases or choose to run multiple single databases on an elastic pool sharing the compute resources like CPU and memory.

- Azure SQL database does not support Microsoft SQL Server features like linked server, SQL agent, SQL data sync, SQL Auditing, Service Broker, and many more. However, you can use Azure SQL Managed Instance in such cases that supports almost all the on-premises SQL Server Enterprise Edition capabilities on Azure.

## CHAPTER 8

Work with Azure Cosmos DB

Modern applications use NoSQL databases for storing data. These databases should be highly scalable and responsive and have very low latency. These applications are globally available, and this needs their databases to be available globally. Data replication should happen in no time across the globe for such applications. Azure Cosmos DB is a cloud-based NoSQL database on Azure that can meet these requirements.

In the previous chapter, we learned the basic concept of the Azure SQL database. We then created a Java-based application and worked with the Azure SQL database. In this chapter, we will learn the details of the Azure Cosmos DB, and then we will provision the Azure Cosmos DB and build a Java application that can perform read and write operations on Azure Cosmos DB.

Structure

In this chapter, we will discuss the following aspects of the Azure Cosmos DB:

- Introduction to Azure Cosmos DB
- Create an SQL API Cosmos DB
- Work with SQL API

Objectives

After studying this chapter, you should be able to do the following:

- Understand the concept of Azure Cosmos DB
- Work with Azure Cosmos DB from Java application

© Abhishek Mishra 2022
A. Mishra, *Microsoft Azure for Java Developers*, https://doi.org/10.1007/978-1-4842-8251-9_8

Introduction to Azure Cosmos DB

Azure Cosmos DB is a Platform-as-a-Service NoSQL database on Azure and is best suited for real-time and near-real-time applications. It ensures very high throughput and ensures elastic read and write scalability. The data stored can be replicated globally and ensures very low latency. The database can be highly available as it can be replicated across multiple Azure regions.

You can access the data stored in Azure Cosmos DB using multiple supported database APIs. The following are the supported APIs:

- *SQL API* helps you access the stored data using SQL queries. You can migrate your relational database workload to Cosmos DB using SQL APIs.

- *API for MongoDB* helps you access data MongoDB queries. You can insert your data in the document structure using the MongoDB-supported BSON format.

- *Cassandra API* helps you store data using column-oriented schema. You can query the data using Cassandra Query Language.

- *Table API* helps you store data in a key-value format.

- *Gremlin API* stores data in a graph database format using edges and vertices. You can query the data using the graph query language.

For Azure Cosmos DB, you get charged for the throughput you need and the storage you consume on an hourly basis. The throughput is defined using Request Units. Request Units are the combination of CPU, memory, and IOPs consumed to perform a database operation. You can create an Azure Cosmos DB account based on your consumption of the Restricted Units. The following are the supported ways to create a Cosmos DB account:

- *Provisioned throughput* mode helps you choose the number of Restricted Units per second you need for your database operations. You can scale by increasing or decreasing the Restricted Units programmatically or manually based on your need.

- You do not choose any Restricted Units using the *Serverless mode,* and you get billed for the number of Restricted Units you have consumed during the billing period.

- *Autoscale mode* helps you scale the Restricted Unit automatically based on the application's need. This mode is best suited for workloads that have unpredictable traffic patterns.

Create an SQL API Cosmos DB

Let us create an Azure Cosmos DB for SQL API using the Azure portal. Go to the Azure portal as shown in Figure 8-1, and click *Create a resource* as in Figure 8-1.

Figure 8-1. *Create a resource*

You will be taken to the Azure Marketplace in Figure 8-2. Click *Databases*. You will get all the database offerings here. Click *Azure Cosmos DB* as in Figure 8-2.

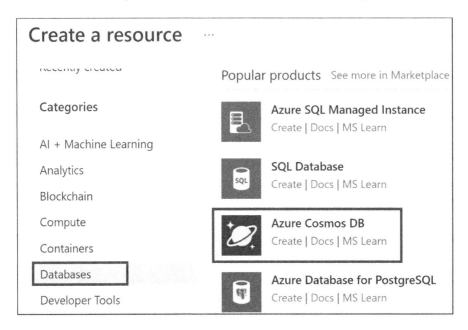

Figure 8-2. *Click Azure Cosmos DB*

Click *Create* for *Core (SQL) – Recommended* as in Figure 8-3.

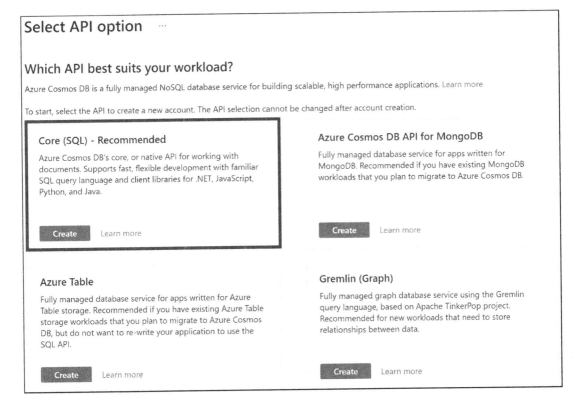

Figure 8-3. *Click Core (SQL) – Recommended*

Provide the subscription and the resource group details. Provide the account name for the Cosmos DB and location. Click *Review + create* as in Figure 8-4.

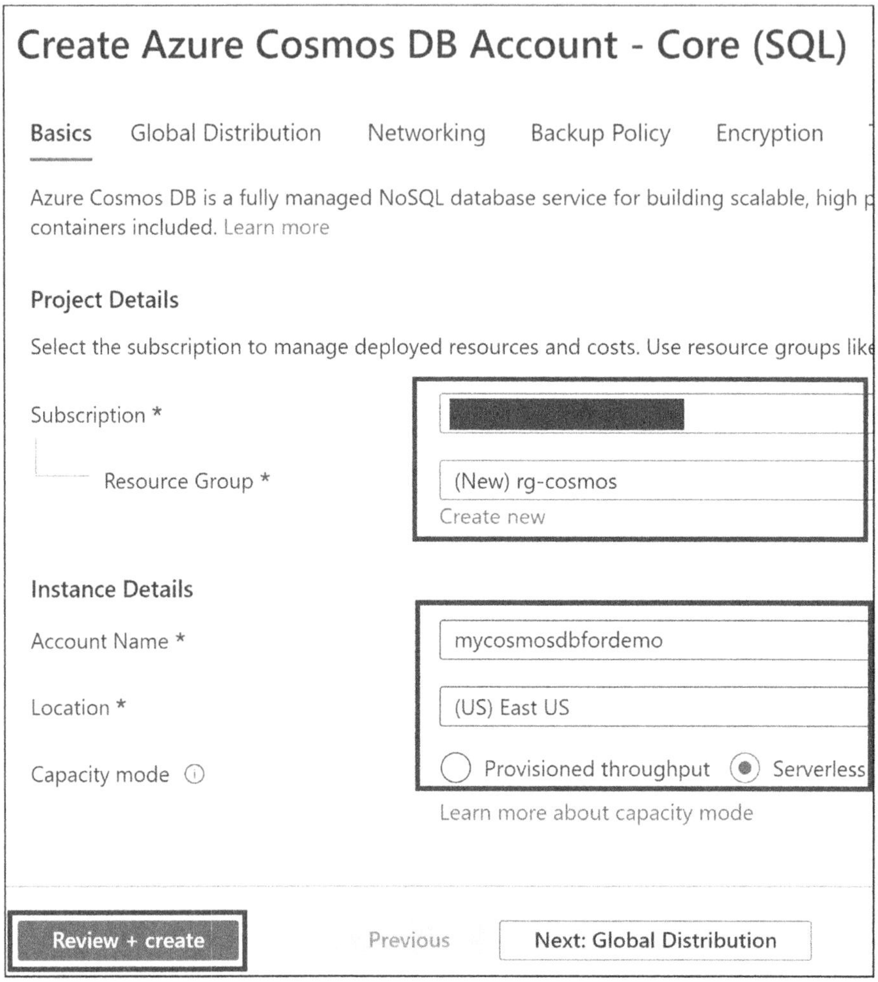

Figure 8-4. *Click Review + create*

Click *Create* as in Figure 8-5. This action will spin up Azure Cosmos DB for you.

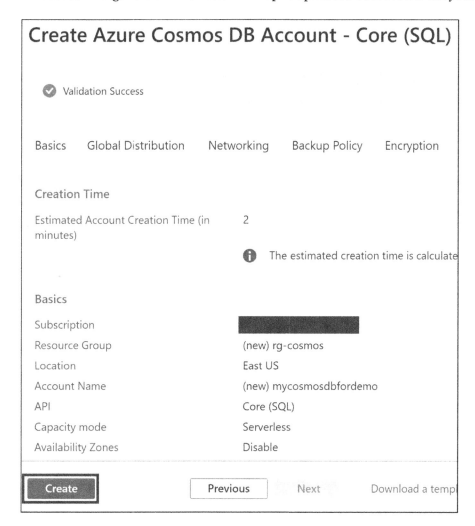

Figure 8-5.   *Click Create*

Once the Cosmos DB gets created, navigate to the Cosmos DB and click *Keys* as in Figure 8-6. We need the endpoint URL and the access key to connect to the Cosmos DB from the Java code.

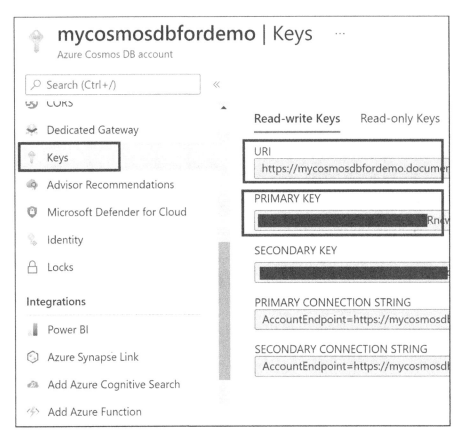

Figure 8-6.   *Click Keys*

Work with SQL API Cosmos DB

Now let us write a Java Maven project and work with SQL API. We need to add the Cosmos DB package to the POM file. Listing 8-1 shows the POM file that you can use.

Listing 8-1. POM.xml

```xml
<?xml version="1.0" encoding="UTF-8"?>
<project xmlns="http://maven.apache.org/POM/4.0.0"
        xmlns:xsi="http://www.w3.org/2001/XMLSchema-instance"
        xsi:schemaLocation="http://maven.apache.org/POM/4.0.0 http://
        maven.apache.org/xsd/maven-4.0.0.xsd">
    <modelVersion>4.0.0</modelVersion>

    <groupId>com.cosmosdb</groupId>
    <artifactId>sqldemo</artifactId>
    <version>1.0-SNAPSHOT</version>

    <dependencies>
        <dependency>
            <groupId>com.azure</groupId>
            <artifactId>azure-cosmos</artifactId>
            <version>4.4.0</version>
        </dependency>
    </dependencies>

    <properties>
        <maven.compiler.source>11</maven.compiler.source>
        <maven.compiler.target>11</maven.compiler.target>
    </properties>

</project>
```

Inside a Cosmos DB database, data is stored inside a container, and the data stored should have a partition key and ID column. Let us create a Java class as in Listing 8-2 having the Main function where we can add the code to create a database, create a container to store student data, insert records to it, and read the records. Let us create a Student class with the data fields for the student data. It must have the *id* and the *partitionKey* fields. The data is stored in partitions for faster data access, and each of the partition is identified by a partition key. A combination of partition key and ID will uniquely identify a record.

Listing 8-2. Student.java

```java
public class Student {

    public Student(){

    }

    private String id;
    private String name;
    private int marks;
    private String partitionKey;

    public String getName() {
        return name;
    }

    public void setName(String name) {
        this.name = name;
    }

    public int getMarks() {
        return marks;
    }

    public void setMarks(int marks) {
        this.marks = marks;
    }

    public String getPartitionKey() {
        return partitionKey;
    }

    public void setPartitionKey(String partitionKey) {
        this.partitionKey = partitionKey;
    }

    public String getId() {
        return id;
    }
```

```
    public void setId(String id) {
        this.id = id;
    }
}
```

Let us add the code shown in Listing 8-3 to the Main method to connect to Azure Cosmos DB. We need to provide the endpoint URL and the key that we copied earlier from the Azure portal.

Listing 8-3. Connect to database

```
String endpoint = "{Provide endpoint URL}";
String key = "{Provide Access Key}";

// Create connection to Database
CosmosClient client = new CosmosClientBuilder()
        .endpoint(endpoint)
        .key(key)
        .buildClient();
```

Let us create a database named *students* using the code from Listing 8-4. The database will only get created if it does not exist.

Listing 8-4. Create a database

```
// Create Database
String databaseName = "students";
CosmosDatabaseResponse databaseDetails = client.createDatabaseIfNotExists
(databaseName);
CosmosDatabase database = client.getDatabase(databaseDetails.
getProperties().getId());
System.out.println("Database created - " + database.getId() );
```

Let us create a container named *class* where we can store student data for different classes as in Listing 8-5. The container will only get created if it does not exist.

Listing 8-5. Create Container

```
// Create Container
String containerName = "class";
CosmosContainerProperties containerProperties = new CosmosContainer
Properties(containerName, "/partitionKey");
CosmosContainerResponse containerResponse = database.createContainerIf
NotExists(containerProperties);
CosmosContainer container = database.getContainer(containerResponse.
getProperties().getId());
System.out.println("Container created " + container.getId());
```

Let us insert data for four students as in Listing 8-6.

Listing 8-6. Insert data

```
//Insert data to the Container
//Insert Student 1
Student student = new Student();
student.setId("1");
student.setMarks(80);
student.setPartitionKey("eight-standard");
student.setName("Abhishek");
CosmosItemResponse item = container.createItem(student, new
PartitionKey(student.getPartitionKey()), new CosmosItemRequestOptions());

//Insert Student 2
student = new Student();
student.setId("2");
student.setMarks(60);
student.setPartitionKey("ninth-standard");
student.setName("Abhijeet");
item = container.createItem(student, new PartitionKey(student.
getPartitionKey()), new CosmosItemRequestOptions());

//Insert Student 3
student = new Student();
student.setId("3");
```

```
student.setMarks(70);
student.setPartitionKey("eight-standard");
student.setName("Sunny");
item = container.createItem(student, new PartitionKey(student.
getPartitionKey()), new CosmosItemRequestOptions());

//Insert Student 4
student = new Student();
student.setId("4");
student.setMarks(60);
student.setPartitionKey("seventh-standard");
student.setName("Abhilash");
item = container.createItem(student, new PartitionKey(student.
getPartitionKey()), new CosmosItemRequestOptions());
```

Let us read the students data stored as in Listing 8-7.

Listing 8-7. Read data

```
//Query data from the container
int pageSize = 10;
CosmosQueryRequestOptions queryOptions = new CosmosQueryRequestOptions();
//  Set populate query metrics to get metrics around query executions
queryOptions.setQueryMetricsEnabled(true);

CosmosPagedIterable<Student> studentPagedIterable = container.queryItems
        (SELECT * FROM class WHERE class.partitionKey IN ('eight-standard',
        'seventh-standard')", queryOptions, Student.class);
studentPagedIterable.iterableByPage(pageSize).forEach(resultItem -> {

    resultItem.getResults().forEach(data -> System.out.println(data.getId()
    + "-" +data.getName()+"-"+data.getMarks()));

});
```

Listing 8-8 is the complete code that interacts with the Azure Cosmos DB.

Listing 8-8. Complete code

```java
import com.azure.cosmos.CosmosClient;
import com.azure.cosmos.CosmosClientBuilder;
import com.azure.cosmos.CosmosContainer;
import com.azure.cosmos.CosmosDatabase;
import com.azure.cosmos.models.CosmosContainerProperties;
import com.azure.cosmos.models.CosmosContainerResponse;
import com.azure.cosmos.models.CosmosDatabaseResponse;
import com.azure.cosmos.models.CosmosItemRequestOptions;
import com.azure.cosmos.models.CosmosItemResponse;
import com.azure.cosmos.models.CosmosQueryRequestOptions;
import com.azure.cosmos.models.PartitionKey;
import com.azure.cosmos.util.CosmosPagedIterable;

public class SQLDemo {

    public static void main(String args[])
    {
        String endpoint = "{Provide endpoint URL}";
        String key = "{Provide Access Key}";

        // Create connection to Database
        CosmosClient client = new CosmosClientBuilder()
                .endpoint(endpoint)
                .key(key)
                .buildClient();

        // Create Database
        String databaseName = "students";
        CosmosDatabaseResponse databaseDetails = client.createDatabaseIfNot
        Exists(databaseName);
        CosmosDatabase database = client.getDatabase(databaseDetails.
        getProperties().getId());
        System.out.println("Database created - " + database.getId() );
```

```java
// Create Container
String containerName = "class";
CosmosContainerProperties containerProperties = new CosmosContainer
Properties(containerName, "/partitionKey");
CosmosContainerResponse containerResponse = database.createContaine
rIfNotExists(containerProperties);
CosmosContainer container = database.
getContainer(containerResponse.getProperties().getId());
System.out.println("Container created " + container.getId());

//Insert data to the Container
//Insert Student 1
Student student = new Student();
student.setId("1");
student.setMarks(80);
student.setPartitionKey("eight-standard");
student.setName("Abhishek");
CosmosItemResponse item = container.createItem(student,
new PartitionKey(student.getPartitionKey()), new
CosmosItemRequestOptions());

//Insert Student 2
student = new Student();
student.setId("2");
student.setMarks(60);
student.setPartitionKey("ninth-standard");
student.setName("Abhijeet");
item = container.createItem(student, new PartitionKey(student.
getPartitionKey()), new CosmosItemRequestOptions());

//Insert Student 3
student = new Student();
student.setId("3");
student.setMarks(70);
student.setPartitionKey("eight-standard");
```

```java
student.setName("Sunny");
item = container.createItem(student, new PartitionKey(student.
getPartitionKey()), new CosmosItemRequestOptions());

//Insert Student 4
student = new Student();
student.setId("4");
student.setMarks(60);
student.setPartitionKey("seventh-standard");
student.setName("Abhilash");
item = container.createItem(student, new PartitionKey(student.
getPartitionKey()), new CosmosItemRequestOptions());

//Query data from the container
int pageSize = 10;
CosmosQueryRequestOptions queryOptions = new
CosmosQueryRequestOptions();
//  Set populate query metrics to get metrics around query
    executions
queryOptions.setQueryMetricsEnabled(true);

CosmosPagedIterable<Student> studentPagedIterable = container.
queryItems(
        "SELECT * FROM class WHERE class.partitionKey IN
        ('eight-standard', 'seventh-standard')", queryOptions,
        Student.class);
studentPagedIterable.iterableByPage(pageSize).
forEach(resultItem -> {

    resultItem.getResults().forEach(data -> System.out.
    println(data.getId() + "-" +data.getName()+"-"+data.
    getMarks()));

});

    }
}
```

Now let us go to the portal and check the data inserted in the Cosmos DB. Click *Data Explorer* as in Figure 8-7. You can see the *students* database.

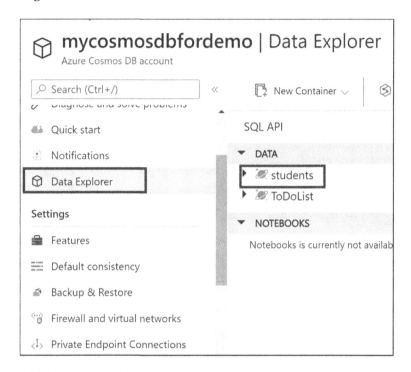

Figure 8-7. *Click Data Explorer*

Expand the Student database, and you can see the *class* container. Click *Items* as in Figure 8-8, and you can see the student records stored.

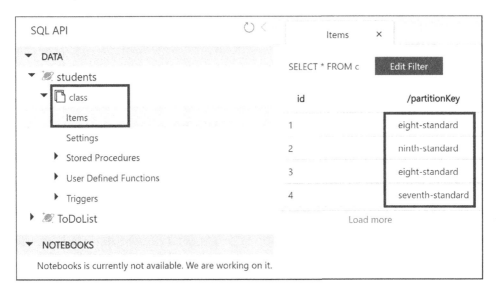

Figure 8-8.   *Click Items*

Click on any of the records to see the data stored as in Figure 8-9.

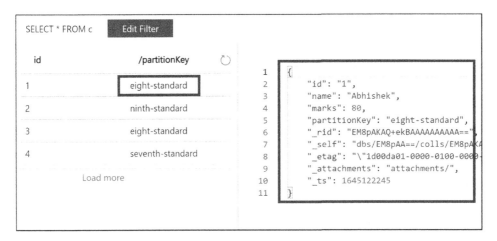

Figure 8-9.   *Click on an item*

Summary

In this chapter, we learned Azure Cosmos DB and how to create an Azure SQL API–based Azure Cosmos DB using the Azure portal. We then developed a Maven-based Java code and performed an insert and read operation on the Azure Cosmos DB. In the next chapter, we will learn how to work with Azure Redis Cache programmatically from Java applications.

The following are the key takeaways from this chapter:

- Azure Cosmos DB is a NoSQL database that supports horizontal data replication across the globe and ensures low latency.

- NoSQL data stored in Azure Cosmos DB can be accessed using the following APIs.

    - SQL API

    - API for MongoDB

    - Cassandra API

    - Table API

    - Gremlin API

- You can create your Azure Cosmos DB account using the following modes:

    - Provisioned throughput

    - Serverless

    - Autoscale

## CHAPTER 9

Storing Runtime Data in Azure Redis Cache

Modern applications generate and work on runtime data. They keep the runtime data either in memory or in a persistent disk or data store. Storing the data in the memory enables you faster access to the temporary runtime data stored. However, it gets slower while accessing data from persistent storage like disk or database than the in-memory store. Azure Redis Cache helps you store and manage runtime data for your application in Azure. Azure Redis Cache helps you access the runtime data quickly and increases your application's performance.

In the previous chapter, we learned the basic concept of the Azure Cosmos DB. We then created a Java-based application and worked with the Azure Cosmos DB SQL API. In this chapter, we will learn the details of the Azure Redis Cache. Then we will provision the Azure Redis Cache and build a Java application that can perform read and write operations on Azure Redis Cache.

Structure

In this chapter, we will discuss the following aspects of the Azure Redis Cache:

- Introduction to Azure Redis Cache
- Create Azure Redis Cache
- Work with Azure Redis Cache
- Using Console to work with Redis Cache

© Abhishek Mishra 2022
A. Mishra, *Microsoft Azure for Java Developers*, https://doi.org/10.1007/978-1-4842-8251-9_9

Objectives

After studying this chapter, you should be able to get the following learnings.

- Understand the concept of the Azure Redis Cache

- Work with Azure Redis Cache from Java application

Introduction to Azure Redis Cache

Redis Cache is an in-memory cache offering that helps you keep frequently accessed runtime data. You can fetch your data once from the data store and keep that in the cache for the first request. The data will get fetched from the cache for all subsequent requests instead of getting it from the data store. When the data in the data store changes, the data in the cache gets refreshed with the new version of data stored in the data store. This approach would ensure that the Redis Cache data is always up to date and the application always gets the latest data.

Azure offers Redis Cache as a Platform-as-a-Service offering. You can spin the Redis Cluster in a few minutes and start using it. You need not set up any infrastructure for Redis Cache on Azure. The underlying Azure platform manages all the infrastructure aspects. Azure Redis Cache can store content, user session, and distributed data and even work as a message broker. The use cases are many. The following are some examples of use cases that you can achieve using Redis Cache:

- You have an application running on Azure WebApp. Whenever a user logs in, the session data for the user can be stored in the Azure Redis Cache so that the data can be available to all the WebApp instances and user requests. During peak hours, the Azure WebApp can scale to multiple instances.

- You have a Web application running either on Azure or on-premises or any cloud-based server, and it uses headers, footers, cascading style sheets, and other static pages. You can store a copy of all these static contents in the Azure Redis Cache. For the first time, the static content can be fetched from the server, and for the following requests, the data can be served from the cache. This approach would increase the performance of the application.

- You have an application that makes frequent database calls to fetch data. In such cases, you can store the frequently accessed and static data in the Azure Redis Cache. The application can fetch the data from the cache instead of the database. However, the data should be fetched from the database and simultaneously stored in the Redis Cache for the first user request. If the data changes in the database, the Redis Cache data should also be updated.

- You can have applications that perform distributed transactions. If all the transactions are successful, then only the data should be committed to the database. In such cases, you can store the intermediate transaction data for all the transactions in the Redis Cache, and if all the transactions are successful, then commit the data in the Redis Cache to the database or invalidate the data stored in cache for failed transactions as a rollback effort.

Azure Redis Cache offers you very low latency and high-throughput data access for your applications. The data is stored in the memory of the Redis server managed by the Azure platform and can serve huge volumes of data requests with ease. The data stored is encrypted and highly secured.

The following are pricing plans available for Azure Redis Cache:

- The *Basic* plan offers an open source Redis Cache version running on a single virtual machine instance. You can use this for development and test purposes. This plan offers no SLAs.

- The *Standard* plan offers an open source Redis Cache version running on two virtual machine instances, and the data gets replicated instantaneously across the virtual machine instances.

- The *Premium* plan offers an open source Redis Cache version running on multiple powerful virtual machine instances. It offers very high throughput, availability, low latency, and many other production-grade features.

- The *Enterprise* plan offers higher performance and availability than the Premium plan and provides Redis Labs-based enterprise offering for Redis Cache. You can run Redis-based modules like Redis Bloom, RediSearch, and Redis Time Series.

- The *Enterprise flash* plan offers a cost-effective Redis Labs-based enterprise version that runs on nonvolatile memory.

Create Azure Redis Cache

Let us create an Azure Redis Cache using the Azure portal. Go to the Azure portal and click *Create a resource* as shown in Figure 9-1. We will perform read and write operations on this Redis Cache using the Java code.

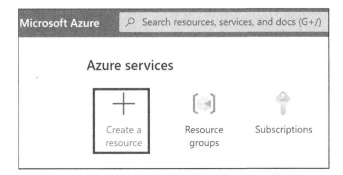

Figure 9-1. *Create a resource*

You will get navigated to Azure Marketplace. Click *Databases* and then click *Azure Cache for Redis*. See Figure 9-2 for an example.

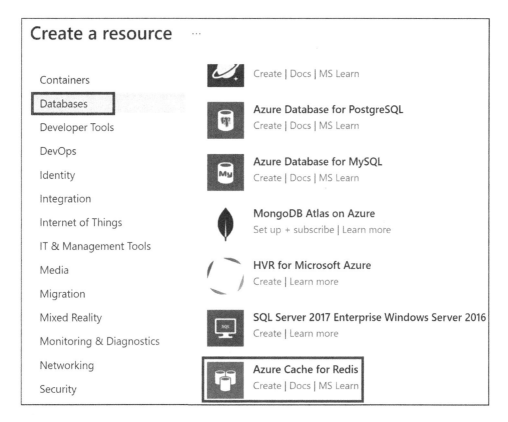

Figure 9-2.   Click Azure Cache for Redis

Provide the basic details to create the Redis Cache. You need to give the subscription and the resource group details, a name for the Redis Cache, the location to create the Redis Cache, and a pricing plan. We are using the Basic C0 plan with no SLA for this demonstration, and this should be used only for development and testing purposes. Click *Next : Networking* to navigate to the Networking tab as in Figure 9-3.

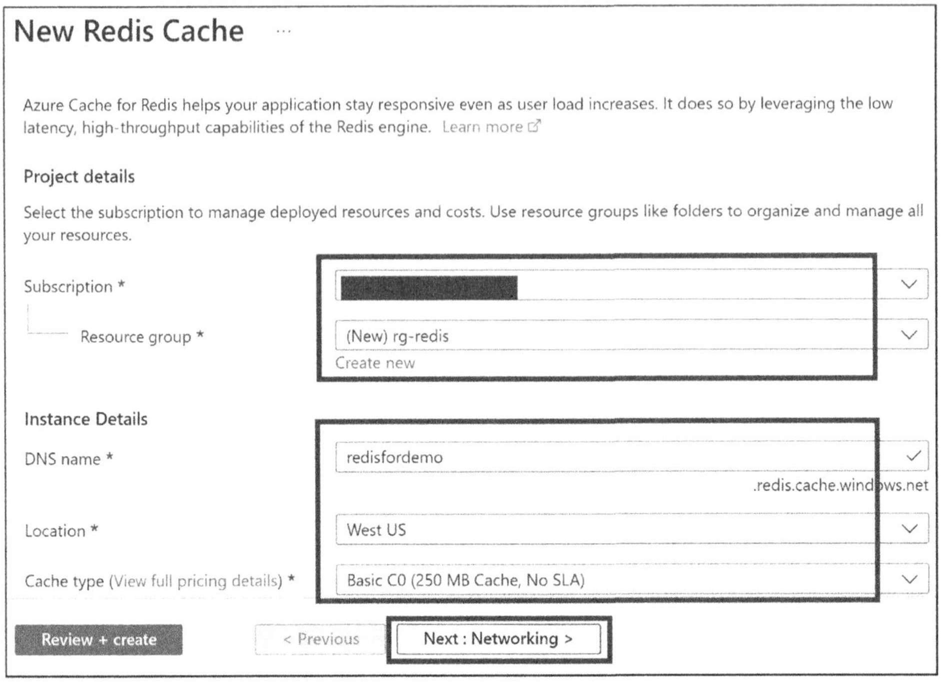

Figure 9-3. *Provide basic details*

Select Public Endpoint. However, you should configure a Private Link Endpoint in the production scenario and set up a Private Endpoint. Using a higher pricing plan, you can integrate the Redis Cache in the Virtual Network. Click *Next : Advanced* as in Figure 9-4.

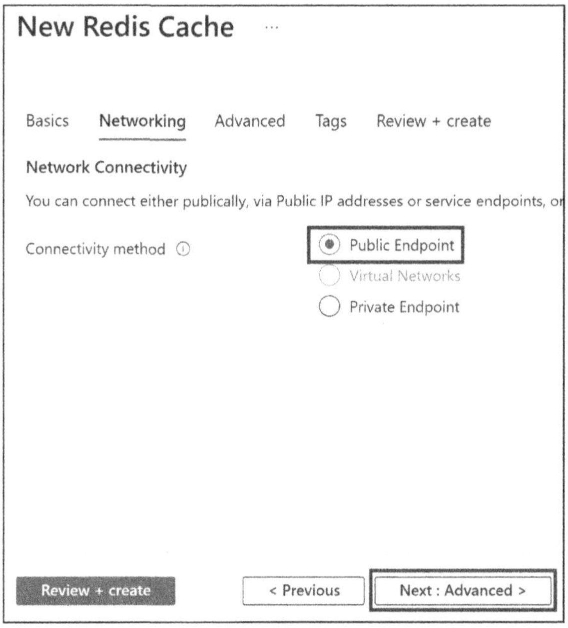

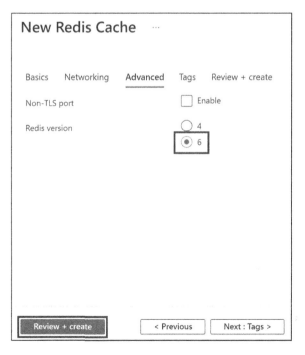

Figure 9-4. *Provide networking details*

Let us select the latest Redis Cache version. Click *Review + create* as in Figure 9-5.

Figure 9-5. *Click Review + create*

Click *Create* as in Figure 9-6. This action will spin up the Redis Cache cluster on Azure.

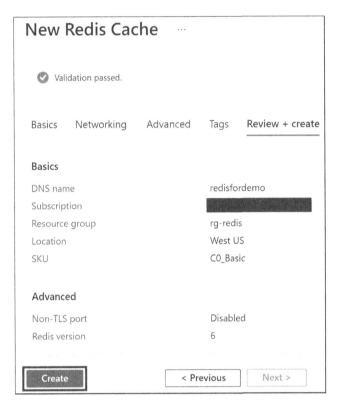

Figure 9-6. *Click Create*

Once the Azure Redis Cache is created, navigate it and go to *Access keys* as in Figure 9-7. Copy the Primary Key to use it as the cache key in the code. Provisioning Azure Redis Cache may take about 15 minutes or more.

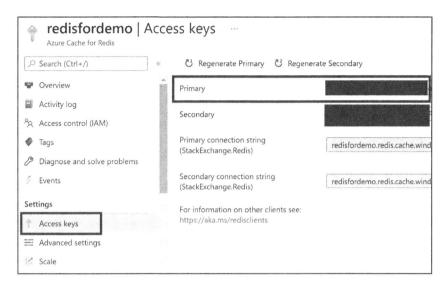

Figure 9-7. *Get the cache key*

Go to the *Properties* section as in Figure 9-8 and copy the hostname. We will use the hostname in the code to connect to the Azure Redis Cache.

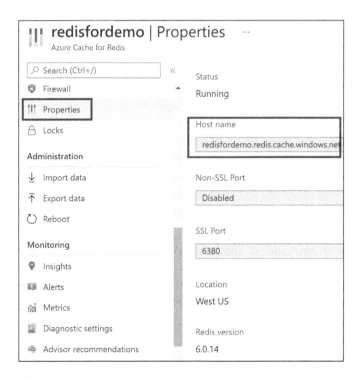

Figure 9-8. *Get the hostname*

Work with Azure Redis Cache

Now let us build a Java code that will insert data to the cache, read from it, set expiry for the cache data, and delete the data from the Redis Cache. We need the *jedis* package to work with the Redis Cache from Java code.

Let us add the jedis package to the *pom.xml* file. Listing 9-1 shows an example.

Listing 9-1. Pom.xml

```
<dependency>
    <groupId>redis.clients</groupId>
    <artifactId>jedis</artifactId>
    <version>3.2.0</version>
    <type>jar</type>
    <scope>compile</scope>
</dependency>
```

We need to connect the Azure Redis Cache from the Java code. We need to provide the hostname and the cache key we copied earlier. Listing 9-2 code builds a connection.

Listing 9-2. Connect to Redis Cache

```
boolean ssl = true;
String hostName = "{Provide Host Name}";
String cacheKey = "{Provide Cache Key}";
//Redis Cache connects on port 6380
int port = 6380;

// Build connection to Redis Cache
JedisShardInfo shardInfo = new JedisShardInfo(hostName, port, ssl);
shardInfo.setPassword(cacheKey);
Jedis jedisCache = new Jedis(shardInfo);
```

You can test if the connection is successful using the *ping* function as in Listing 9-3. You will get a response as *Pong* if the connection is successful.

Listing 9-3. Ping Redis Cache

```
// Check if you are able to connect/ping to Redis Cache
System.out.println( "Ping Result : " + jedisCache.ping());
```

You can use the *set* function to set data in the cache as in Listing 9-4. You can set the data as key-value pairs.

Listing 9-4. Set data in Redis Cache

```
// Set Data 1 Key : Data 1, Value : This is value for Data1
jedisCache.set("Data1", "This is value for Data1");

// Set Data 2 Key : Data 2, Value : This is value for Data2
jedisCache.set("Data2", "This is value for Data2");
```

You can use the *get* function and pass on the data key to fetch the data from the Azure Redis Cache as in Listing 9-5.

Listing 9-5. Read data from Redis Cache

```
// Read Data 1 from Redis Cache
System.out.println( "Value for Data 1 : " + jedisCache.get("Data1"));

// Read Data 2 from Redis Cache
System.out.println( "Value for Data 2 : " + jedisCache.get("Data2"));
```

You can choose to expire the cache data for a key using the *expire* function as in Listing 9-6. You can specify the number of seconds after the cache data expires.

Listing 9-6. Expire data in Redis Cache after 60 seconds

```
// Set Expiry for Data 1
jedisCache.expire("Data1", 60);
```

You can delete the data in the cache using the *del* function as in Listing 9-7.

Listing 9-7. Delete the data in Redis Cache

```
// Delete Data 2
jedisCache.del("Data2");
```

Listing 9-8 is the complete code to work with Azure Redis Cache.

Listing 9-8. Complete code

```java
import redis.clients.jedis.*;

public class RedisDemo {
    public static void main(String args[])
    {
        boolean ssl = true;
        String hostName = "{Provide Host Name}";
        String cacheKey = "{Provide Cache Key}";
        //Redis Cache connects on port 6380
        int port = 6380;

        // Build connection to Redis Cache
        JedisShardInfo shardInfo = new JedisShardInfo(hostName, port, ssl);
        shardInfo.setPassword(cacheKey);
        Jedis jedisCache = new Jedis(shardInfo);

        // Check if you are able to connect/ping to Redis Cache
        System.out.println( "Ping Result : " + jedisCache.ping());

        // Set Data 1 Key : Data 1, Value : This is value for Data1
        jedisCache.set("Data1", "This is value for Data1");

        // Set Data 2 Key : Data 2, Value : This is value for Data2
        jedisCache.set("Data2", "This is value for Data2");

        // Read Data 1 from Redis Cache
        System.out.println( "Value for Data 1 : " + jedisCache.
        get("Data1"));

        // Read Data 2 from Redis Cache
        System.out.println( "Value for Data 2 : " + jedisCache.
        get("Data2"));
```

```
        // Set Expiry for Data 1
        jedisCache.expire("Data1", 60);

        // Delete Data 2
        jedisCache.del("Data2");

        jedisCache.close();

    }
}
```

Figure 9-9 shows the output for the code execution. You can use Console to verify the data. You can use the *Get* command to see the data inserted in the Redis Cache. The next section demonstrates how to use Azure Redis Cache Console from the Azure portal.

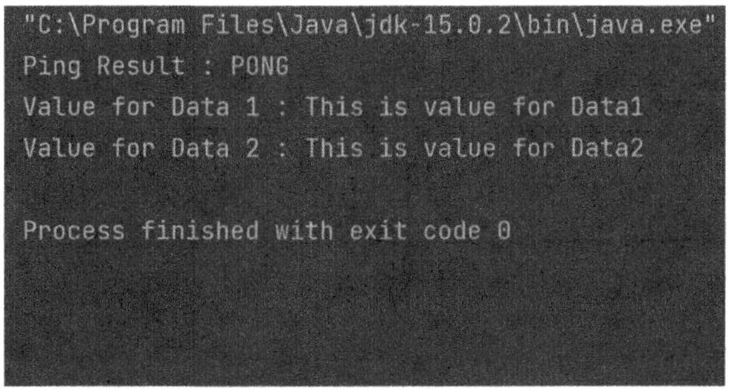

Figure 9-9. *Code execution output*

Using Console to Work with Redis Cache

You may have scenarios where you may need to explore the data stored in the Azure Redis Cache. You can use the Redis Console that is available in the Azure portal to perform all necessary operations on Redis Cache. Go to the *Overview* section and click *Console* as in Figure 9-10.

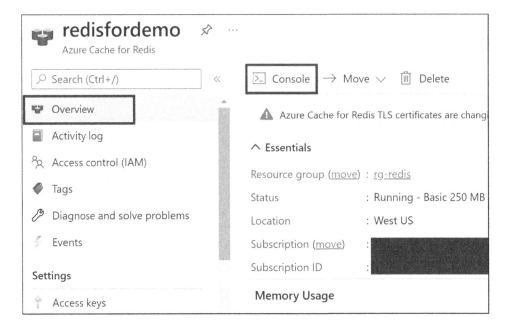

Figure 9-10. *Go to Redis Console*

You can insert data to the cache using the *SET* command. You can read data from the cache using the *GET* command. You can execute any Redis command on this console and work with the Redis Cache cluster. The use of these commands is shown in Figure 9-11.

```
(PREVIEW) Redis Console    📌  ...
redisfordemo

Welcome to secure redis console!

This console connects to your live redis server and all commands are run on the server.

WARNING: Use expensive commands with caution as they can impact your server load!

>SET Data3 "My Test Data"
OK
>GET Data3
"My Test Data"
>█
```

Figure 9-11. *Perform Get and Set operations on Redis Console*

Summary

In this chapter, we learned Azure Redis Cache basics and how to create an Azure Redis Cache using the Azure portal. We then developed a Maven-based Java code and performed read, write, expire, and delete operations on the Azure Redis Cache. In the next chapter, we will learn how to send emails programmatically from Java applications using Graph APIs in the Azure environment.

The following are the key takeaways from this chapter:

- Redis Cache is an in-memory cache offering that helps you keep frequently accessed runtime data.

- Azure offers Redis Cache as a Platform-as-a-Service offering. You can spin the Redis Cluster in a few minutes and start using it. You need not set up any infrastructure for Redis Cache on Azure.

- Azure Redis Cache offers you very low latency and high-throughput data access for your applications.

- The data stored is Azure Redis Cache encrypted and highly secured.

- Azure supports both the open source Redis Cache version and the Redis Lab Enterprise version.

- The following are pricing plans available for Azure Redis Cache:

  - Basic

  - Standard

  - Premium

  - Enterprise

  - Enterprise flash

## CHAPTER 10

Sending Emails Using Graph API

Modern applications need to send emails to the stakeholders, customers, or developers or anyone related to the application. There can be a scenario where the customer is placing an order in an e-commerce application. And once the order gets placed, it will let the customer know the order and the dispatch status. If the order fails, it should notify the operations team to look into it. You can configure your SMTP server for mailing needs on a virtual machine on Azure. However, you will end up maintaining the virtual machine and spend cost and effort to keep the SMTP server up and running. To address this issue, Microsoft provides Graph API deployed on Azure and helps you interact with Microsoft 365 Core services. Using the Graph API, you can send emails.

In the previous chapter, we learned the basic concept of the Azure Redis Cache. We then created a Java-based application and worked with the Azure Redis Cache. In this chapter, we will learn the details of the Graph API. Then we will build a Java application that can send mails using Graph API.

Structure

In this chapter, we will discuss the following aspects of the Graph API:

- Introduction to Graph API

- Steps to send mail using Graph API

- Send mail using Microsoft Graph API

- Microsoft Graph API Explorer

© Abhishek Mishra 2022
A. Mishra, *Microsoft Azure for Java Developers*, https://doi.org/10.1007/978-1-4842-8251-9_10

Objectives

After studying this chapter, you should be able to get the following learnings:

- Understand the concept of the Graph API

- Send mail from Java application using Graph API

Introduction to Graph API

Microsoft Graph API provides you with a set of RESTful endpoints that you can use to interact with Microsoft 365 Core services, Enterprise Mobility and Security services, Windows 10 services, and Dynamics 365 services. Microsoft Graph API is hosted on Azure and can be easily used by developers. Developers can build a variety of applications using Graph API. The following are a few examples.

- You can send and read emails, set meetings, and perform email-related operations using Microsoft 365 Core services. You can use Graph API endpoints to help you interact with Microsoft 365 Core services.

- You can build applications that revolve around Azure AD, Intune, Advanced Threat Protection, and many more using Graph API for Enterprise Mobility and Security services.

- You can automate controlling and applying the latest patches to your Windows server using Graph API for Windows 10 services.

- You can build applications that interact with Dynamics 365 using Graph API for Dynamics 365 Business Central.

Figure 10-1 depicts the interaction between Microsoft services and customer applications using Graph API.

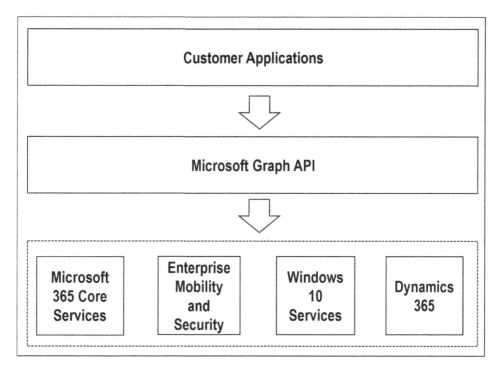

Figure 10-1. *Microsoft Graph API and Microsoft services*

Now let us explore a Microsoft 365 Core use case for Graph API. A developer needs to set up a meeting invite with his supervisor whenever an application fails. He needs to attach a log file from the OneDrive in the invite. This log file is generated by the application and stored in the one-drive. All these actions should be automated. The developer need not monitor the one-drive 24×7 and keep scheduling meetings. We can build a solution to help the developer using Microsoft Graph API. The solution will use Graph API to read Lead's calendar and find a free slot available. It will then access the developer's mailbox and set up an invite with the Lead. The solution will use the Graph API to access the log stored in one-drive and attach it to the invite. Figure 10-2 demonstrates the use case we discussed.

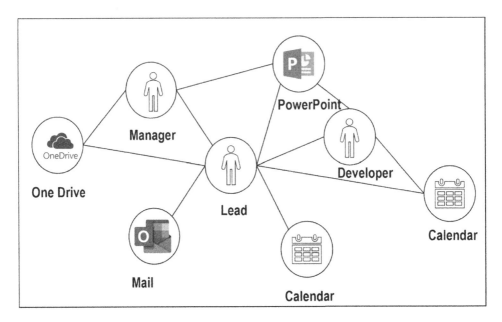

Figure 10-2. *Microsoft Graph API and Microsoft 365 use case*

Steps to Send Mail Using Graph API

As a prerequisite, you should have a Microsoft 365 E5 Developer license. This license would help you configure the mailbox for the user or service account to send mails.

Note   You can get a free Microsoft 365 E5 Developer License at `https://developer.microsoft.com/en-us/microsoft-365/dev-program`. You can create your own sandbox environment that you can use for the demonstration in this chapter.

Once you have purchased the Microsoft 365 Developer E5 license, you can follow the following steps to configure Graph API and invoke the Graph API to send email from your application:

1. Create a user in your Azure tenant.

2. Assign Microsoft 365 E5 license to the user to use a Microsoft 365 mailbox.

3. Create a service principal and provide necessary Graph API permission to the service principal to send mail.

4. Configure your Java application to send mail.

Send Mail Using Microsoft Graph API

Let us create a user in the Azure tenant. We will use this user to send emails using the Java application. Go to the Azure portal and click *Azure Active Directory* as shown in Figure 10-3.

Figure 10-3. *Click Azure Active Directory*

Click *Users* and then click *New user* as shown in Figure 10-4. We can create a new user in the tenant here.

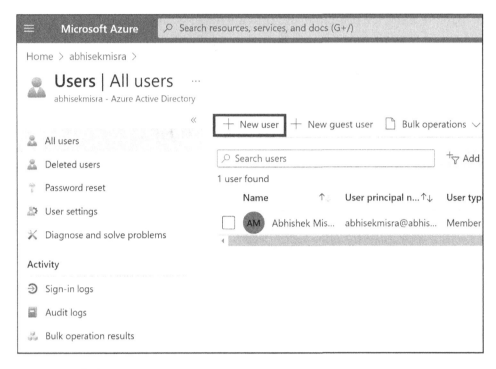

Figure 10-4. *Click New user*

Select *Create user* as shown in Figure 10-5.

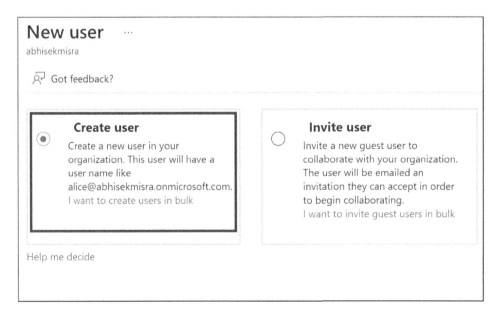

Figure 10-5. *Create user*

Provide username, password details, and other necessary information for the user as shown in Figure 10-6.

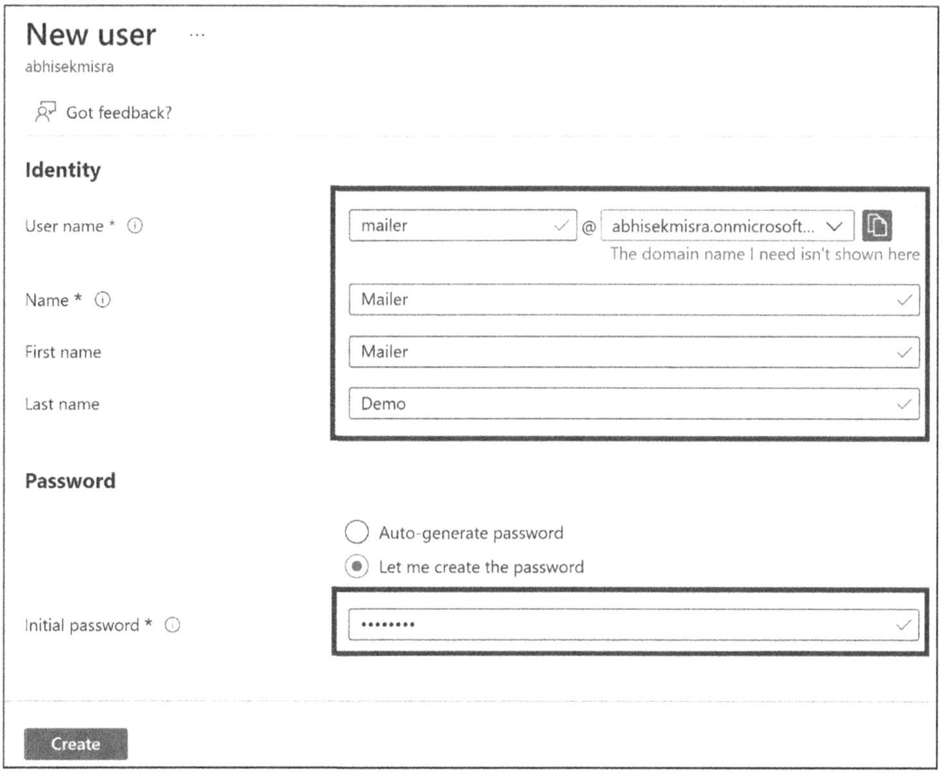

Figure 10-6. *Provide user details*

Make sure you provide the usage location for the user you are creating. Click *Create* as shown in Figure 10-7. The user will get created.

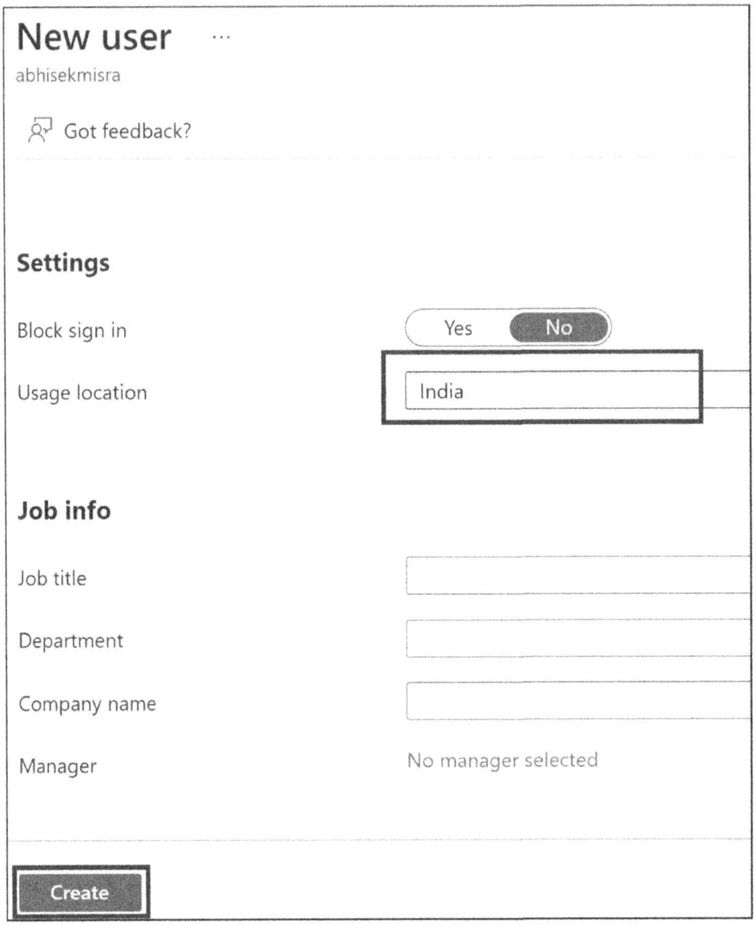

New user   ...
abhisekmisra

    Got feedback?

Settings

Block sign in   Yes   No

Usage location   India

Job info

Job title

Department

Company name

Manager   No manager selected

Create

Figure 10-7. *Provide usage location*

Once the user gets created, click on the user, and this action will navigate you to the user details section, where we can assign a license. Figure 10-8 demonstrates this action.

Figure 10-8. *Click on the user created*

Click *Licenses* and then click *Assignments* as shown in Figure 10-9.

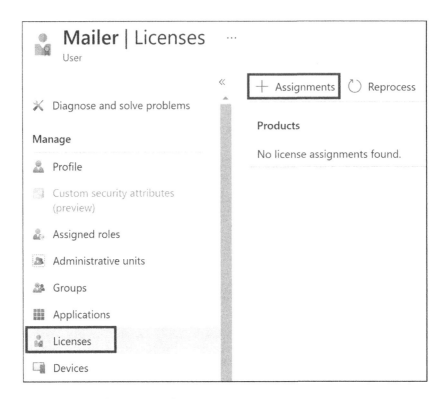

Figure 10-9. *Assign a license to the user*

Select the Microsoft 365 E5 Developer license. You will get this license listed here only if you have purchased the subscription for it. Click *Save* as shown in Figure 10-10.

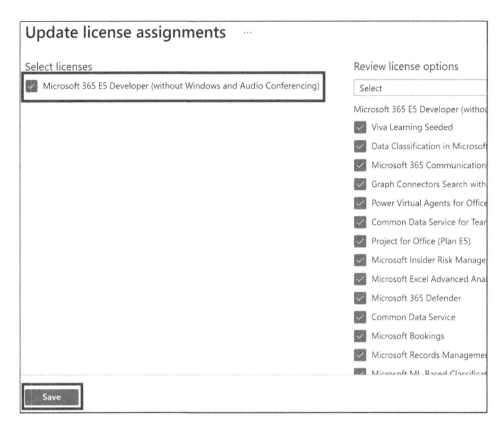

Figure 10-10. *Select Microsoft 365 E5 Developer license*

Now that the user is ready, we can send a mail using the user from the Java application. We need a service principal to authenticate with the Azure tenant and send an email. In Azure Active Directory, click *App registrations*. Then click *New registration* as shown in Figure 10-11.

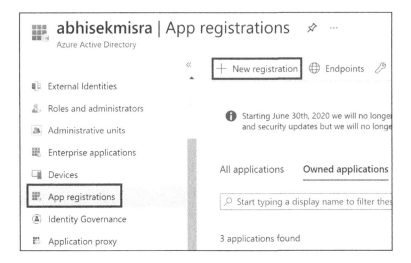

Figure 10-11. *Click App registrations*

Provide a name for the service principal and click *Register* as shown in Figure 10-12.

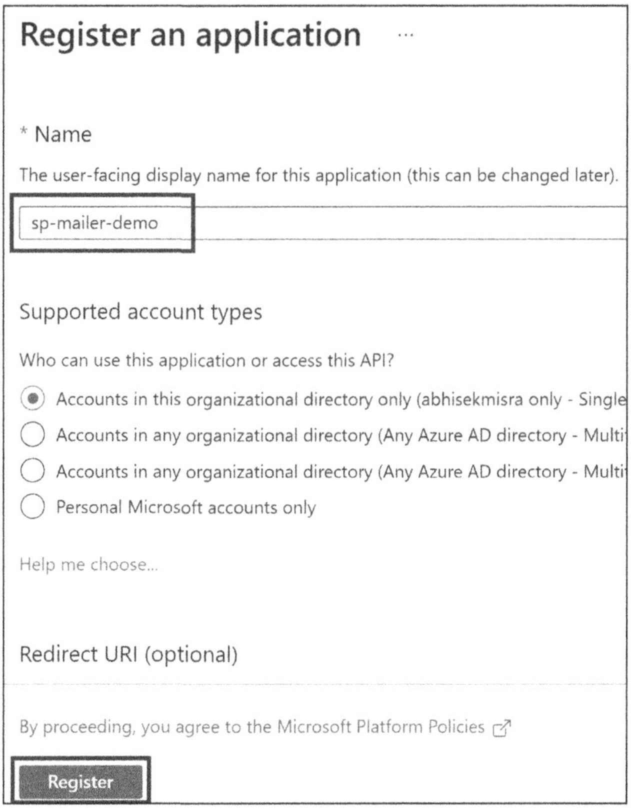

Figure 10-12. *Create a new service principal*

Once the service principal gets created, open the service principal and click *API permissions*. Click *Add a permission* and add the *Mail.Send* permission for Microsoft Graph as shown in Figure 10-13. Make sure that you provide the admin consent to the permission you added.

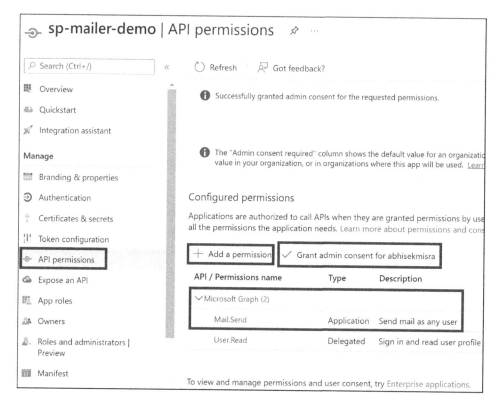

Figure 10-13. *Provide API permissions*

Now we need to generate a secret for the service principal. Go to *Certificates & secrets* and click *New client secret* as shown in Figure 10-14. Generate a secret and copy the value for the secret you created. You will use this value in the Java code to authenticate and send mail.

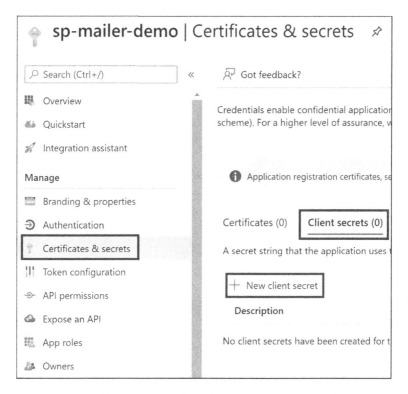

Figure 10-14. *Generate client secrets for the service principal*

Go to the *Overview* page and copy *Application (client) ID* and *Directory (tenant) ID* as shown in Figure 10-15. We will use these values in the Java code.

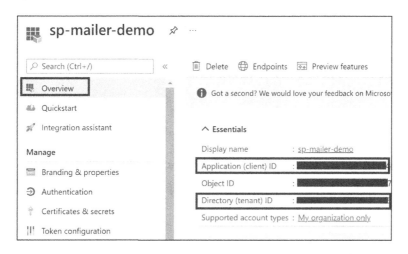

Figure 10-15. *Copy client ID and tenant ID for the service principal*

Now we have the user and the service principal ready. Let us create the Maven-based Java console application to send emails.

Let us add the Microsoft Graph API and the Identity packages to the *pom.xml* file as in Listing 10-1.

Listing 10-1. Pom.xml

```
<dependency>
    <groupId>com.microsoft.graph</groupId>
    <artifactId>microsoft-graph</artifactId>
    <version>[5.0,)</version>
</dependency>
<dependency>
    <groupId>com.azure</groupId>
    <artifactId>azure-identity</artifactId>
    <version>[1.3,)</version>
</dependency>
```

Go to the *main* function in the Java class file as in Listing 10-2 and add the following code. We need to create the authentication provider that will use the service principal client secret to authenticate and authorize the code to send mail using the user we created.

Listing 10-2. Build the authentication provider

```
String clientId="{Provide Client ID for Service Principal}";
String clientSecret = "Provide Secret value for Service Principal";
String tenantId = "Provide Tenant ID";

//You can send using the default scope.
List<String> SCOPES = List.of("https://graph.microsoft.com/.default");

//Build Client Credential based on the Service Principal
final ClientSecretCredential clientCredential = new
ClientSecretCredentialBuilder()
        .clientId(clientId)
        .clientSecret(clientSecret)
        .tenantId(tenantId)
```

```
        .build();
```

```
//Build a Token Credential Auth provider that can authenticate using the
Service Principal
final TokenCredentialAuthProvider tokenProvider =
        new TokenCredentialAuthProvider(SCOPES, clientCredential);
```

Build the graph client to use the authentication provider we created and send mail using the user as in Listing 10-3.

Listing 10-3. Build the Graph Client object

```
//Build the Graph Client
final GraphServiceClient graph = GraphServiceClient
        .builder()
        .authenticationProvider(tokenProvider)
        .buildClient();
```

Now let us construct the mail body and subject and provide the recipient list to whom we need to send the mail as in Listing 10-4.

Listing 10-4. Construct the mail method

```
//Construct the message
Message message = new Message();
message.subject = "Order Status - IX1234";
ItemBody body = new ItemBody();
body.contentType = BodyType.HTML;
body.content = "Dear Customer <br/><br/> You order is ready. It will be
dispatched soon <br/><br/> Thanks<br/>OPs Team";
message.body = body;
LinkedList<Recipient> to = new LinkedList<Recipient>();
Recipient toReceiver = new Recipient();
EmailAddress email = new EmailAddress();
email.address = "abhisek.misra@thecloudcompute.com";
toReceiver.emailAddress = email;
to.add(toReceiver);
message.toRecipients = to;
```

Let us use the graph client object and send mail using the user we created earlier as in Listing 10-5.

Listing 10-5. Send mail

```
//Send mail. Provide the mail address of the user we created in the
Azure AD
//and have assigned Microsoft365 Developer E5 license
graph.users("mailer@abhisekmisra.onmicrosoft.com")
        .sendMail(UserSendMailParameterSet
                .newBuilder()
                .withMessage(message)
                .withSaveToSentItems(false)
                .build())
        .buildRequest()
        .post();
```

The following is the complete code to send mail using Graph API from the Java application as in Listing 10-6.

Listing 10-6. Complete code

```
import com.azure.identity.ClientSecretCredential;
import com.azure.identity.ClientSecretCredentialBuilder;
import com.microsoft.graph.authentication.TokenCredentialAuthProvider;
import com.microsoft.graph.models.*;
import com.microsoft.graph.requests.GraphServiceClient;
import java.util.LinkedList;
import java.util.List;

public class SendMail {
    public static void main(String args[])
    {
        String clientId="{Provide Client ID for Service Principal}";
        String clientSecret = "Provide Secret value for Service Principal";
        String tenantId = "Provide Tenant ID";

        //You can send using the default scope.
```

```java
List<String> SCOPES = List.of("https://graph.microsoft.com/.
default");

//Build Client Credential based on the Service Principal
final ClientSecretCredential clientCredential = new
ClientSecretCredentialBuilder()
        .clientId(clientId)
        .clientSecret(clientSecret)
        .tenantId(tenantId)
        .build();

//Build a Token Credential Auth provider that can authenticate
using the Service Principal
final TokenCredentialAuthProvider tokenProvider =
        new TokenCredentialAuthProvider(SCOPES, clientCredential);

//Build the Graph Client
final GraphServiceClient graph = GraphServiceClient
        .builder()
        .authenticationProvider(tokenProvider)
        .buildClient();

//Construct the message
Message message = new Message();
message.subject = "Order Status - IX1234";
ItemBody body = new ItemBody();
body.contentType = BodyType.HTML;
body.content = "Dear Customer <br/><br/> You order is ready. It
will be dispatched soon <br/><br/> Thanks<br/>OPs Team";
message.body = body;
LinkedList<Recipient> to = new LinkedList<Recipient>();
Recipient toReceiver = new Recipient();
EmailAddress email = new EmailAddress();
email.address = "abhisek.misra@thecloudcompute.com";
toReceiver.emailAddress = email;
to.add(toReceiver);
message.toRecipients = to;
```

```
//Send mail. Provide the mail address of the user we created in the
Azure AD
//and have assigned Microsoft365 Developer E5 license
graph.users("mailer@abhisekmisra.onmicrosoft.com")
        .sendMail(UserSendMailParameterSet
                .newBuilder()
                .withMessage(message)
                .withSaveToSentItems(false)
                .build())
        .buildRequest()
        .post();
    }
}
```

Microsoft Graph API Explorer

You may need to find out the right Graph API that can exactly fit into your use case. Microsoft Graph API Explorer can help you find out the right API. It provides you with all the available Microsoft Graph APIs. You can test the Graph API and see the response using the Microsoft Graph API Explorer. Listing 10-7 shows the URL for the Microsoft Graph API Explorer.

Listing 10-7. The Microsoft Graph API Explorer URL

```
https://developer.microsoft.com/en-us/graph/graph-explorer
```

Now let us go to the Microsoft Graph API Explorer and try out a popular Graph API that will get the user profile. Log in to the Microsoft Graph API using your Azure credentials. You will be able to see the available Graph APIs. Figure 10-16 displays a few of the Graph APIs available.

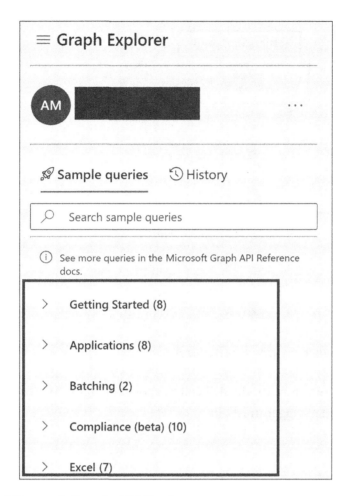

Figure 10-16. *Microsoft Graph API Explorer*

Expand the *Getting Started* node and click *my profile* Graph API as shown in Figure 10-17.

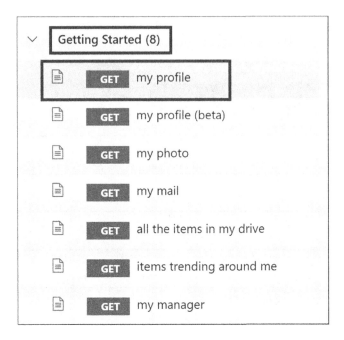

Figure 10-17. *Trigger my profile Graph API*

You will get the response for the API call as shown in Figure 10-18. You can modify the API call here and retrigger the API.

Figure 10-18. *my profile Graph API response*

Summary

In this chapter, we learned Microsoft Graph API basics and how to configure permissions for Azure AD users to send mails using Microsoft Graph API. We then developed a Maven-based Java code and sent mail using Microsoft Graph API. In the next chapter, we will learn how to monitor Java applications using Azure Monitor and Application Insights.

The following are the key takeaways from this chapter:

- Microsoft Graph API provides you with a set of RESTful endpoints that you can use to interact with Microsoft 365 Core services, Enterprise Mobility and Security services, Windows 10 services, and Dynamics 365 services.

- You should have a Microsoft 365 E5 Developer license to send mails using Graph API as a prerequisite. This license would help you configure the mailbox for the user or service account to send mails.

- The following are the steps to configure Graph API and invoke the Graph API to send email from your application:

  - You need to create a user in your Azure tenant.

  - Assign Microsoft 365 E5 license to the user to use a Microsoft 365 mailbox.

  - Create a service principal and provide necessary Graph API permission to the service principal to send mail.

  - Configure your Java application to send mail.

CHAPTER 11

Debugging and Monitoring Using Azure Monitor and Application Insights

Applications may get sluggish at times, and you may need to troubleshoot performance issues. There can be various reasons for the degradation of application performance. For example, the CPU or memory utilization can get high while the application is processing a long-running request. We need a mechanism to periodically monitor the application performance metrics like CPU, memory, and disk utilization and alert the operations team whenever the application reaches the threshold performance level. You may also need logs to debug your application failures. Azure Monitor helps you track application metrics, and Azure Application Insights helps you analyze the logs for your application running on Azure or on-premises or any other public cloud.

In the previous chapter, we learned the basic concept of the Microsoft Graph APIs. We then created a Java-based application and configured Microsoft Graph API to send mails. In this chapter, we will learn the details of the Azure Monitor and Azure Application Insights. Then we will build a Java application that can Azure Monitor to generate performance metrics and Azure Application Insights that can generate logs for the application.

Structure

In this chapter, we will discuss the following aspects of the Azure Monitor and Application Insights:

© Abhishek Mishra 2022
A. Mishra, *Microsoft Azure for Java Developers*, https://doi.org/10.1007/978-1-4842-8251-9_11

- Introduction to Azure Monitor and Application Insights

- Configure Azure Monitor Metrics and Dashboard

- Create performance alerts

- Work with Application Insights for Java application

Objectives

After studying this chapter, you should be able to get the following learnings:

- Understand the concept of Azure Monitor and Application Insights

- Configure Azure Monitor and Application Insights for Java application

Introduction to Azure Monitor and Application Insights

Azure Monitor helps you collect performance metrics and logs data from your applications and infrastructure on Azure, on-premises, or any other cloud platforms. It collects data from Azure Services, Azure Subscription, and Azure Tenant. The stored logs and metrics in the Azure Monitor can be analyzed and used further based on your needs. You can gather the following insights from the logs and metrics ingested collected by Azure Monitor:

- Using Application Insights, you can get insights into your applications.

- Using Container Insights, you can get insights into your containers.

- Using Virtual Machine Insights, you can get insights for your Virtual Machines.

- You can get insights into your network and storage.

You can analyze the ingested logs using Log Analytics and analyze the metrics using Metrics Explorer. You can build dashboards and workbooks to visualize the analytics and insights for the ingested logs and metrics data. You can respond to the logs and metrics based on your analysis by creating alerts and auto-scale settings. You can integrate with Logic Apps workflows and perform actions based on your analytics. Figure 11-1 demonstrates Azure Monitor.

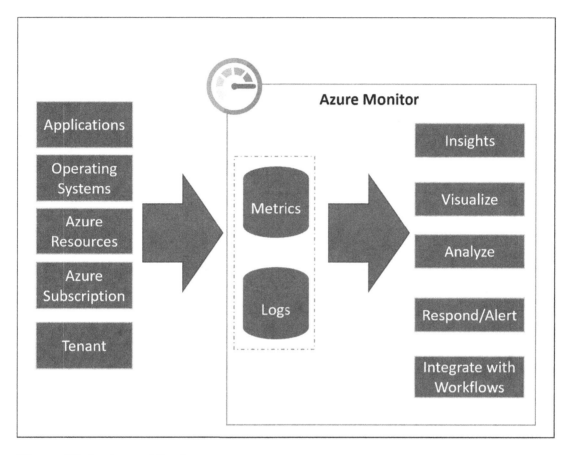

Figure 11-1. *Azure Monitor*

Application Insights helps you monitor and gather insights for your logs and performance metrics data for your applications running on Azure, on-premises, or any other cloud. It can be integrated with applications developed using various programming languages and frameworks like .NET, Java, Python, PHP, and many more. Figure 11-2 demonstrates Application Insights.

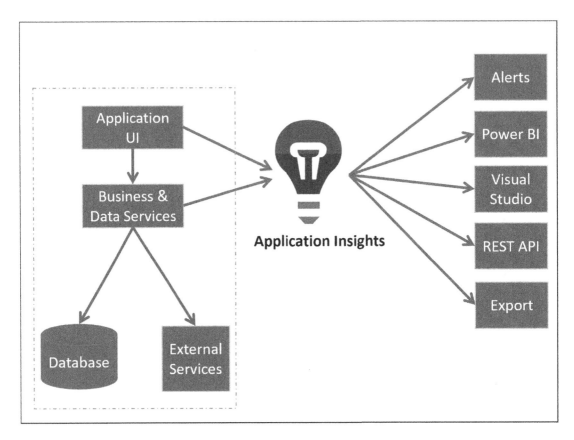

Figure 11-2. *Application Insights*

Note   Azure Monitor collects and analyzes data for application, infrastructure, operating system, Azure services, tenants, and Azure subscriptions. Application Insights is a subset of Azure Monitor and helps you analyze and gather insights from application data.

Configure Azure Monitor Metrics and Dashboard

Let us configure Metrics for an Azure WebApp using Azure Monitor. We will then create a private dashboard to display the metrics. As a prerequisite, we should have a WebApp created beforehand. Refer to Chapter 2 to learn how to create WebApp. Go to the Azure portal and search for *Monitor*. Click *Monitor* in the search results as in Figure 11-3.

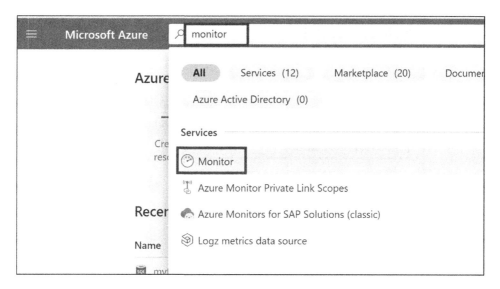

Figure 11-3. *Search for Monitor*

Click *Metrics* in the Azure Monitor as in Figure 11-4.

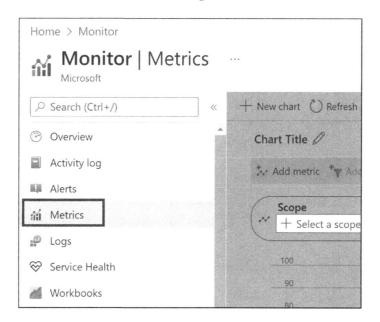

Figure 11-4. *Go to Metrics*

Select Subscription and expand the resource group where the Azure WebApp is created as in Figure 11-5.

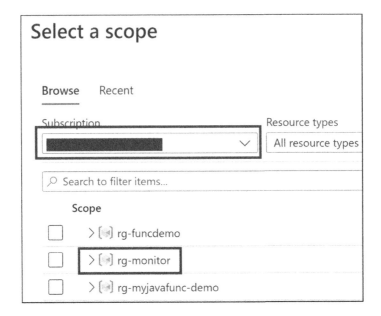

Figure 11-5. *Select the resource group*

Select the WebApp and click *OK* as in Figure 11-6.

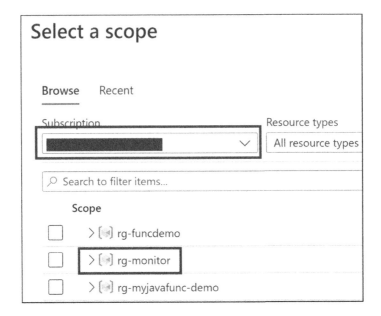

Figure 11-6. *Select the WebApp*

Select the Metric details for the sum of CPU time as in Figure 11-7.

Figure 11-7. *Configure Metrics*

Let us add this metric to the Dashboard. Once you have added the metric to the Dashboard, click *New chart* to create a new metric. First, let us add the existing metric to the Dashboard and then create a new metric. Click *Save to Dashboard* and *Pin to Dashboard* as in Figure 11-8.

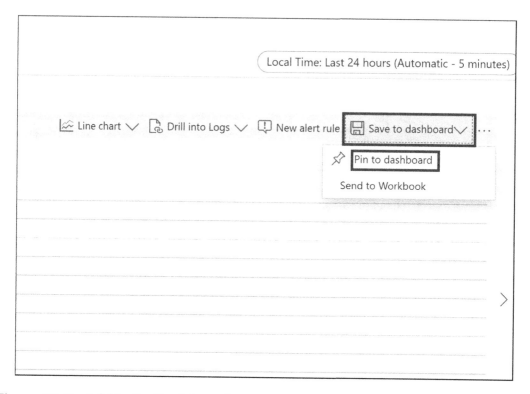

Figure 11-8. *Add to the Dashboard*

Go to the *Create new* tab and provide a dashboard name. Click *Create and pin* as in Figure 11-9.

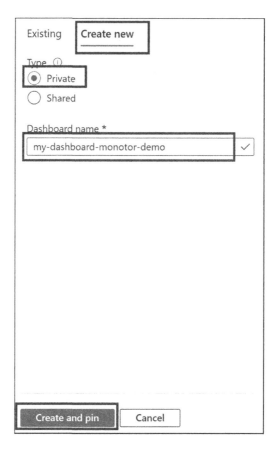

Figure 11-9. *Create the Dashboard*

Now click *New chart* and add a metric for the sum of the requests as in Figure 11-10.

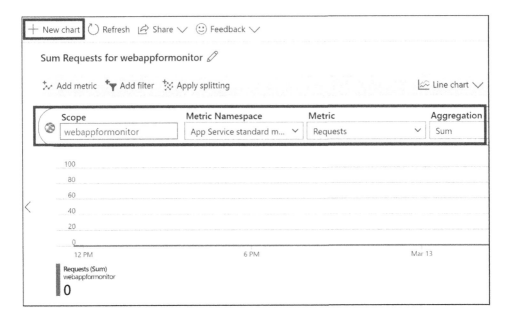

Figure 11-10. *Configure Metrics*

Pin this metric to the Dashboard we created earlier as in Figure 11-11.

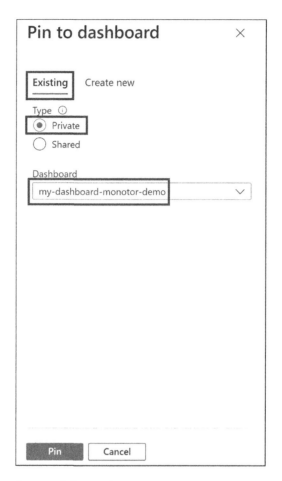

Figure 11-11. *Pin to the Dashboard*

Let us add one more metric for response time by clicking on the *New chart* as in Figure 11-12. Pin this to the Dashboard we created earlier.

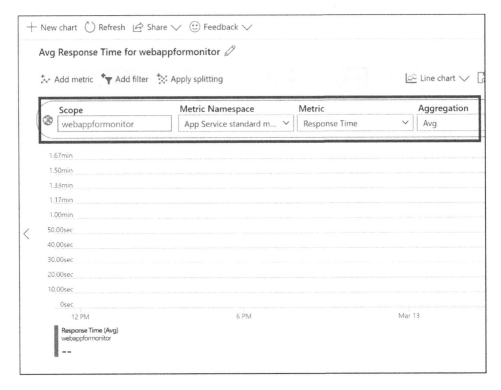

Figure 11-12. *Configure Metrics*

Go to *Dashboard* in the portal menu as in Figure 11-13.

Figure 11-13. *Go to Dashboard*

Select the Dashboard we created earlier as in Figure 11-14.

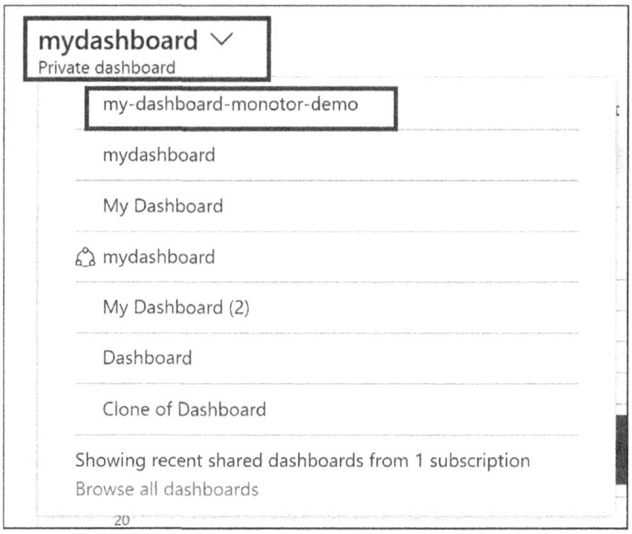

Figure 11-14. *Select the Dashboard*

Click *Edit* as in Figure 11-15 and arrange the placements of the charts so that the Dashboard looks good.

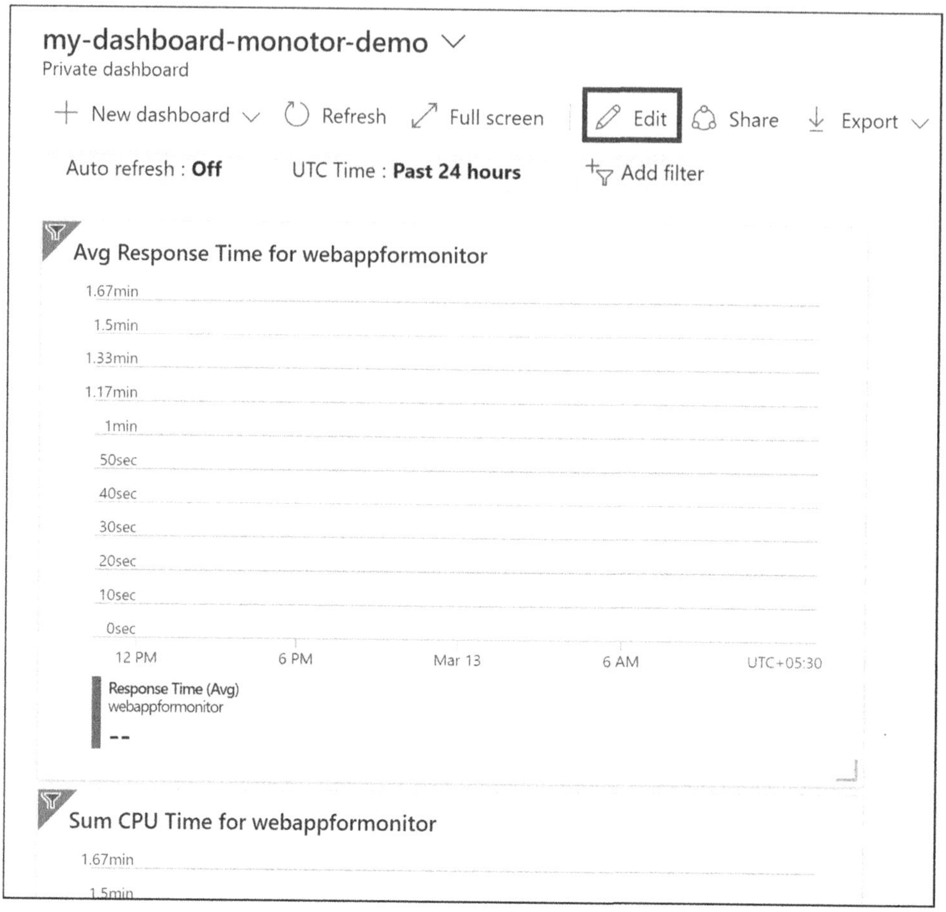

Figure 11-15. *Edit the Dashboard*

Click *Save* as in Figure 11-16.

Figure 11-16. *Save the Dashboard*

Browse the WebApp URL, and you can see the metrics being generated in the Dashboard as in Figure 11-17.

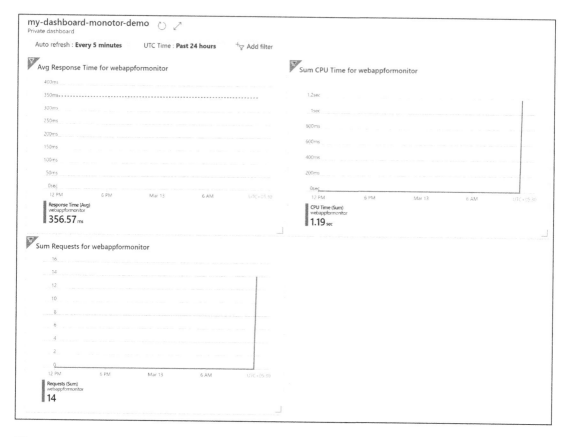

Figure 11-17. *Metrics data in the Dashboard*

Create Performance Alerts

Let us create performance alerts for Azure Storage Account. Go to *Metrics* in Azure Monitor. Configure a metric for the blob container count as in Figure 11-18.

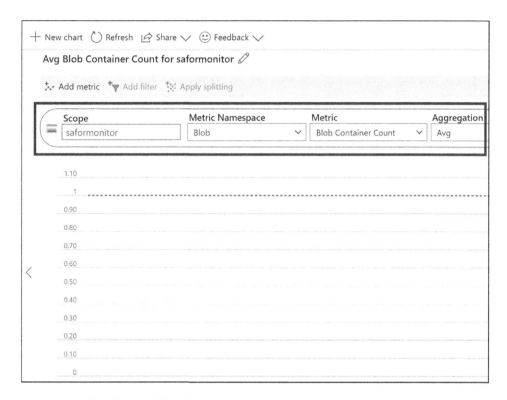

Figure 11-18. *Configure Metrics*

Let us create an alert for the metric configured. Click *New alert rule* as in Figure 11-19.

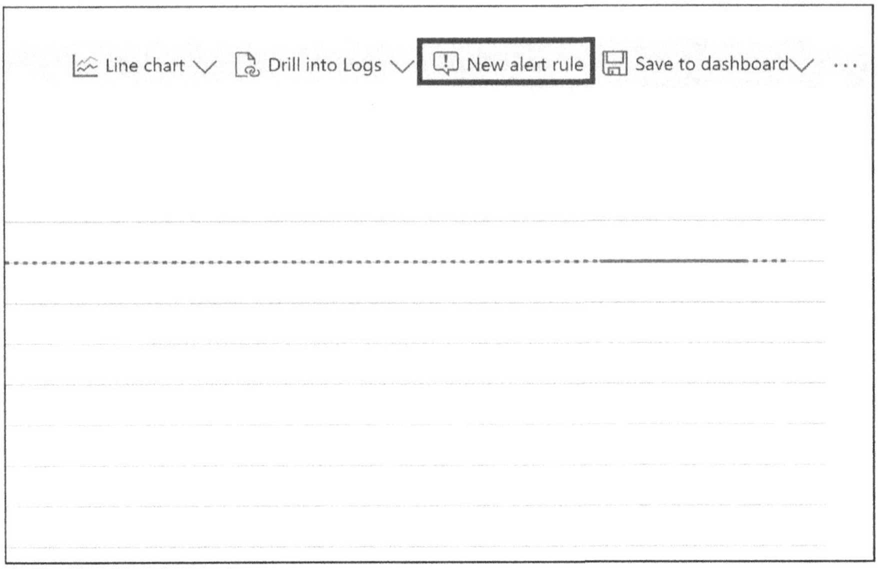

Figure 11-19. *New alert rule*

We need to configure a condition when the alert is raised. Click *Condition* as in Figure 11-20. Click on the default listed condition.

Figure 11-20. *Configure the alert condition*

Configure the alert condition. In this condition, we are configuring an alert when the average number of containers exceeds 10. Click *Done* as in Figure 11-21.

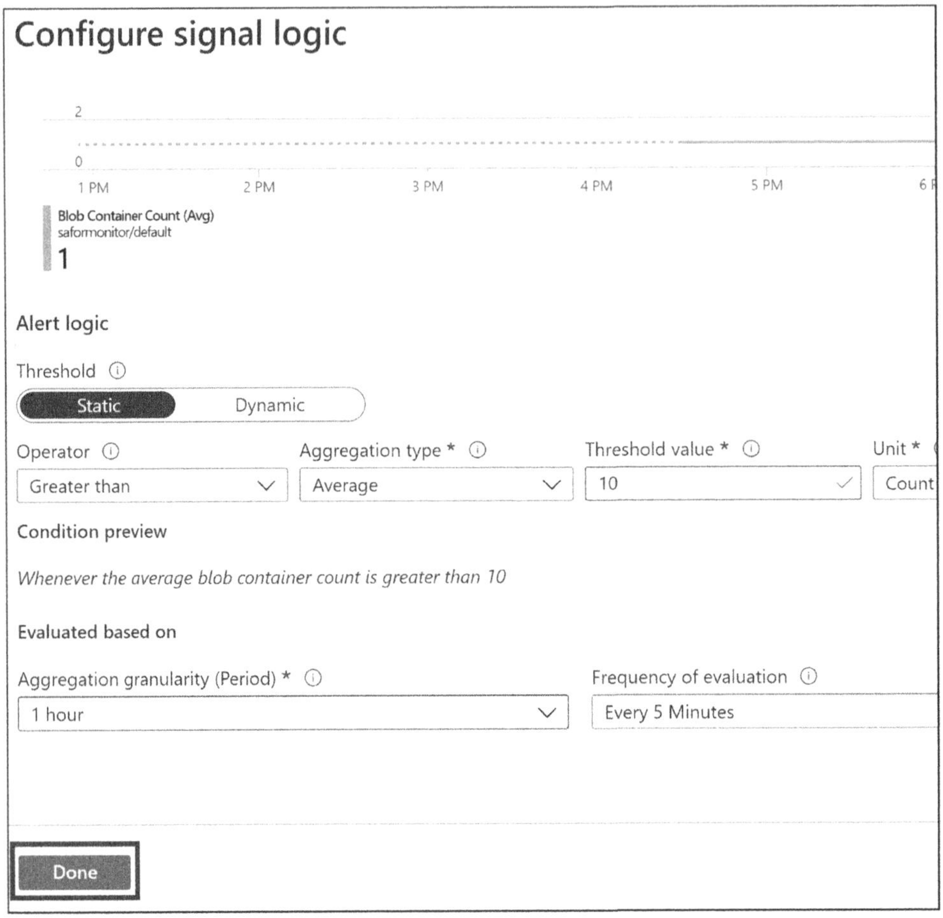

Figure 11-21. *Provide condition details*

Go to the *Actions* tab and click *Create action group* as in Figure 11-22.

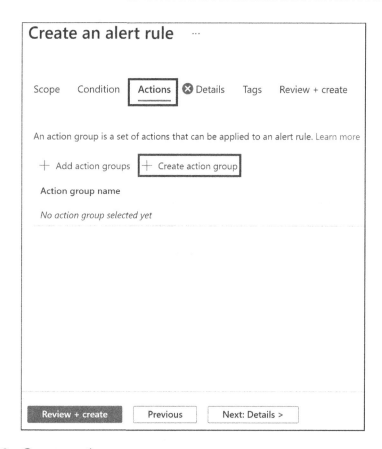

Figure 11-22. *Create action group*

Provide subscription, resource group, name, and other details. Click *Next: Notifications* as in Figure 11-23.

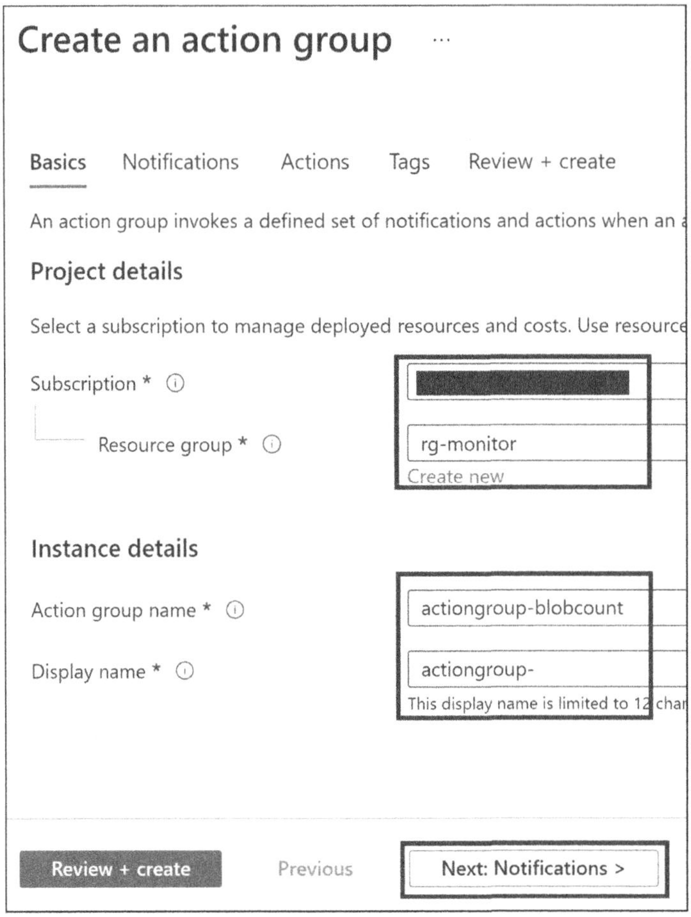

Figure 11-23. *Provide basic details for the action group*

Let us notify the users using an email when the alert is raised. Select email as the notification type as in Figure 11-24.

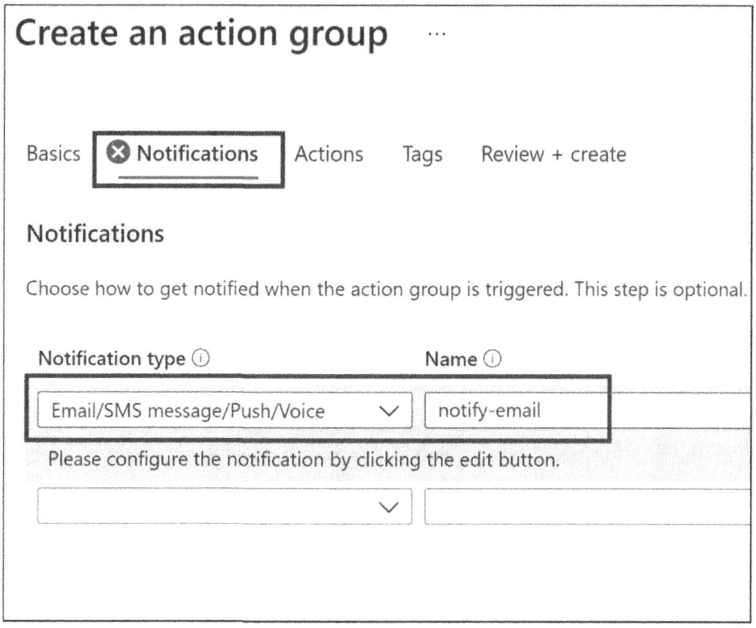

Create an action group   ···

Basics   ⊗ Notifications   Actions   Tags   Review + create

Notifications

Choose how to get notified when the action group is triggered. This step is optional.

Notification type ⓘ	Name ⓘ
Email/SMS message/Push/Voice ⌄	notify-email

Please configure the notification by clicking the edit button.

⌄	

Figure 11-24. *Configure email notification*

Provide your email address to which you need to send a notification when an alert is raised. Click *OK* as in Figure 11-25.

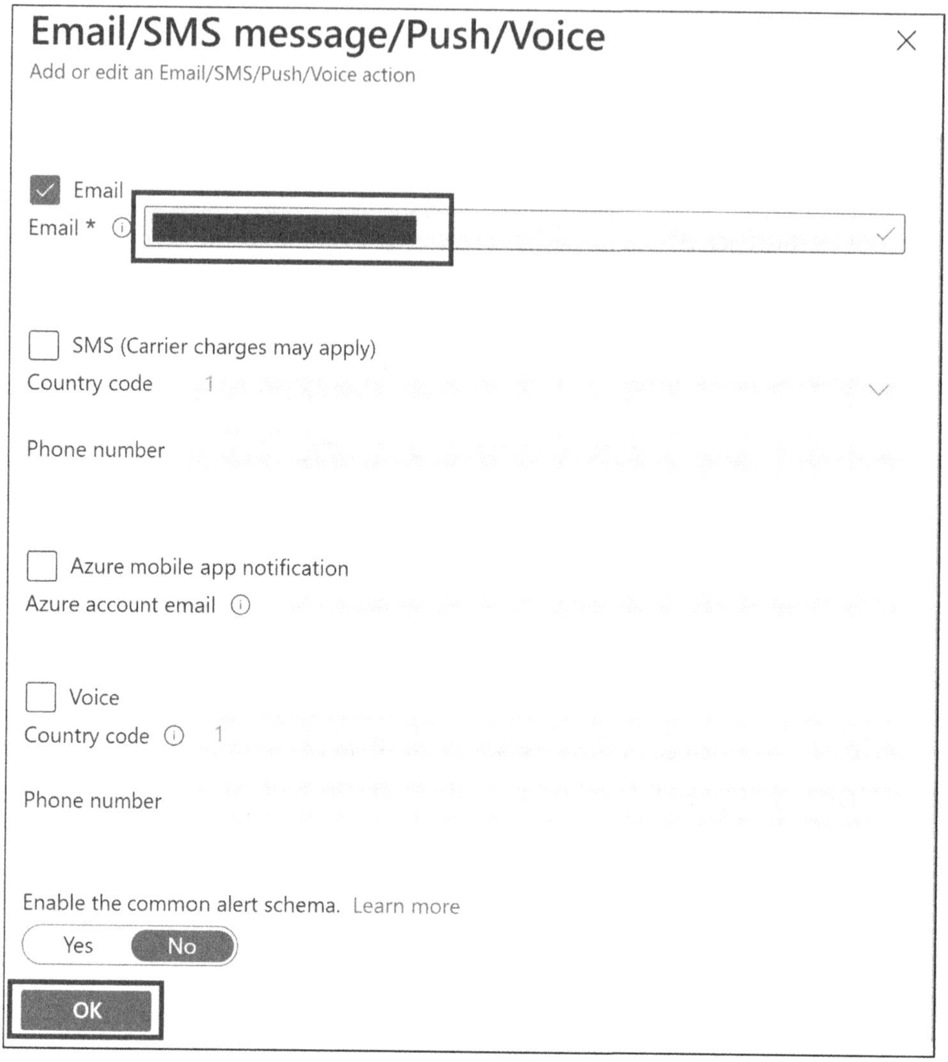

Figure 11-25. *Provide an email address to be notified*

Go to the *Actions* tab and configure an action. You can choose one of the listed actions to execute when the alert is raised. The most popular is *ITSM,* where you can log an issue or a service request in an ITSM tool whenever there is an alert. Click *Review + create* as in Figure 11-26.

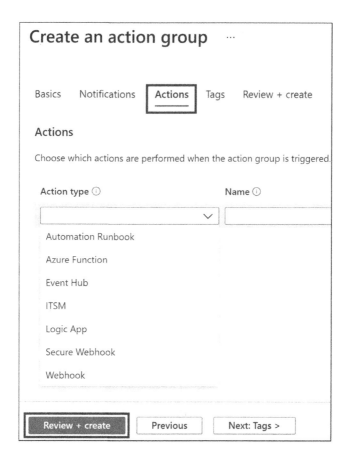

Figure 11-26. *Click Review + create*

Click *Create* to spin up the action group as in Figure 11-27.

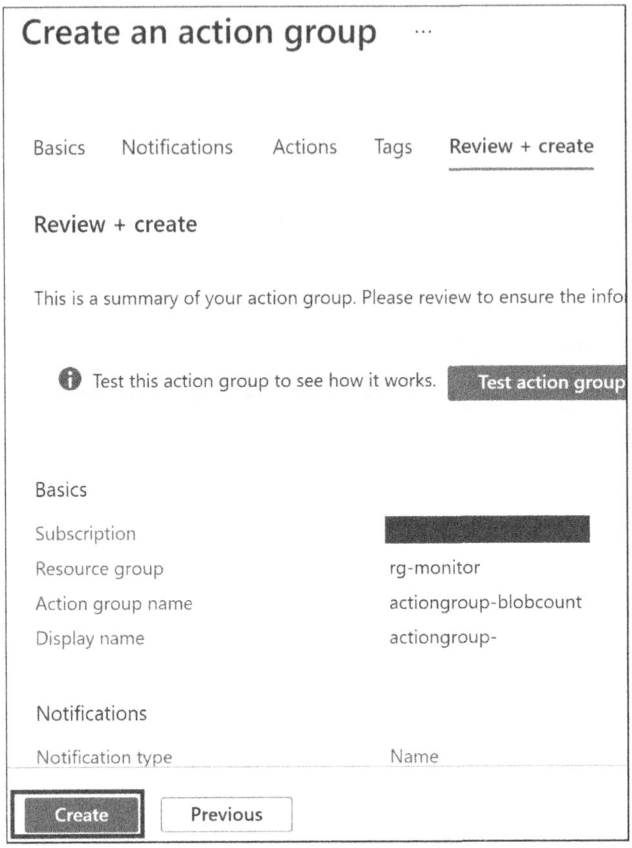

Figure 11-27. *Click Create*

Whenever the average number of blob containers in the Storage Account exceeds 10, an alert will get raised. Go to the *Details* tab for the alert rule and provide the necessary basic details. Click *Review + create* and then click *Create to configure the alert* as in Figure 11-28.

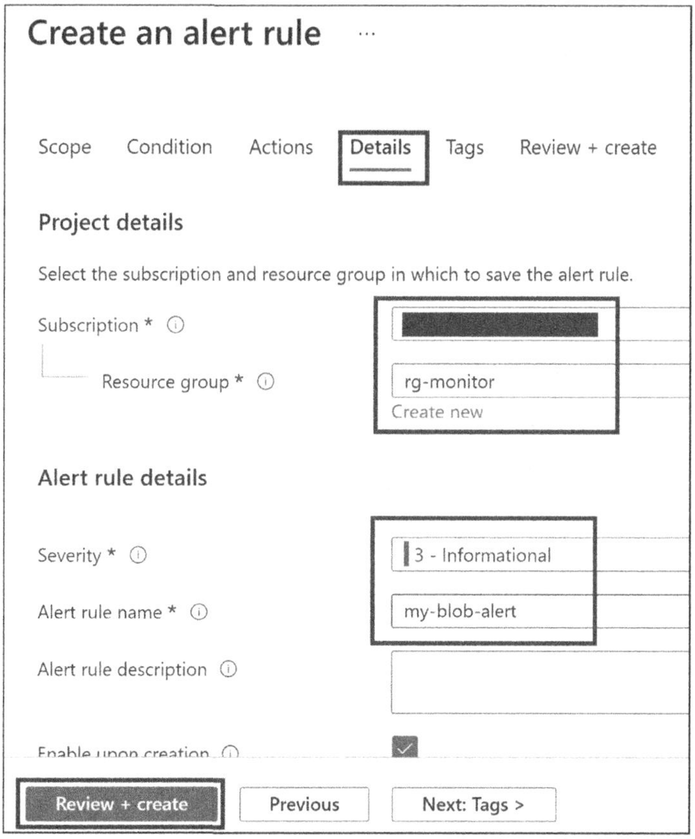

Figure 11-28.   *Create alert*

Work with Application Insights for Java Application

Now let us spin up an Application Insights resource and push some Java logs to it. You need to package the Application Insights agent for Java with the application and pass it as the JVM argument. This action would automatically push application logs and performance metrics to Application Insights for popular Java-based loggers like Log4j, java.util.logging, and SLF4J without any additional configuration.

Let us create an Application Insights. Go to the Azure portal and search for *Application Insights*. Click *Application Insights* in the search result as in Figure 11-29.

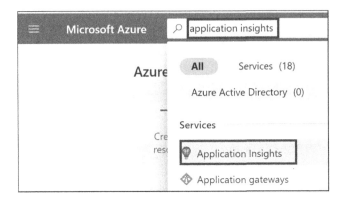

Figure 11-29. *Search for Application Insights*

Click *Create* to spin up an Application Insights as in Figure 11-30.

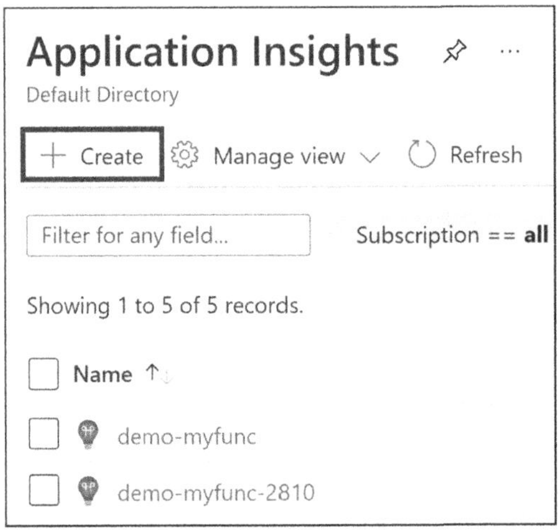

Application Insights

Figure 11-30. *Create Application Insights*

Provide the basic details for Application Insights. We need to keep the logs in a Log Analytics workspace, and hence, we need to create one or use an existing one. Application Insights will connect to this Log Analytics workspace and get the log insights. Click *Review + create* and then click *Create* as in Figure 11-31.

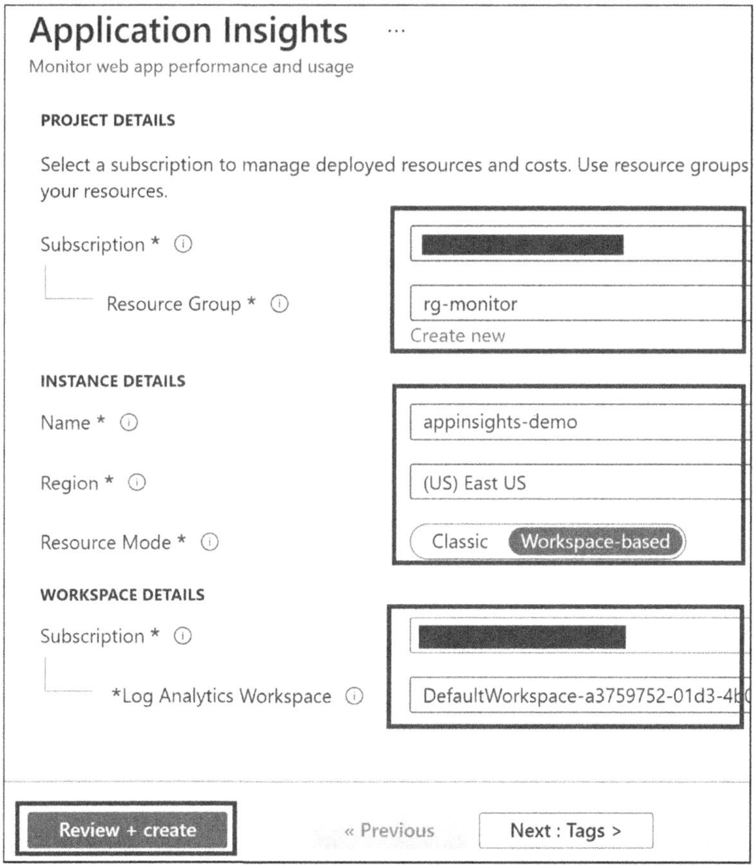

Figure 11-31. *Provide basic details*

Once the Application Insights spins up, copy the connection string. We will use the connection string in the Java code as in Figure 11-32.

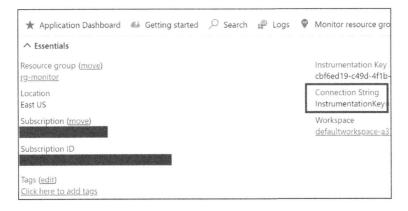

Figure 11-32. *Copy the connection string*

Now let us create a Maven-based Java console application. Go to the class file where the Main method is there and add a few logging statements using java.util.logging as in Listing 11-1.

Listing 11-1. Main method

```
import java.util.logging.Level;
import java.util.logging.Logger;

//https://github.com/microsoft/ApplicationInsights-Java/releases
public class AppInsightsLoggingDemo {

    private static final Logger logger = Logger.getLogger("AppInsightsLogg
    ingDemo");
    public static void main(String args[])
    {
        logger.setLevel(Level.ALL);
        logger.log(Level.INFO,"This is ERROR");
        logger.log(Level.WARNING,"This is WARNING");
        logger.log(Level.SEVERE, "This is SEVERE");
    }
}
```

Create an *applicationinsights.json* file and keep it in the same folder where the *pom. xml* file is present. We need to provide the Application Insights connection string here as in Listing 11-2.

Listing 11-2. Application insights.json

```
{
  "connectionString": "Provide your connection string"
}
```

Download the Application Insights agent file *applicationinsights-agent-3.2.8.jar* from the Microsoft GitHub location as in Listing 11-3. Keep it in the same folder as *pom.xml*.

Listing 11-3. Download the URL for applicationinsights-agent-3.2.8.jar

```
https://github.com/microsoft/ApplicationInsights-Java/releases
```

Compile the application and run the application with the JVM argument as `-javaagent:[Your Path]/applicationinsights-agent-3.2.8.jar`. Replace [Your Path] with the path on your system where this file is there.

After a few minutes, go to Application Insights and click *Transaction search* as in Figure 11-33. You can see your ingested logs.

Figure 11-33. *Logs in Application Insights*

Summary

In this chapter, we learned Application Insights and Azure Monitor basics. We learned how to configure dashboard and alerts for Azure Monitor metrics. We then developed a Maven-based Java code and pushed logs to Application Insights. In the next chapter, we will learn how to authenticate application users using Azure Monitor.

The following are the key takeaways from this chapter:

- Azure Monitor helps you collect performance metrics and logs data from your applications and infrastructure on Azure, on-premises, or any other cloud platforms.

- Application Insights helps you monitor and gather insights for your logs and performance metrics data for your applications running on Azure, on-premises, or any other cloud.

- Application Insights can be integrated with applications developed using various programming languages and frameworks like .NET, Java, Python, PHP, etc.

CHAPTER 12

Authentication and Authorization Using Azure Active Directory

Applications should allow access to authenticated users. The authenticated users should access the application modules that they are authorized for and perform the allowed activities in the application. Azure Active Directory is an identity provider on Azure that can be used for authentication and authorization by applications either hosted on Azure or on-premises or on any other public or private cloud.

In the previous chapter, we learned the basic concept of Azure Monitor and Application Insights. We then created a Java application that can use Azure Monitor to generate performance metrics and Azure Application Insights that can generate logs for the application. In this chapter, we will secure a Java application using Spring Security and Azure Active Directory.

Structure

In this chapter, we will discuss the following aspects of Azure Active Directory.

- Introduction to Azure Active Directory
- Configure Azure Active Directory for authentication and authorization
- Configure a Java Spring Boot application
- Authentication scenarios for Azure AD

© Abhishek Mishra 2022
A. Mishra, *Microsoft Azure for Java Developers*, https://doi.org/10.1007/978-1-4842-8251-9_12

Objectives

After studying this chapter, you should be able to get the following learnings:

- Understand the concept of Azure Active Directory

- Work with Azure Active Directory

- Configure authentication and authorization for Java Spring Boot application using Azure Active Directory

Introduction to Azure Active Directory

Azure Active Directory is an Identity-as-a-Service (IDaaS) offering on Azure. It provides an enterprise-grade identity management solution on Azure. Azure Active Directory offers multitenant directory management service. You can also integrate on-premises Active Directory to Azure Active Directory using AD Connect and sync all the users, groups, and roles in the on-premises directory to Azure. You can use it as a Domain Controller on Azure and join your Azure Virtual Machines to it.

Azure Active Directory helps you manage user authentication and authorization for your applications running on Azure or on-premises or any other cloud. It offers functionalities like Single Sign-On, Multifactor Authentication, and other modern identity management and governance offerings. You can use SAML, OAuth, OpenID Connect, or WS-Federation to authenticate and authorize the application users.

It supports integrating B2B scenarios where another business organization can authenticate, collaborate, and consume services of the business organization. It also supports B2C scenarios where the end customers can authenticate, collaborate, and consume services of the business organization.

Azure Active Directory is a Platform-as-a-Service offering, and you just need to configure and use the domain and identity services without needing to build and manage any infrastructure.

Configure Azure Active Directory for Authentication and Authorization

Let us configure Azure Active Directory and use it to authenticate a user and authorize it to use a Java Web API. The following are the steps we will perform. We will use the default tenant. However, you may prefer to create a new tenant and use it. The following are the steps we will execute to configure Azure Active Directory for authentication and authorization.

1. Create a user in Azure Active Directory.

2. Register an application in Azure Active Directory.

3. Assign the user to the application role.

Create a User in Azure Active Directory

Let us create a user in the default tenant. Go to the Azure portal. Search for *Azure Active Directory*. Click *Azure Active Directory* in the search results as in Figure 12-1.

Figure 12-1. *Search for Azure Active Directory*

You will get navigated to the Default tenant or directory. Click *Users* as in Figure 12-2. We need to create a User using which we can perform authentication and authorization.

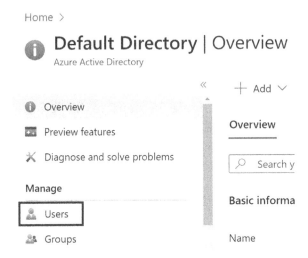

Figure 12-2. *Click Users*

Click *New user* to create a user as in Figure 12-3. We need this new user to perform authentication and authorization on the application.

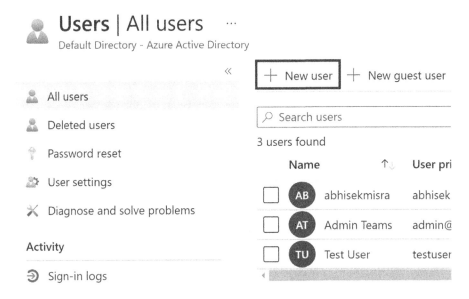

Figure 12-3. *Click New user*

Select *Create user* as in Figure 12-4. We need to create a user in the default directory or tenant and do not need a guest user.

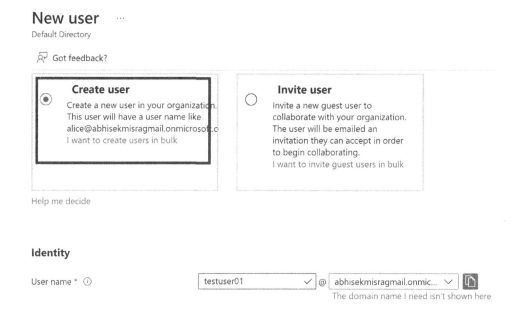

Figure 12-4. *Select Create user*

Provide the user's name, password, and other necessary details. Click *Create* as in Figure 12-5. A new user will get created.

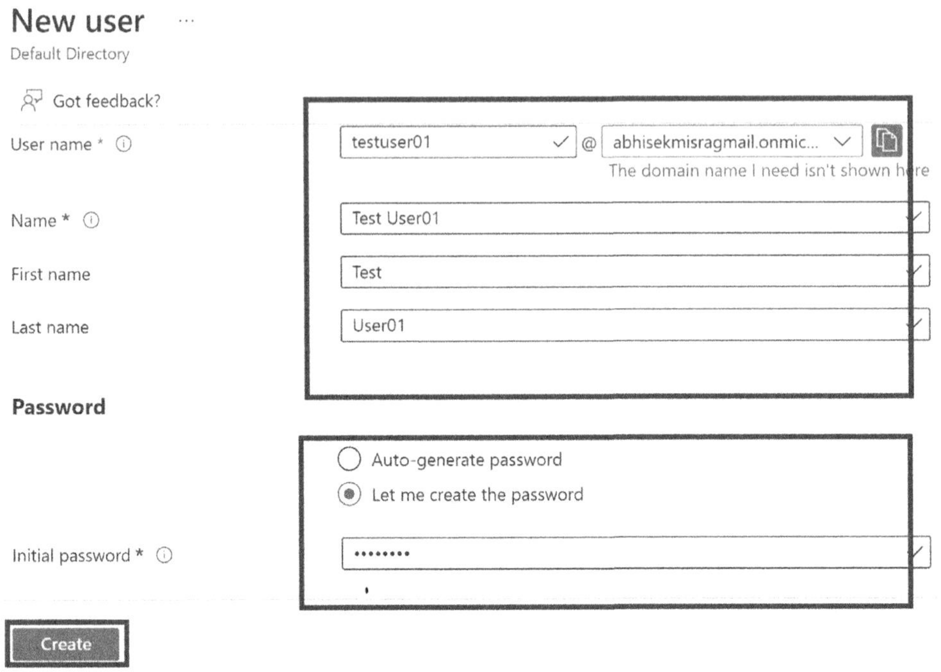

Figure 12-5. *Create a user*

Register an Application in Azure Active Directory

Now let us create an application in the default tenant. We will use this application for configuring authentication and authorization for the Java application. Go to Azure Active Directory in the Azure portal and click *App registrations* as in Figure 12-6.

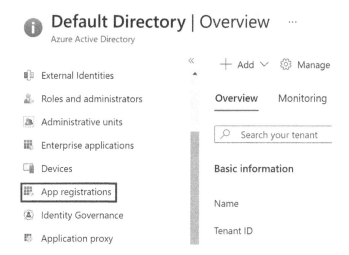

Figure 12-6. *Click App registrations*

Click *New registration* to register a new application as in Figure 12-7.

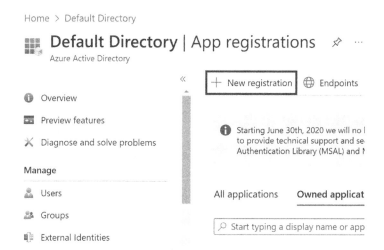

Figure 12-7. *Click New registration*

Provide a unique name for the application and click *Register* as in Figure 12-8.

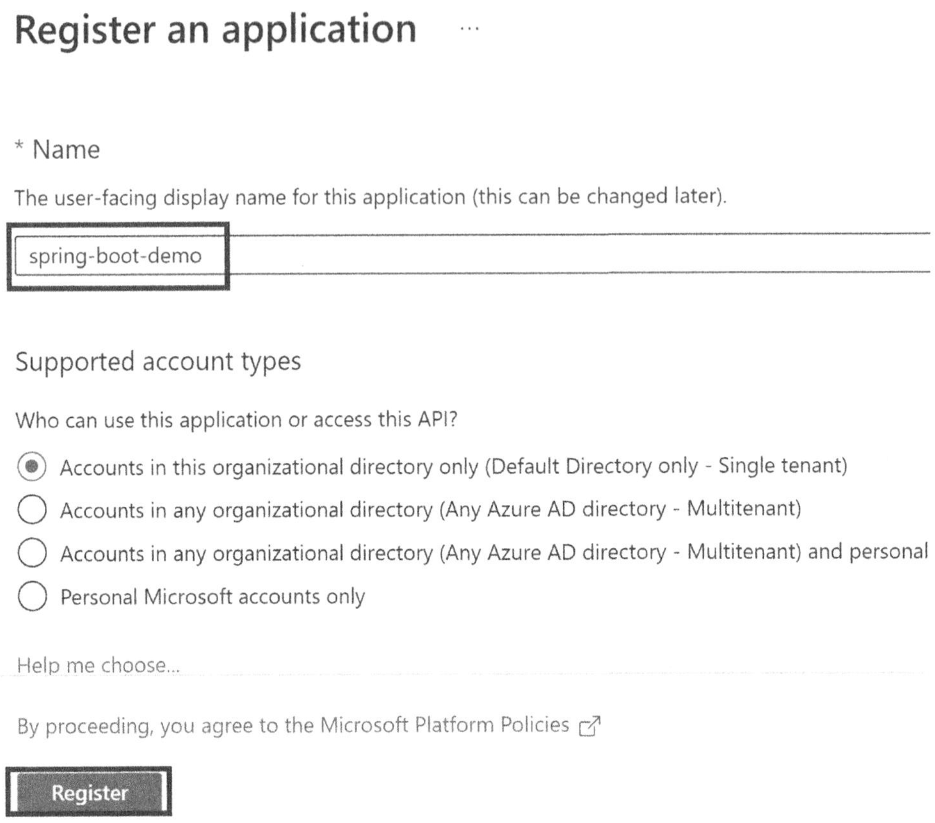

Register an application   ⋯

* Name

The user-facing display name for this application (this can be changed later).

```
spring-boot-demo
```

Supported account types

Who can use this application or access this API?

(●) Accounts in this organizational directory only (Default Directory only - Single tenant)

( ) Accounts in any organizational directory (Any Azure AD directory - Multitenant)

( ) Accounts in any organizational directory (Any Azure AD directory - Multitenant) and personal

( ) Personal Microsoft accounts only

Help me choose...

By proceeding, you agree to the Microsoft Platform Policies ⤤

```
Register
```

Figure 12-8. *Register application*

Once the application gets created, copy the tenant or directory ID and the
application or client ID for the application. We will use them later in the Java application.
Let us configure a Redirect URI for the application. Click *Add a Redirect URI* as in
Figure 12-9.

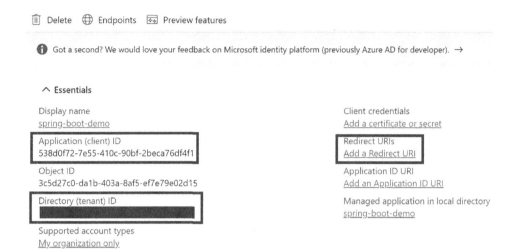

Figure 12-9. *Add a redirect URI*

Click *Add a platform* as in Figure 12-10. We need to add a web platform as we are dealing with a web application.

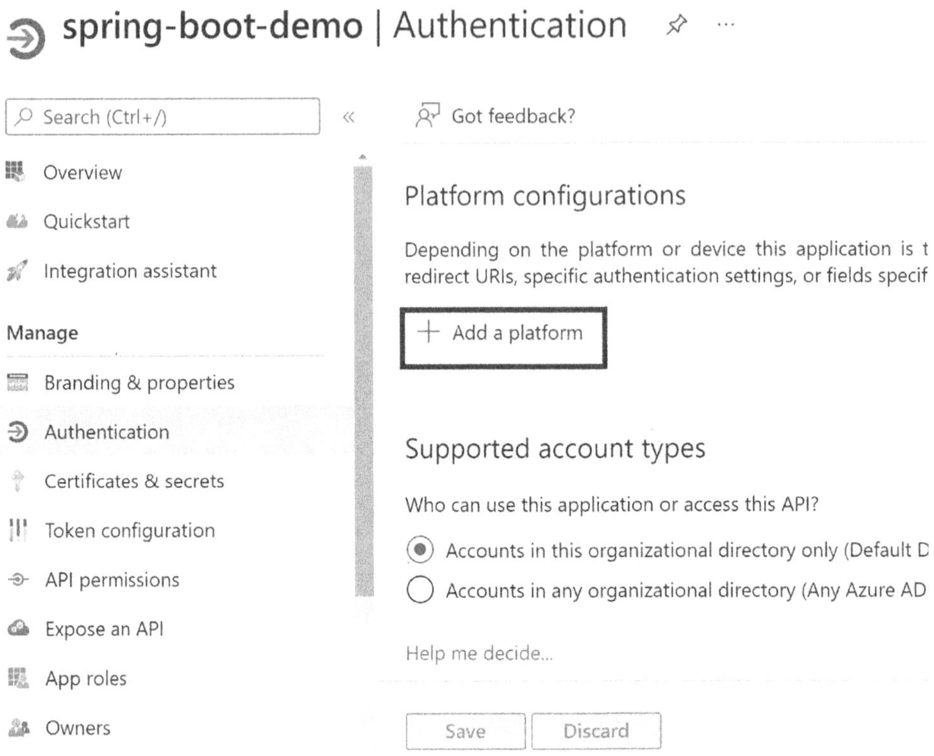

Figure 12-10. *Add a platform*

Select *Web* as we are going to use this application in a Java-based API project. Figure 12-11 demonstrates this action.

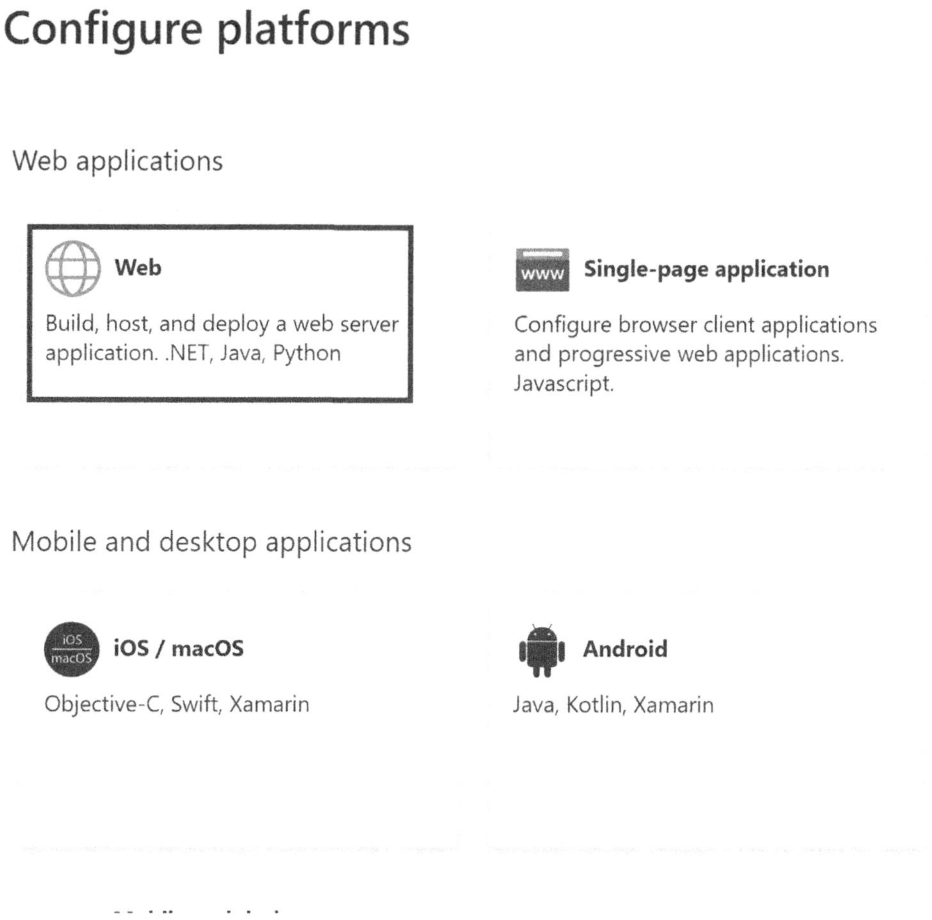

Configure platforms

Web applications

 Web

Build, host, and deploy a web server application. .NET, Java, Python

 Single-page application

Configure browser client applications and progressive web applications. Javascript.

Mobile and desktop applications

 **iOS / macOS**

Objective-C, Swift, Xamarin

Android

Java, Kotlin, Xamarin

Figure 12-11. *Select Web*

Provide Redirect URIs as `http://localhost:8080/login/oauth2/code/`. Click *Configure* as in Figure 12-12. The application gets created in the default tenant.

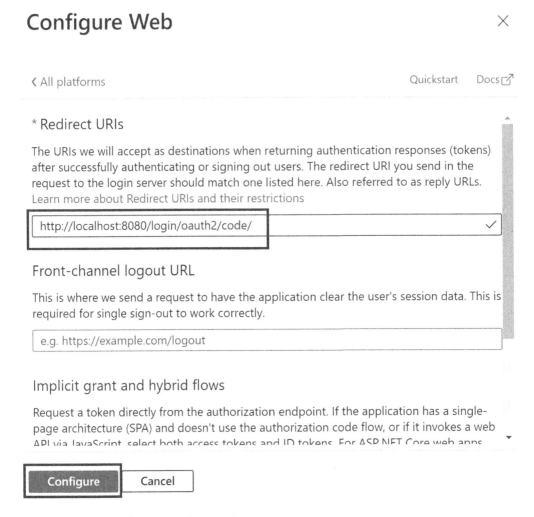

Figure 12-12. *Configure Redirect URI*

Now let us create an application role for the user. We will assign this role to the user we created. Click the *App roles* section and then click *Create app role* as in Figure 12-13.

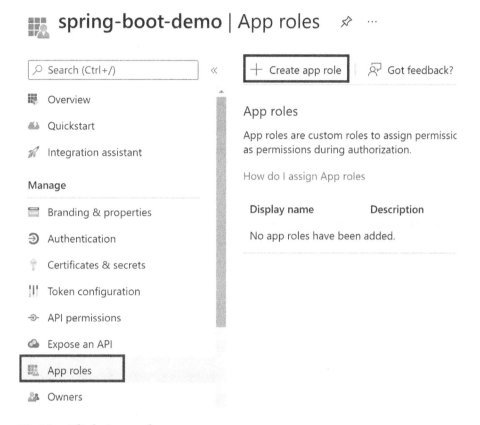

Figure 12-13. *Click App roles*

Provide the role details. We will use the value for the role in the Java code. Click *Apply* as in Figure 12-14. The role gets created in the application.

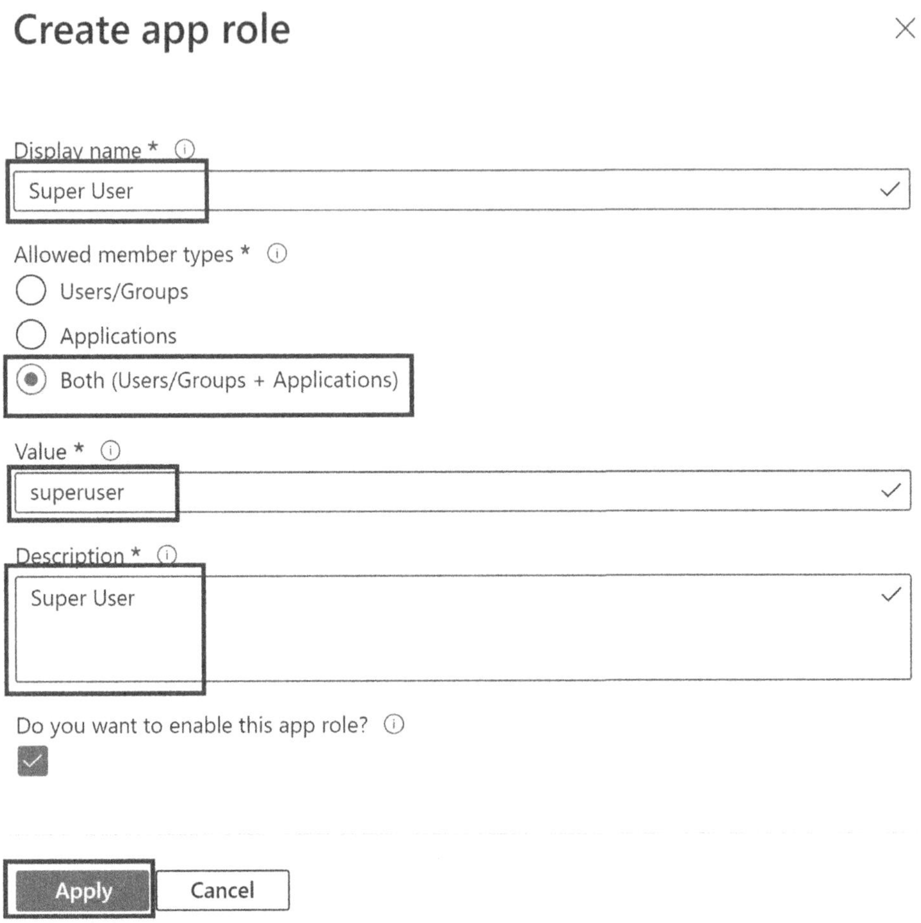

Create app role

Display name * ⓘ

Super User

Allowed member types * ⓘ

○ Users/Groups

○ Applications

◉ Both (Users/Groups + Applications)

Value * ⓘ

superuser

Description * ⓘ

Super User

Do you want to enable this app role? ⓘ

☑

Apply   Cancel

Figure 12-14. *Create a role*

We need to generate a secret for the application. We will use it in the Java code along with the tenant ID and client ID for the application. Click *Certificates & secrets* as in Figure 12-15. Then click *New client secret*. Copy the value of the secret once you have created it. You will be able to see the value once, and this value will not be available to you once you leave this page.

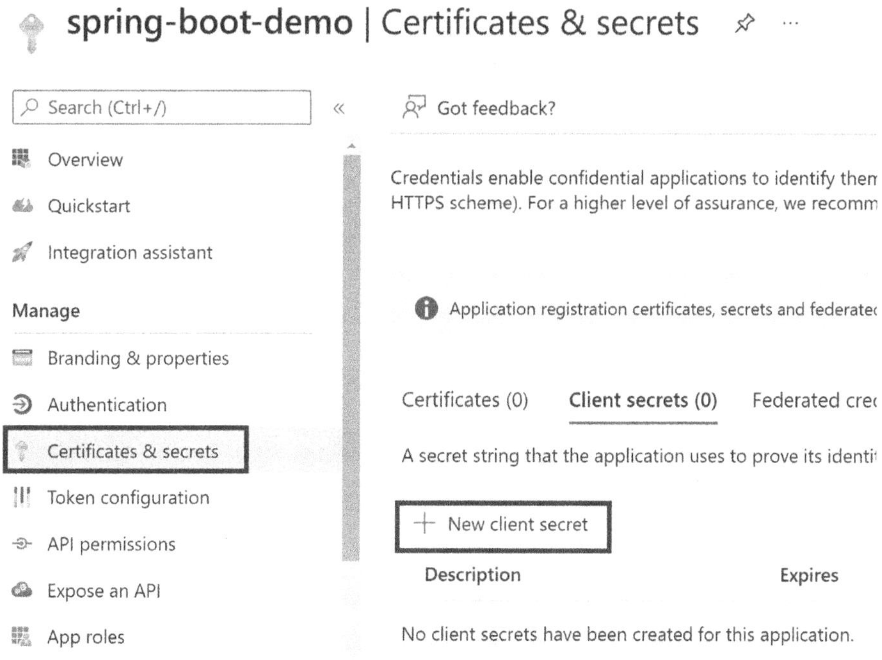

spring-boot-demo | Certificates & secrets 📌 ⋯

⌕ Search (Ctrl+/)   «   ☿ Got feedback?

▦ Overview
        Credentials enable confidential applications to identify them
🐤 Quickstart   HTTPS scheme). For a higher level of assurance, we recomm

🚀 Integration assistant

Manage   ⓘ Application registration certificates, secrets and federated

▦ Branding & properties

⊙ Authentication   Certificates (0)   **Client secrets (0)**   Federated cre

⎷ Certificates & secrets   A secret string that the application uses to prove its identi

⎟⎟ Token configuration   ┌──────────────────────────┐
        │ + New client secret   │
⟜ API permissions   └──────────────────────────┘

☁ Expose an API   Description   Expires

▦ App roles   No client secrets have been created for this application.

Figure 12-15. *Generate a secret for the application*

Assign the User to the Application Role

Now let us assign the user to the role we created for the application. We need to make this configuration in the *Enterprise applications* section in the tenant. Click *Enterprise applications* as in Figure 12-16.

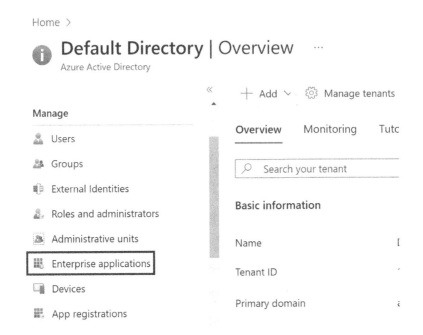

Figure 12-16. *Click Enterprise applications*

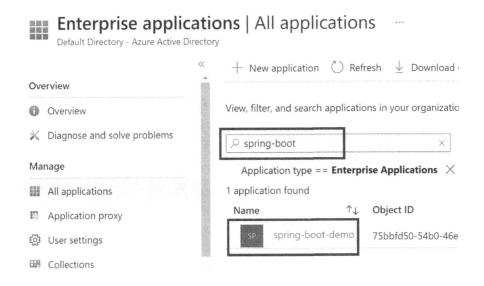

Figure 12-17. *Search for the application*

Search for the application we created earlier and then click on the application in the search results as in Figure 12-17.

Go to *Users and groups*. Click *Add user/group* as in Figure 12-18. We need to search for the user and do a role assignment.

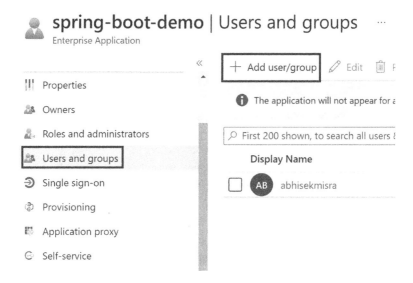

Figure 12-18. *Click Add user/group*

Let us add the user against the role we created. Click *None Selected* as in Figure 12-19.

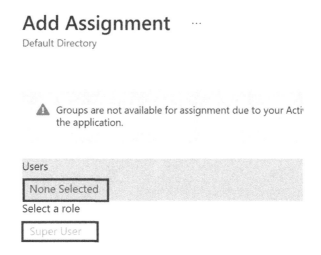

Figure 12-19. *Click None Selected*

Select the user and click *Select* as in Figure 12-20.

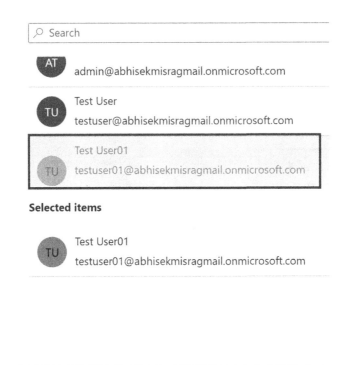

Figure 12-20.   *Select the user*

Click *Assign* as in Figure 12-21 to complete the role assignment for the user.

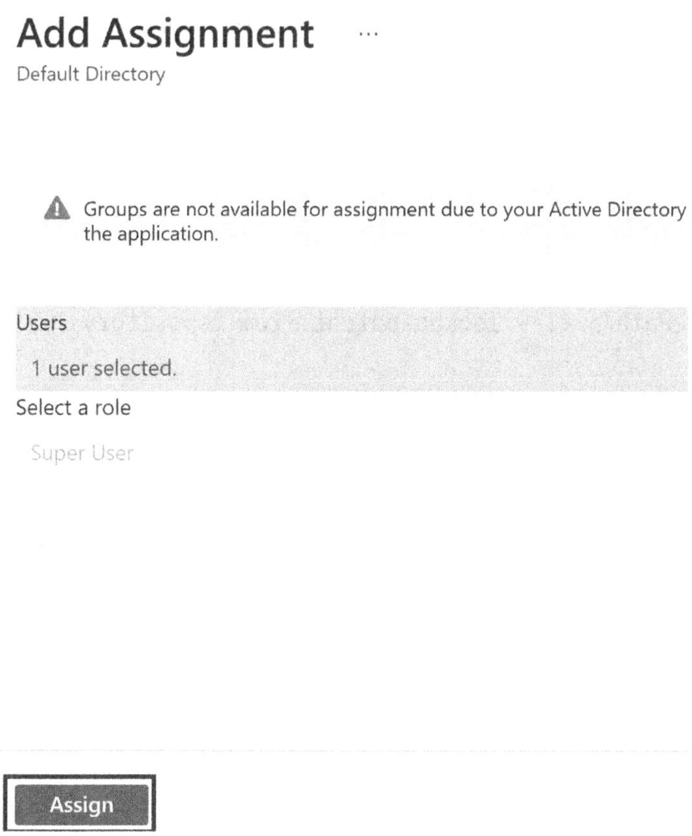

Add Assignment   ⋯

Default Directory

⚠ Groups are not available for assignment due to your Active Directory the application.

Users

1 user selected.

Select a role

Super User

Assign

Figure 12-21. *Assign the role to the user*

Configure a Spring Boot Application

Now let us configure authentication and authorization for Java Spring Boot application to perform authentication and authorization. Create a Spring Boot application that can expose an API. You can use *Spring Intializr* to generate the project as we did in the previous chapters. Make sure that the *pom.xml* file contains the packages as listed in the following code. We need to configure Spring Security along with Azure Active Directory for the API project. Listing 12-1 demonstrates the changes in the pom.xml file.

Listing 12-1. Pom.xml

```
<?xml version="1.0" encoding="UTF-8"?>
<project xmlns="http://maven.apache.org/POM/4.0.0" xmlns:xsi="http://www.
w3.org/2001/XMLSchema-instance"
```

```xml
xsi:schemaLocation="http://maven.apache.org/POM/4.0.0 https://maven.
apache.org/xsd/maven-4.0.0.xsd">
<modelVersion>4.0.0</modelVersion>
<parent>
    <groupId>org.springframework.boot</groupId>
    <artifactId>spring-boot-starter-parent</artifactId>
    <version>2.6.4</version>
    <relativePath/> <!-- lookup parent from repository -->
</parent>
<groupId>com.azure.azuread</groupId>
<artifactId>authdemo</artifactId>
<version>0.0.1-SNAPSHOT</version>
<name>authdemo</name>
<description>Demo project for Spring Boot</description>
<properties>
    <java.version>11</java.version>
    <azure.version>3.14.0</azure.version>
</properties>
<dependencies>
    <dependency>
        <groupId>org.springframework.boot</groupId>
        <artifactId>spring-boot-starter-oauth2-client</artifactId>
    </dependency>
    <dependency>
        <groupId>org.springframework.boot</groupId>
        <artifactId>spring-boot-starter-web</artifactId>
    </dependency>
    <dependency>
        <groupId>com.azure.spring</groupId>
        <artifactId>azure-spring-boot-starter-active-directory</
        artifactId>
    </dependency>

    <dependency>
        <groupId>org.springframework.boot</groupId>
        <artifactId>spring-boot-starter-test</artifactId>
```

```xml
                <scope>test</scope>
            </dependency>
        </dependencies>
        <dependencyManagement>
            <dependencies>
                <dependency>
                    <groupId>com.azure.spring</groupId>
                    <artifactId>azure-spring-boot-bom</artifactId>
                    <version>${azure.version}</version>
                    <type>pom</type>
                    <scope>import</scope>
                </dependency>
            </dependencies>
        </dependencyManagement>

        <build>
            <plugins>
                <plugin>
                    <groupId>org.springframework.boot</groupId>
                    <artifactId>spring-boot-maven-plugin</artifactId>
                </plugin>
            </plugins>
        </build>

</project>
```

Let us create an *application.properties* file in the resources folder. We need to provide the application or the client ID, tenant ID, and the client secret that we copied earlier while creating the application registration in Azure Active Directory. Listing 12-2 demonstrates the changes in the application.properties file.

Listing 12-2. application.properties

```
# Specifies your Active Directory ID:
azure.activedirectory.tenant-id={Provide Tenant ID}
# Specifies your App Registration's Application ID:
azure.activedirectory.client-id={Provide App Id}
# Specifies your App Registration's secret key:
azure.activedirectory.client-secret={Provide client secret}
```

Go to the class file having the *Main* method. Convert the class as REST Controller as in Listing 12-3. Add a REST method as *SuperUser*. In the *PreAuthorize* attribute, provide the Role value in the format *APPROLE_{RoleValue}* where *RoleValue* is the value of the Role you create in the Azure Active Directory application.

Listing 12-3. Class file for the Main method

```
import org.springframework.boot.SpringApplication;
import org.springframework.boot.autoconfigure.SpringBootApplication;
import org.springframework.security.config.annotation.method.configuration.
EnableGlobalMethodSecurity;
import org.springframework.security.config.annotation.web.configuration.
EnableWebSecurity;
import org.springframework.web.bind.annotation.RestController;
import org.springframework.web.bind.annotation.GetMapping;
import org.springframework.web.bind.annotation.ResponseBody;
import org.springframework.web.bind.annotation.RestController;
import org.springframework.security.access.prepost.PreAuthorize;

@SpringBootApplication
@RestController
public class AuthedApplication {

    public static void main(String[] args) {
        System.out.println("Hello");
        SpringApplication.run(AuthedApplication.class, args);
    }

    @GetMapping("SuperUser")
    @ResponseBody
    @PreAuthorize("hasAuthority('APPROLE_superuser')")
    public String SuperUser() {
        return "This is a Super User !! You have all kinds of Access in the
        WORLD !!";
    }

}
```

Build and run the application. Browse the URL as in Listing 12-4 once that application starts up.

Listing 12-4. URL to browse

```
http://localhost:8080/SuperUser
```

You will get prompted to provide the sign-in credentials as in Figure 12-22. You need to provide the credentials for the user we created. For all other users, the authorization will not be successful, and you will get *Forbidden* response.

Figure 12-22. *Provide credentials*

Once you have provided the correct credentials, you get the following output rendered in the browser as in Figure 12-23.

This is a Super User !! You have all kinds of Access in the WORLD !!

Figure 12-23. *API response*

Authentication Scenarios for Azure AD

Azure AD supports the following authentication scenarios:

- Web Browser to Web Application

- Single Page Application

- Native Application to Web API

- Web Application to Web API

- Server Application to Web API

Let us discuss each of these scenarios in detail.

Web Browser to Web Application

When the user requests the home page of the application in the browser, then the user will get redirected to the Azure AD login page. The user signs in to the Azure AD and if the sign-in is successful, the browser gets a security token as Reply URL. The browser then sends this security token to the application. The security token contains the claims for the user. The application validates this token and starts a session. The application can check for the claims and allow the user to perform the actions on the application as mentioned in the claims. The supported protocols for this sign-on are OpenID Connect, SAML 2.0, and WS-Federation. You can use MSAL Azure AD SDKs to perform the authentication.

Single Page Application

A Single Page Application uses the OAuth 2.0 implicit authentication mechanism to grant users access to the application and its back-end APIs. Developers can use ADAL JavaScript libraries to perform the authentication. The user requests for the Single Page Application in the browser. The browser loads the application sign-in page on the browser. Once the user clicks the sign-in button, the browser fires a GET request to the Azure AD authorization endpoint and requests for an ID token. The GET query passes on client ID and Reply URL as per your configuration for the application in the portal as query string parameters. Then Azure AD will validate the request and the Reply URL. Then it asks the user to sign in. If the user is able to sign in successfully, Azure AD returns the ID token as part of the Reply URL. The application can then extract the token and accordingly allow access to the back-end APIs based on the user claims.

Native Application to Web API

In this case, a native application calls a Web API on behalf of the user. It uses the OAuth 2.0 authorization code grant type with a public token. The native application requests for the authorization code from the Azure AD authorization endpoint, and then the user is asked to sign in. Once the user signs in, the application gets an authorization code. Then the application sends the authorization code to the Azure AD Token endpoint and gets the JWT token. It then passes on the JWT token to the Web API in the request authorization header. The Web API validates the JWT token and then allows the application to access the Web API.

Web Application to Web API

Here, you can use either Delegated User Identity or Application Identity to access the Web API. In the case of Application Identity, you use the OAuth 2.0 client credentials grant. The user signs in to the Web Application as in the Browser to Web Application scenario. Then the Web Application tries to get the access token by requesting the Azure AD Token endpoint. Azure AD authenticates the request, and if the authentication is successful, the application gets a JWT token. The JWT token is used to call the Web API. The Web API validates the JWT token and provides access.

In this scenario, the Web API does not get the user details in the JWT token as the Web Application is driving the authentication. Delegated User Identity helps the Web Application to authenticate as the user, and the JWT will have user details that can be used by the Web API.

Server Application to Web API

The Server application can be a daemon or a batch application that cannot authenticate like a human. It needs to pass on the credentials that can be a password or a certificate to Azure AD along with application URI and client ID. It uses either Application Identity with the credentials grant or Delegated User Identity with OAuth 2.0 on-behalf-of flow for authentication purposes.

Summary

In this chapter, we learned Azure Active Directory basics. We learned how to create a user and register an application in Azure Active Directory. We then developed a Maven-based Java code and used the application in Azure Active Directory. In the next chapter, we will learn how to provision Azure resources using Azure DevOps and Azure CLI.

The following are the key takeaways from this chapter:

- Azure Active Directory is an Identity-as-a-Service (IDaaS) offering on Azure.

- Azure Active Directory helps you manage user authentication and authorization for your applications running on Azure or on-premises or any other cloud.

- Azure Active Directory supports integrating B2B and B2C scenarios.

- You can integrate on-premises Active Directory to Azure Active Directory using AD Connect and sync all the users, groups, and roles in the on-premises directory to Azure.

PART III

DevOps and Best Practices

## CHAPTER 13

Provisioning Resources with Azure DevOps and Azure CLI

Infrastructure as Code (IaC) is a widely adopted practice in a cloud-based enterprise. You automate the creation of cloud infrastructure using scripts and DevOps tools. You need to create these scripts or solutions once and reuse them across multiple environments. This approach saves a lot of time and effort for you. There are many Infrastructure-as-Code (IaC) utilities and tools available that will help you automate provisioning the Azure infrastructure.

In the previous chapter, we learned the basic concept of Azure Active Directory. We then created a Java application that can use Azure Active Directory to perform user authentication and authorization. In this chapter, we will explore the Infrastructure-as-Code (IaC) options for Azure and then spin up an Azure WebApp using Azure CLI and Azure DevOps.

Structure

In this chapter, we will discuss the following aspects of infrastructure creation using Azure DevOps and Azure CLI:

- Introduction to Infrastructure as Code (IaC) on Azure

- Create an Azure CLI script to spin up Azure WebApp

- Create an Azure DevOps pipeline to spin up Azure WebApp

© Abhishek Mishra 2022
A. Mishra, *Microsoft Azure for Java Developers*, https://doi.org/10.1007/978-1-4842-8251-9_13

Objectives

After studying this chapter, you should be able to get the following learnings:

- Explore the options available to create Azure infrastructure using automation

- Create Azure resources using Azure DevOps and Azure CLI

Introduction to Infrastructure as Code (IaC) on Azure

The Azure portal helps you create Azure resources with ease. You get an intuitive and wizard-based user interface using which you can create your resources. However, you need to manually log in to the Azure portal and then provide the resource details in the portal and create your resource. This approach works well if you have a single environment. However, enterprises have multiple environments like development, testing, acceptance, and production. If you use the Azure portal to create resources across these environments, you may end up in many repetitive activities. You will create the resources for the application in the development environment and then create the same set of resources in other environments. This approach is effort-intensive and risks introducing errors due to the manual efforts involved. However, you can automate the resource creation activity and trigger the automation across multiple environments. This approach would save much time for you and would be error-free. You can get your environments created faster than the approach of creating resources using the Azure portal.

The following are some popular Infrastructure-as-Code (IaC) offerings to automate the creation of Azure resources:

- Azure CLI

- Azure PowerShell

- ARM Templates

- Terraform

- Bicep

Azure CLI is a cross-platform offering where you can spin up Azure resources either from Windows, Linux, or Mac systems. You can run the Azure CLI scripts from a command prompt, bash prompt, or PowerShell prompt.

Azure PowerShell offers you PowerShell modules that will help you spin up Azure resources. If you use Azure PowerShell Core that can run on PowerShell 6 and above, you can build cross-platform scripts.

Using ARM Templates, you can represent the Azure infrastructure as a JSON template and then deploy the template to the Azure environment and spin up your Azure resources. Both Azure CLI and Azure PowerShell expose commands that you can use to deploy these templates.

Azure PowerShell, Azure CLI, and ARM Templates are Microsoft offerings to create Azure resources. Terraform is a third-party offering that would help you script Azure resources creation.

You can use Azure DevOps pipelines to invoke the scripts developed using Azure CLI, PowerShell, Terraform, or ARM Templates to spin up Azure infrastructure. In this case, you can build release pipelines to spin up infrastructure across various environments. This approach will help you build single-click automation that will spin up Azure infrastructure and deploy an application.

Create an Azure CLI Script to Spin Up Azure WebApp

Let us create an Azure CLI script to spin up Azure WebApp. As a prerequisite, you should install the Azure CLI in your system. Follow the installation steps provided in Listing 13-1.

Listing 13-1. Azure CLI Installation URL

```
https://docs.microsoft.com/en-us/cli/azure/install-azure-cli
```

Let us open PowerShell or command prompt or bash prompt. We need to log in to Azure as the first step using the command as in Listing 13-2.

Listing 13-2. Log in to Azure

```
az login
```

You will get prompted in your browser to provide your credentials as in Figure 13-1.

Figure 13-1. *Log in to Azure*

Once you have logged in to Azure, you need to select a subscription where you need to create your resources. Execute the command as in Listing 13-3 to select your subscription. Replace {subscription} with your subscription name or subscription ID. You can use the `az account show` command to list out all the subscriptions in the chapter.

Listing 13-3. Select a subscription

```
az account set -s "{subscription}"
```

You need to create a resource group inside which you can create a WebApp. You may choose to use an existing resource group. In that case, you can ignore this step. Replace {name} with the resource group name. Here, we are creating the resource group in the eastus location. You may choose to have an Azure location matching your need. Listing 13-4 demonstrates the command to create a resource group.

Listing 13-4. Create a resource group

```
az group create --location eastus --name {name}
```

We need an App Service Plan for our WebApp. Execute the command as in Listing 13-5 to explore how to use the create command for the App Service Plan. You will also learn about the various App Service Plan SKUs available here and other details.

Listing 13-5. Create App Service Plan Help

```
az appservice plan create --help
```

Execute the command as in Listing 13-6 to create an App Service Plan in the region eastus and with standard SKU (S1). Replace {resourcegroup-name} with the name of the resource group and {name} with the name of the App Service Plan.

Listing 13-6. Create an App Service Plan

```
az appservice plan create --resource-group {resourcegroup-name} --name {name} --sku S1 --location eastus
```

Execute the command as in Listing 13-7 to create a WebApp. Replace {name} with the name of the WebApp, {resourcegroup-name} with the name of the resource group, and {plan-name} with the name of the App Service Plan.

Listing 13-7. Create a WebApp

```
az webapp create --name {name} --resource-group {resourcegroup-name} --plan {plan-name}  --runtime "java:11:Java SE:11"
```

Your WebApp gets created in the resource group provided. You can use the command `curl -s -o /dev/null -w "%{http_code}" https://{name}.azurewebsites.net/` where {name} is the name of the WebApp. You should get response code as 200.

Create an Azure DevOps Pipeline to Spin Up Azure WebApp

Let us create an Azure WebApp using Azure DevOps. We will invoke the Azure CLI script to create the WebApp from the Azure DevOps task. Let us log in to the Azure DevOps portal using the URL as in Listing 13-8.

Listing 13-8. Azure DevOps login URL

```
https://dev.azure.com
```

Once you have logged in to Azure DevOps, we can create a new DevOps project. Click *New project* as in Figure 13-2.

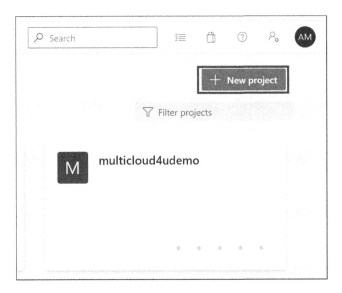

Figure 13-2. *Create a new project*

Provide the project's name, mark it as a private project, and click *Create* as in Figure 13-3.

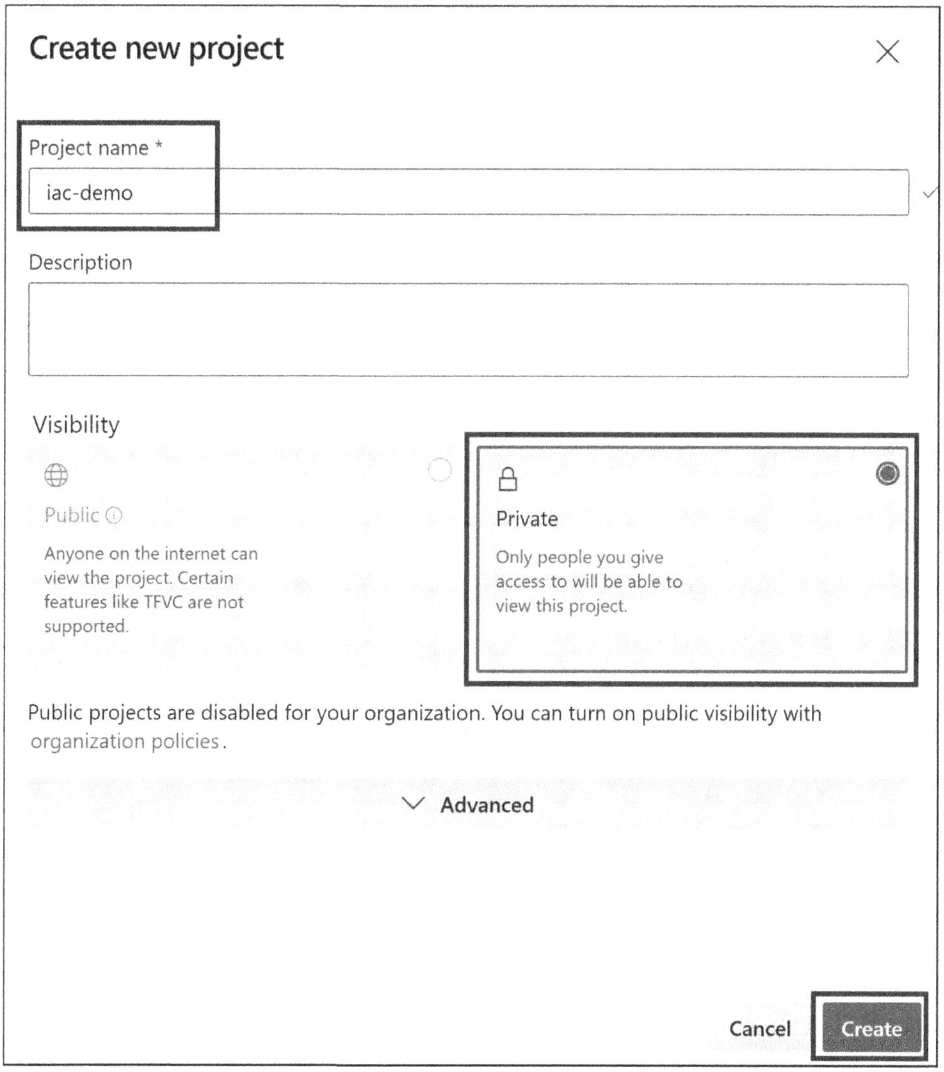

Figure 13-3. *Click Create*

Hover on *Pipelines* as in Figure 13-4. This action will list out the menu items for the Pipelines.

***Figure 13-4.** Hover on Pipelines*

Click *Releases* as in Figure 13-5. You will get navigated to the release pipelines.

***Figure 13-5.** Click Releases*

Let us create a new release pipeline. Click *New pipeline* as in Figure 13-6.

Figure 13-6. *Click New pipeline*

You will get prompted to select a job template. Select *Empty job* as in Figure 13-7.

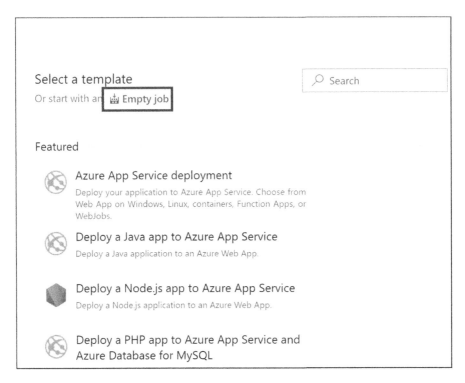

Figure 13-7. *Select the Empty job template*

We need to add the Azure CLI task to the Stage. Click *1 job, 0 task* as in Figure 13-8.

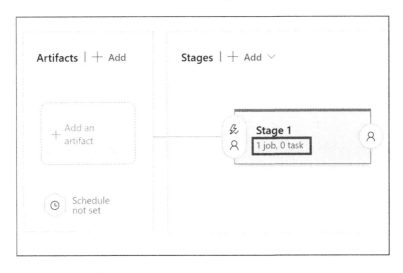

Figure 13-8. *Add the task*

We need to add the Azure CLI task. Click on the + icon as in Figure 13-9.

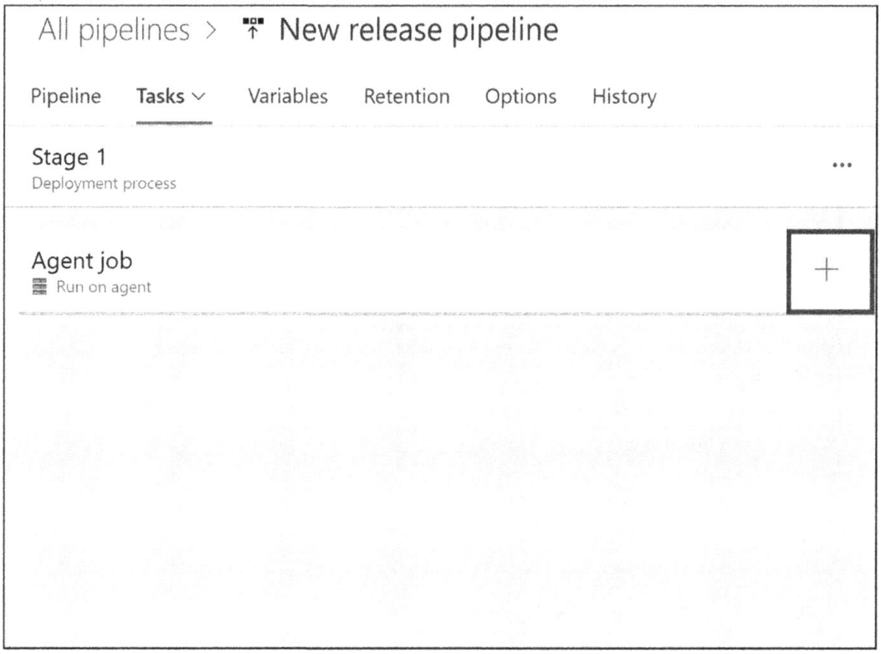

Figure 13-9.   *Click on the + icon*

Search for *Azure CLI* and select *Azure CLI* as in Figure 13-10.

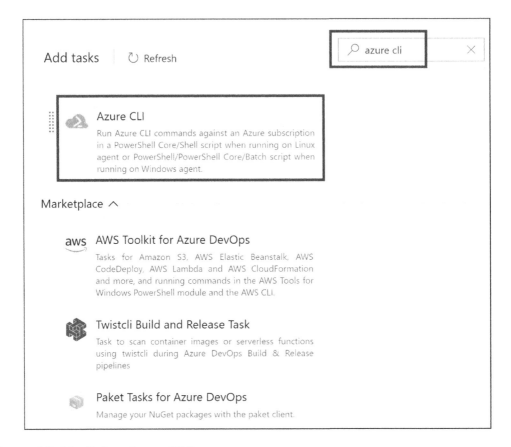

Figure 13-10. *Select Azure CLI*

Click *Add* to include this task in the agent job as in Figure 13-11.

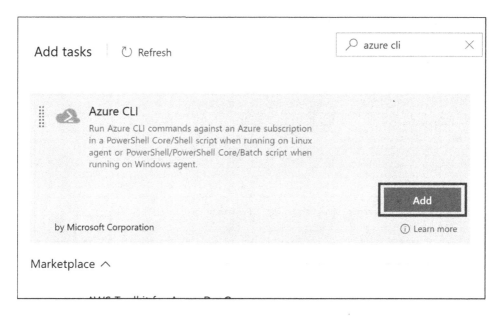

Figure 13-11. *Select Add*

Click the *Azure CLI* task as in Figure 13-12. We need to configure this task to create WebApp.

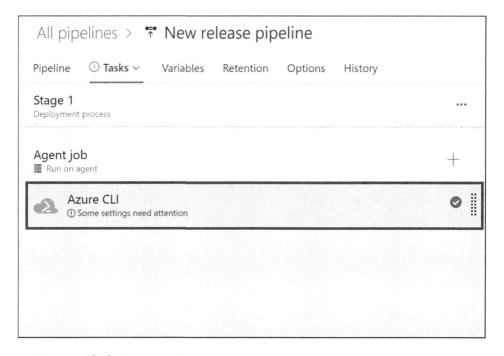

Figure 13-12. *Click Azure CLI*

Select an Azure subscription where you need to create the WebApp as in Figure 13-13.

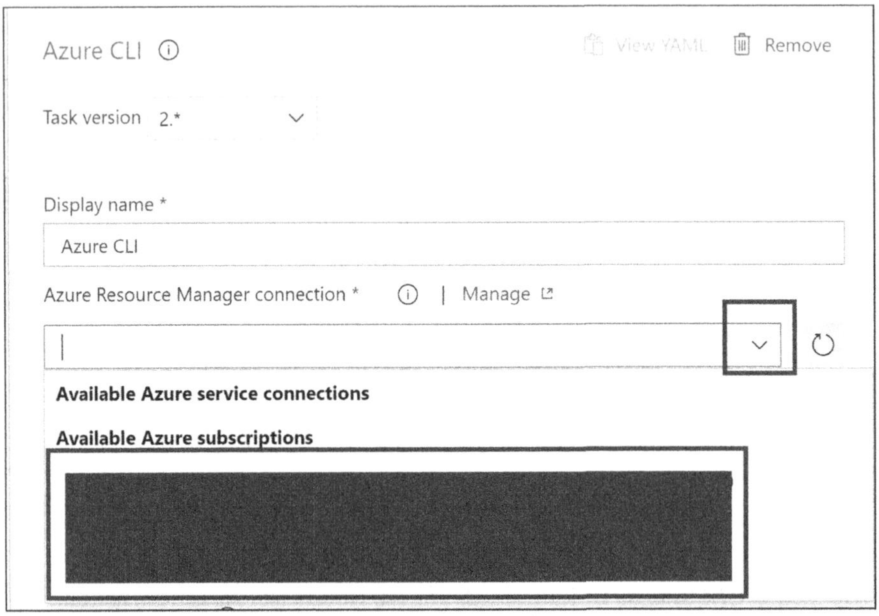

Figure 13-13. *Select an Azure subscription*

Click *Authorize* as in Figure 13-14. This action will authorize the pipeline to connect to the Azure environment and create the WebApp.

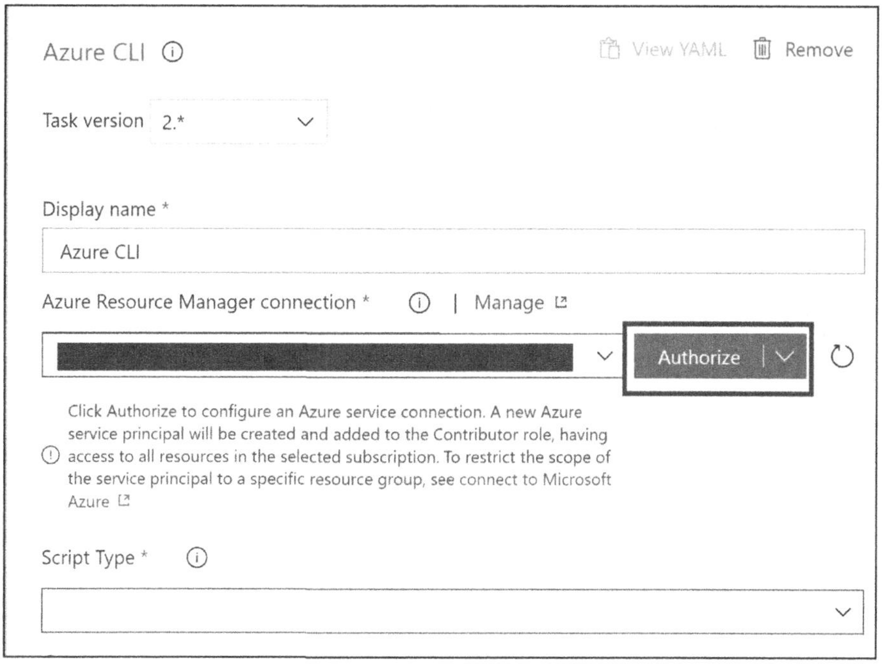

Figure 13-14. *Authorize connection*

You will be prompted to provide your login credentials as in Figure 13-15.

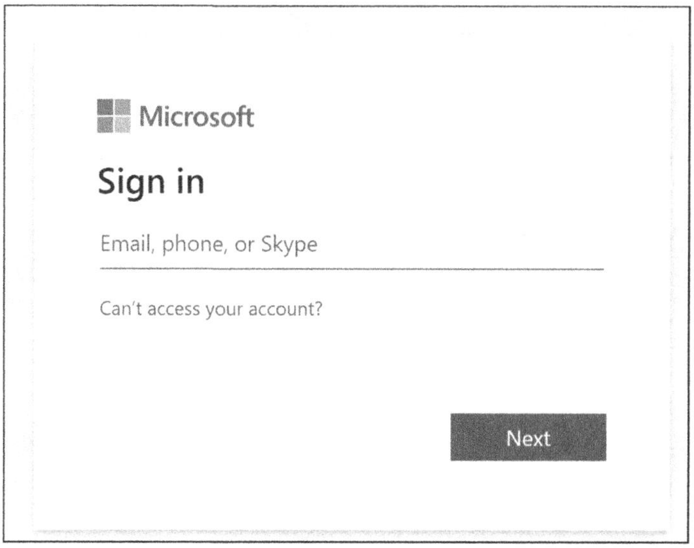

Figure 13-15. *Provide login credentials*

You can provide the command to create a resource group, an App Service Plan, and the WebApp. Select *PowerShell* as *Script Type* and *Inline script* as *Script Location* as in Figure 13-16. We need not log in to the Azure portal and select a subscription.

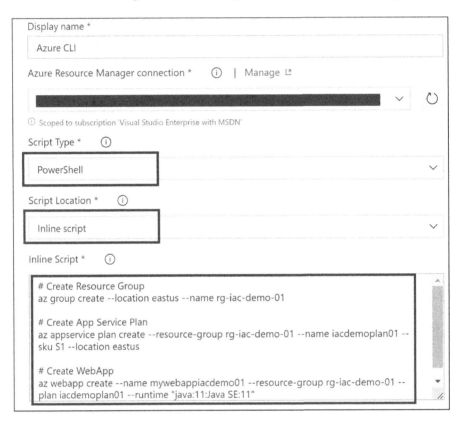

Figure 13-16. *Configure the Azure CLI task*

Provide a meaningful name to the pipeline as in Figure 13-17.

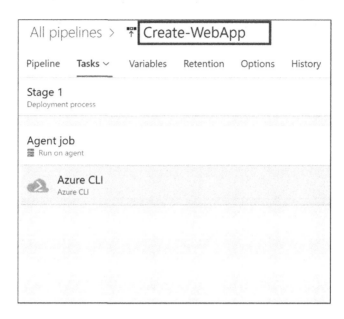

Figure 13-17. *Provide a pipeline name*

Click *Save* as in Figure 13-18. This action will save the pipeline.

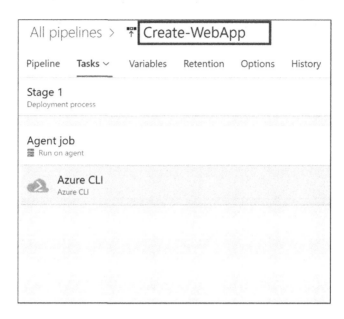

Figure 13-18. *Save the pipeline*

Click *Create release* to create a new release as in Figure 13-19.

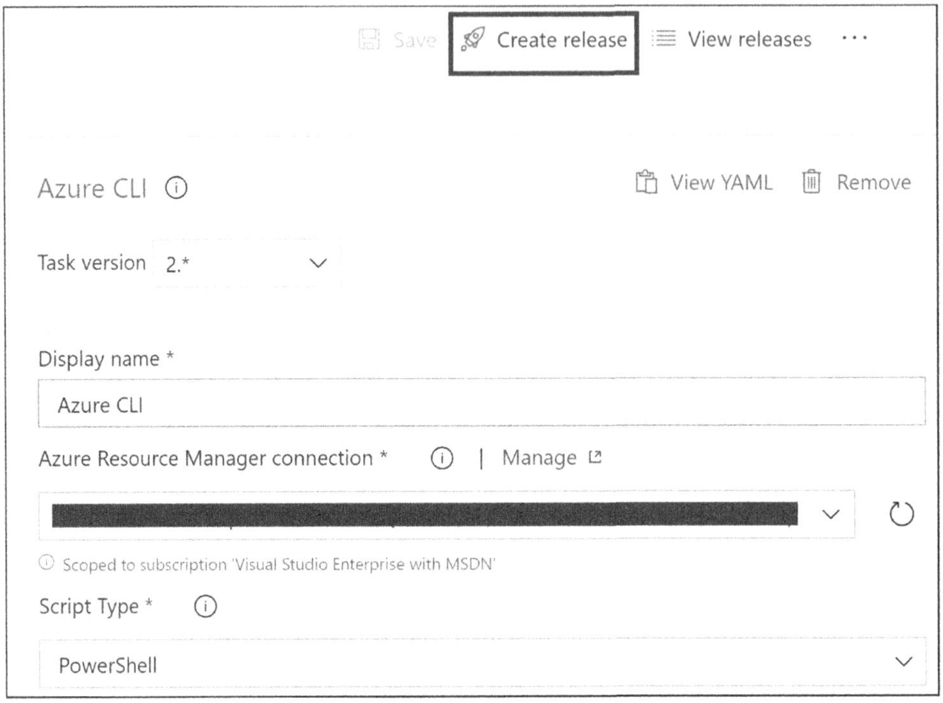

Figure 13-19. *Create a release*

Select the stage and click *Create* as in Figure 13-20.

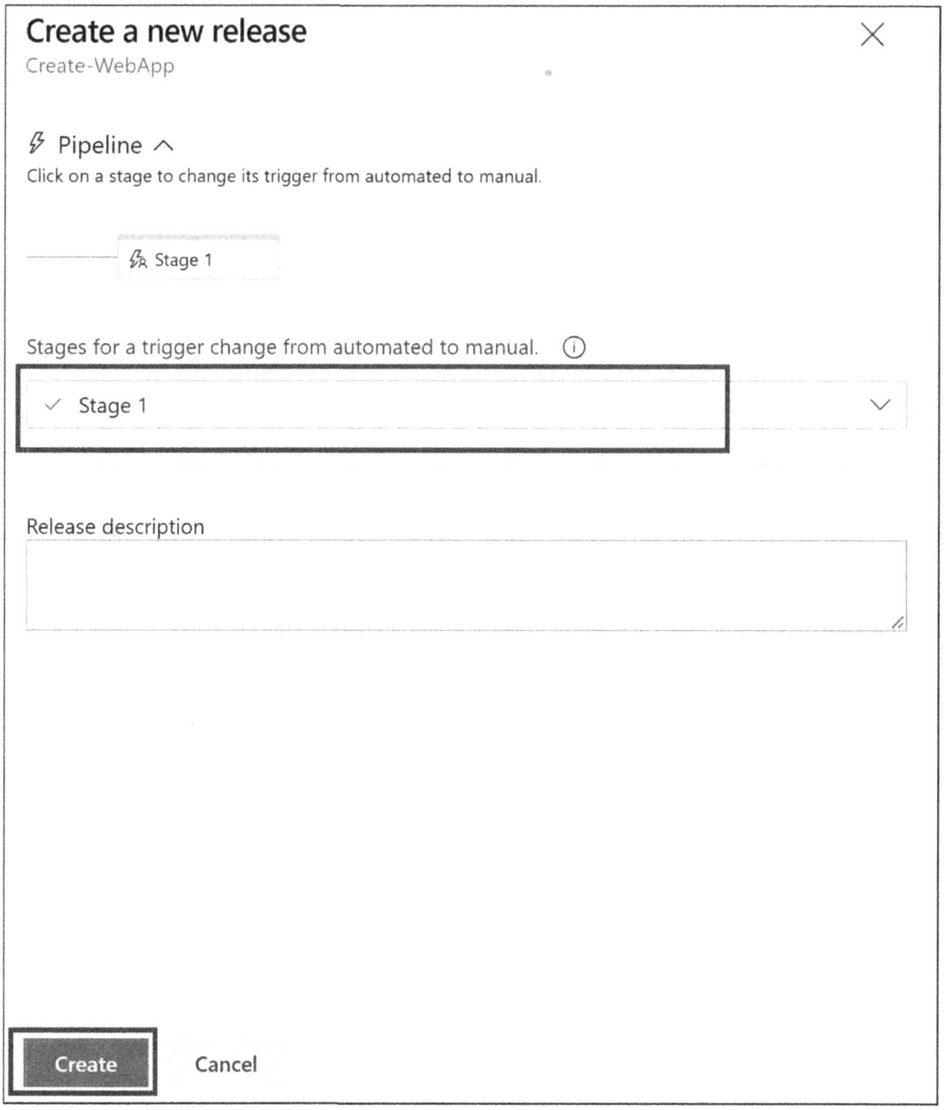

Figure 13-20. *Click Create*

Click on the release that got created as in Figure 13-21.

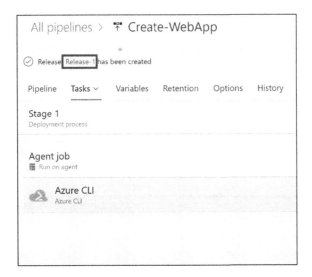

Figure 13-21. *Click on the release created*

Click *Deploy* as in Figure 13-22.

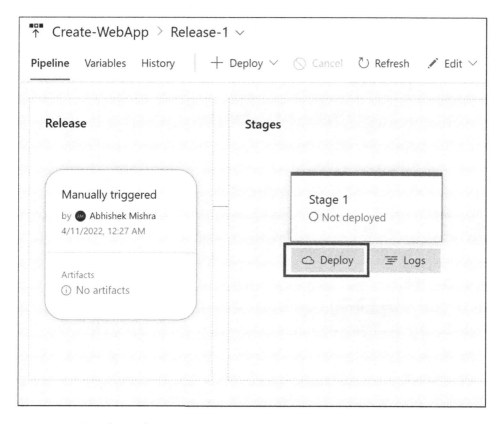

Figure 13-22. *Deploy release*

Click *Deploy* to start creating the WebApp as in Figure 13-23. Once the pipeline completes successfully, the WebApp gets created.

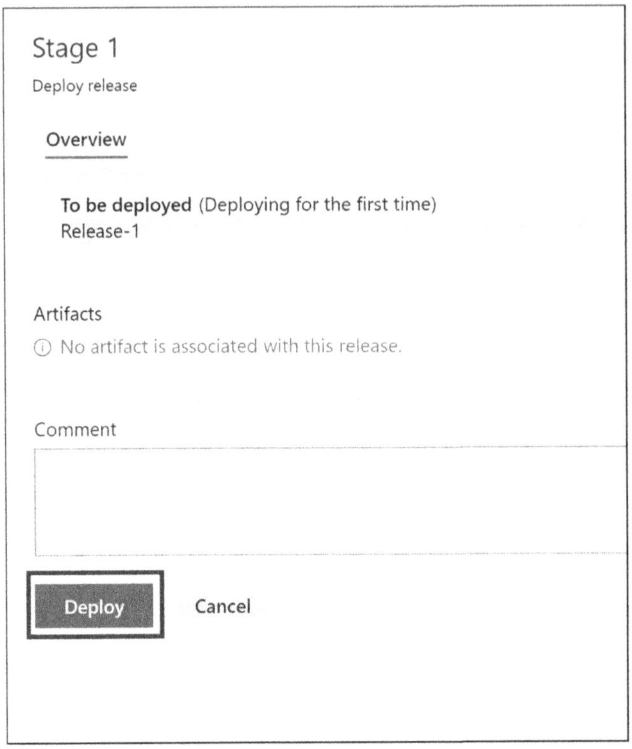

Figure 13-23. *Click Deploy*

For verification, you can use the command `curl -s -o /dev/null -w "%{http_code}" https://mywebappiacdemo01.azurewebsites.net/` and check for the status code as 200.

Summary

This chapter taught us how to create Azure resources using Azure CLI and Azure DevOps. We created a resource group, an App Service Plan, and an Azure WebApp using Azure CLI and Azure DevOps. In the next chapter, we will learn how to deploy Java applications to Azure using Azure DevOps.

The following are the key takeaways from this chapter:

- Creating Azure resources using the Azure portal is effort-intensive and risks introducing errors due to the manual efforts involved. You can automate the resource creation activity and trigger the automation across multiple deployment environments. This approach would save much time for you and would be error-free.

- The following are some popular Infrastructure-as-Code (IaC) offerings to automate the creation of Azure resources:

    - Azure CLI

    - Azure PowerShell

    - ARM Templates

    - Terraform

    - Bicep

CHAPTER 14

Building and Deploying Using Azure DevOps

Continuous Integration Pipelines build the application, and Continuous Deployment Pipelines deploy the applications on the target hosting environment. This DevOps approach automates an application's build and deployment methodology and is adopted across all modern enterprises. These pipelines reduce manual errors during the deployment process and ensure faster market release. We can use Azure DevOps Pipelines to build an application and deploy it to Azure.

In the previous chapter, we learned the basic concept of Infrastructure as Code (IaC). We then created an Azure CLI script to spin up Azure resources. We also used the Azure DevOps CLI task to create a WebApp. In this chapter, we will learn how to deploy a Java application to Azure using Azure DevOps Pipeline.

Structure

In this chapter, we will discuss the following DevOps-based application deployment concepts:

- Create a Java application and commit it to Git-based Azure Repos
- Create a YAML-based pipeline to build the application and deploy it to Azure WebApp

Objectives

After studying this chapter, you should be able to get the following learnings:

- Learn how to work with Azure Repos

© Abhishek Mishra 2022
A. Mishra, *Microsoft Azure for Java Developers*, https://doi.org/10.1007/978-1-4842-8251-9_14

- • Learn how to build and deploy Java applications to Azure using Azure
  DevOps Pipeline

Create a Java Application and Commit It to Git-Based Azure Repos

Let us build a simple Java Spring Boot API that will return a string. You can generate the application using Spring Initializr. Listing 14-1 shows the POM file for the application. We need to include the *Spring Web* dependency as in Listing 14-1.

Listing 14-1. POM.xml

```
<?xml version="1.0" encoding="UTF-8"?>
<project xmlns="http://maven.apache.org/POM/4.0.0" xmlns:xsi="http://www.
w3.org/2001/XMLSchema-instance"
    xsi:schemaLocation="http://maven.apache.org/POM/4.0.0 https://maven.
    apache.org/xsd/maven-4.0.0.xsd">
    <modelVersion>4.0.0</modelVersion>
    <parent>
        <groupId>org.springframework.boot</groupId>
        <artifactId>spring-boot-starter-parent</artifactId>
        <version>2.6.6</version>
        <relativePath/> <!-- lookup parent from repository -->
    </parent>
    <groupId>com.iac</groupId>
    <artifactId>demo</artifactId>
    <version>0.0.1-SNAPSHOT</version>
    <name>demo</name>
    <description>Demo project for Spring Boot</description>
    <properties>
        <java.version>11</java.version>
    </properties>
    <dependencies>
        <dependency>
            <groupId>org.springframework.boot</groupId>
```

```
        <artifactId>spring-boot-starter-web</artifactId>
    </dependency>

    <dependency>
        <groupId>org.springframework.boot</groupId>
        <artifactId>spring-boot-starter-test</artifactId>
        <scope>test</scope>
    </dependency>
</dependencies>

<build>
    <plugins>
        <plugin>
            <groupId>org.springframework.boot</groupId>
            <artifactId>spring-boot-maven-plugin</artifactId>
        </plugin>
    </plugins>
</build>

</project>
```

You can generate a class file with the Main method and a REST API. Listing 14-2 shows the content of the class file.

Listing 14-2. Class file

```
package com.iac.demo;

import org.springframework.boot.SpringApplication;
import org.springframework.boot.autoconfigure.SpringBootApplication;
import org.springframework.web.bind.annotation.GetMapping;
import org.springframework.web.bind.annotation.RestController;

@SpringBootApplication
@RestController
public class DemoApplication {

    public static void main(String[] args) {
        SpringApplication.run(DemoApplication.class, args);
    }
```

```
@GetMapping("/")
public String index() {
    return "Hello Spring Boot on WebApp !!";
}

}
```

Once the application builds successfully, you can check in the code to the Azure Repos. As a prerequisite, you should have Git installed on your system. We can use the Azure DevOps project we created in the previous chapter. Open the Azure DevOps URL and navigate to the project. Click *Repos* and then click *Generate Git Credentials* as in Figure 14-1.

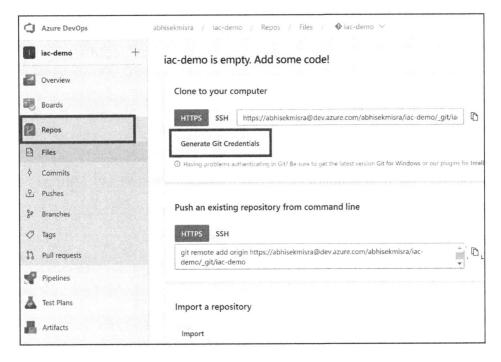

Figure 14-1. *Generate Git credentials*

Copy the HTTPS URL, Git username, and password as in Figure 14-2.

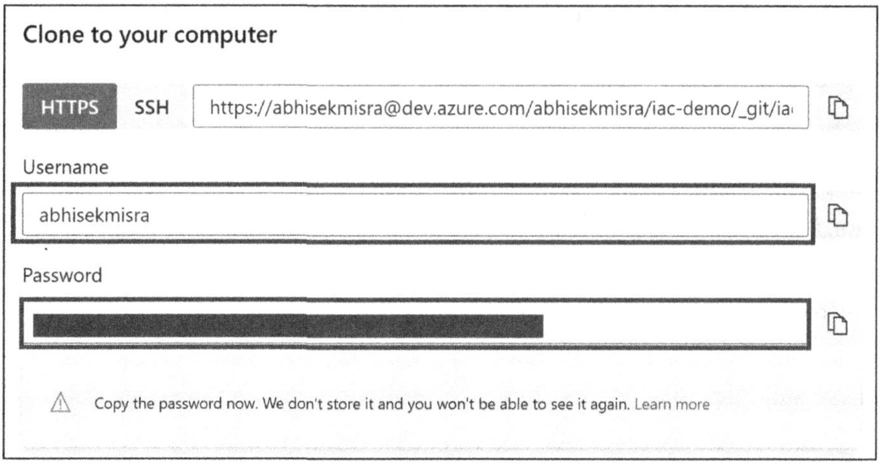

Figure 14-2. Copy Git credentials

Navigate to the Java project root folder in the Windows Explorer with the POM file. Execute the command from Listing 14-3 to initiate a local Git repository.

Listing 14-3. Initialize a local Git repository

```
git init
```

Execute the command as in Listing 14-4 to add the folder content to the local Git repository.

Listing 14-4. Add local changes to the Git repository

```
git add .
```

Execute the command as in Listing 14-5 to commit the added files in the local Git repository.

Listing 14-5. Commit added files to the local Git repository

```
git commit -m "Initial commit"
```

Execute the commands as in Listing 14-6 to connect to the Git repository in Azure DevOps and push the local Git changes to it. Replace [HTTPS_URL] with the URL you copied earlier while generating the Git credentials.

Listing 14-6. Push local Git repository changes to Azure Repos

```
git remote add origin [HTTPS_URL]
git push -u origin --all
```

You will get prompted to provide credentials for Git. You can provide the username and password you copied while generating Git credentials. Ensure you provide the username and the domain—for example, abc@xyx.onmicrosoft.com. The Java project will get checked into the Azure DevOps Repo as in Figure 14-3.

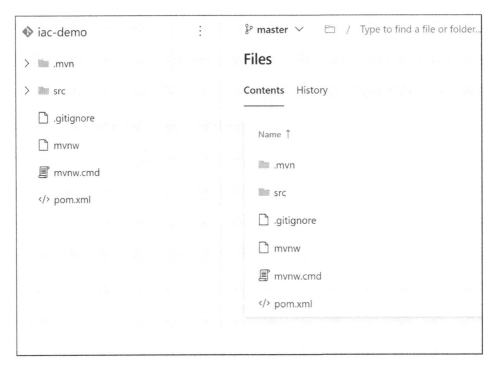

Figure 14-3. *Added project to Git Repo*

Create a YAML-Based Pipeline

Let us create a YAML-based pipeline to build the Java project from the Azure Repos and deploy it on Azure WebApp. As a prerequisite, you should have created a Linux-based Azure WebApp for Java 11 applications. You can refer to Chapter 13 on more details here. Click *Pipelines* as in Figure 14-4.

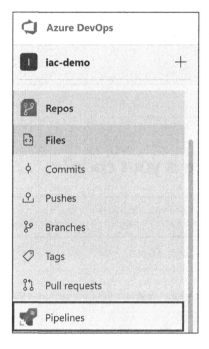

Figure 14-4. *Click Pipelines*

Click *Create Pipeline* as in Figure 14-5 to create a YAML-based pipeline.

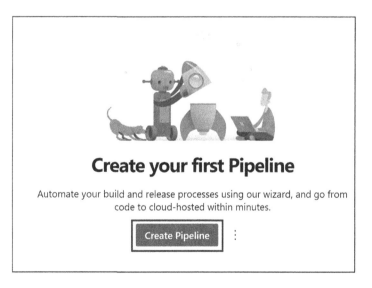

Figure 14-5. *Click Create Pipeline*

You will be asked to provide the source code repository details where the Java code is checked in. We have checked in to Azure Repos Git. So select *Azure Repos Git* as in Figure 14-6.

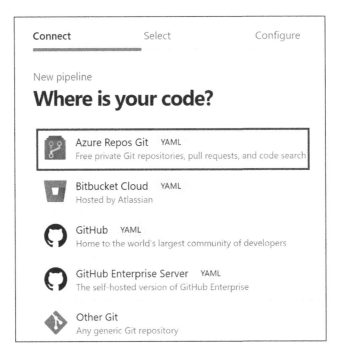

Figure 14-6. *Select Azure Repos Git*

Select the repository where you have checked in the code as in Figure 14-7.

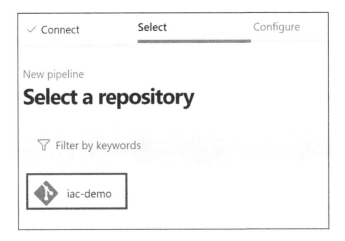

Figure 14-7. *Select the code repository*

You can select the template *Maven package Java project Web App to Linux on Azure* as in Figure 14-8. If you do not see this template listed, click *Show More* and search for it.

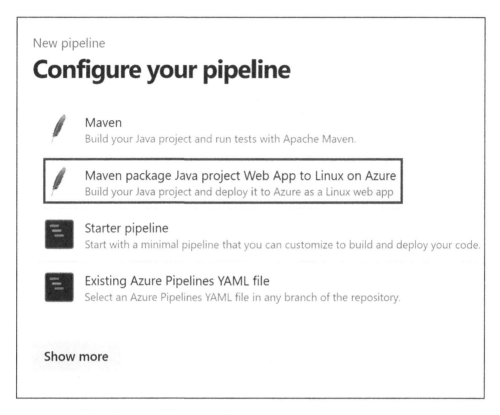

Figure 14-8. *Select the pipeline template*

Select the Azure subscription where you have created the Azure WebApp. Click *Continue* as in Figure 14-9.

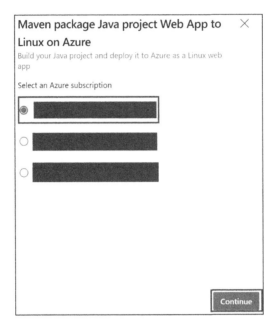

Figure 14-9. *Select a subscription*

You will be prompted to provide your login credentials as in Figure 14-10. Provide your credentials to log in to the system.

Figure 14-10. *Provide your credentials*

Select the name of the WebApp where you are planning to deploy the Java code. Click *Validate and configure* as in Figure 14-11. You need to wait for some time for the

WebApp to get reflected here in the Azure DevOps environment after creating it. At times, it may take a few hours.

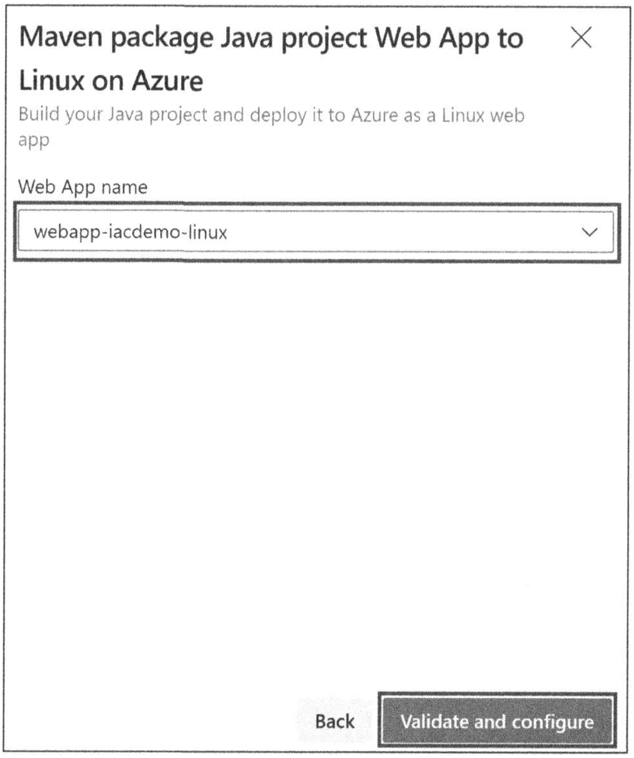

Figure 14-11. *Click Validate and configure*

The YAML pipeline will get generated for you. Listing 14-7 demonstrates the YAML pipeline content.

Listing 14-7. YAML code generated

```
# Maven package Java project Web App to Linux on Azure
# Build your Java project and deploy it to Azure as a Linux web app
# Add steps that analyze code, save build artifacts, deploy, and more:
# https://docs.microsoft.com/azure/devops/pipelines/languages/java

trigger:
- master

variables:
```

```
  # Azure Resource Manager connection created during pipeline creation
  azureSubscription: '3956cc05-4215-45e5-98f9-6d3eef83b0d8'

  # Web app name
  webAppName: 'webapp-iacdemo-linux'

  # Environment name
  environmentName: 'webapp-iacdemo-linux'

  # Agent VM image name
  vmImageName: 'ubuntu-latest'

stages:
- stage: Build
  displayName: Build stage
  jobs:
  - job: MavenPackageAndPublishArtifacts
    displayName: Maven Package and Publish Artifacts
    pool:
      vmImage: $(vmImageName)

    steps:
    - task: Maven@3
      displayName: 'Maven Package'
      inputs:
        mavenPomFile: 'pom.xml'

    - task: CopyFiles@2
      displayName: 'Copy Files to artifact staging directory'
      inputs:
        SourceFolder: '$(System.DefaultWorkingDirectory)'
        Contents: '**/target/*.?(war|jar)'
        TargetFolder: $(Build.ArtifactStagingDirectory)

    - upload: $(Build.ArtifactStagingDirectory)
      artifact: drop

- stage: Deploy
  displayName: Deploy stage
```

```
dependsOn: Build
condition: succeeded()
jobs:
- deployment: DeployLinuxWebApp
  displayName: Deploy Linux Web App
  environment: $(environmentName)
  pool:
    vmImage: $(vmImageName)
  strategy:
    runOnce:
      deploy:
        steps:
        - task: AzureWebApp@1
          displayName: 'Azure Web App Deploy: webapp-iacdemo-linux'
          inputs:
            azureSubscription: $(azureSubscription)
            appType: webAppLinux
            appName: $(webAppName)
            package: '$(Pipeline.Workspace)/drop/**/target/*.?(war|jar)'
```

Click *Save and run* as in Figure 14-12. This will save the pipeline changes and navigate you to the next screen where you can execute the pipeline.

Figure 14-12. *Click Save and run*

Click *Save and run* as in Figure 14-13 to execute the pipeline.

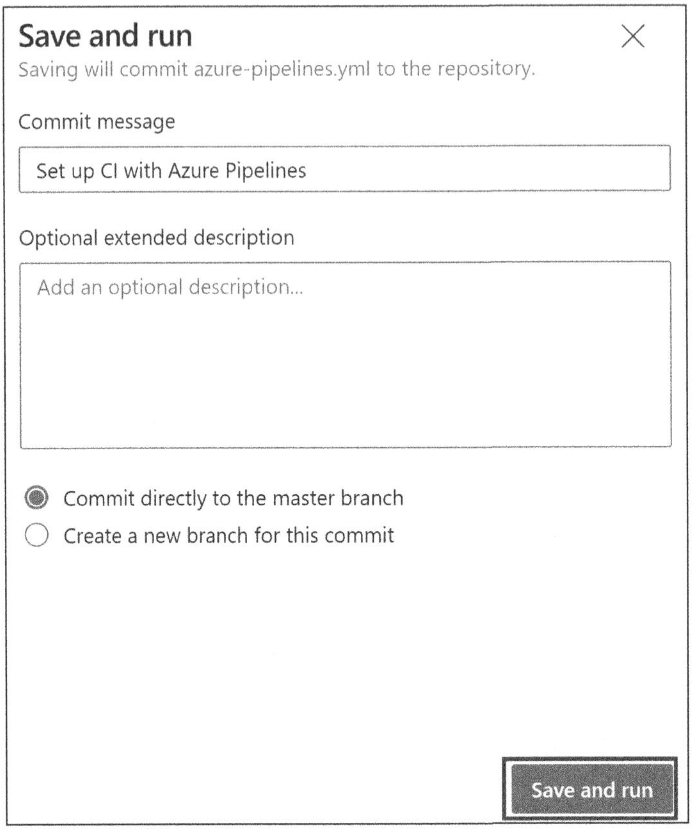

Figure 14-13. *Execute the pipeline*

Once the build stage completes, the pipeline will ask you for permissions to deploy to Azure WebApp. Click *View* as in Figure 14-14 and provide permissions.

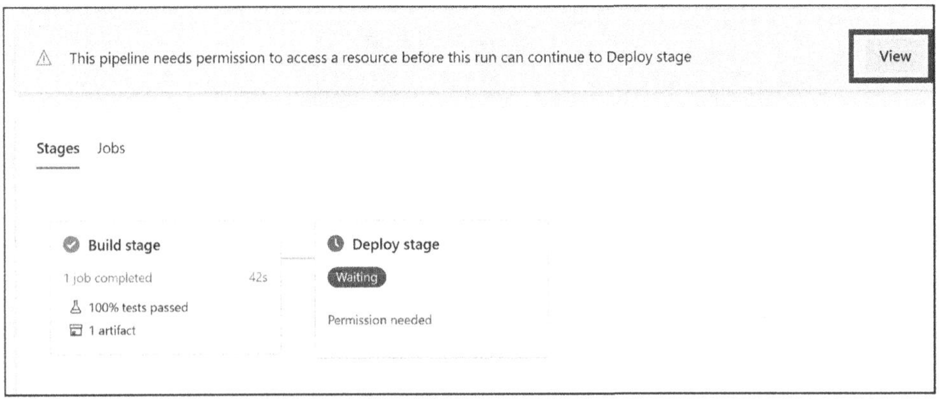

Figure 14-14. *Provide permissions for deployment*

Once the pipeline completes, the Java application gets deployed to Azure WebApp. You can browse the WebApp URL and see the response on the browser as in Figure 14-15.

Figure 14-15. *Response output on the browser*

Summary

This chapter showed how to build and deploy a Java Spring Boot application to Azure WebApp using Azure DevOps. We used Git commands to check in the Java code to Azure Repos. We then created a YAML-based pipeline to build and deploy the Java application from Azure Repos to Azure WebApp. In the next chapter, we will learn the best cases and explore a real-time Java application on Azure.

The following are the key takeaways from this chapter:

- Azure Repos provides a Git repository, and you can execute Git commands to check in to Azure Repos.

- You can also create a TFS-based code repository using Azure DevOps.

- You can create a YAML-based pipeline to build Java code and deploy it to Azure.

## CHAPTER 15

A Near-Production Azure-Based Java Application

Now we have come to the end of the book. We have learned the basics of the essential Azure services that will come in handy while working with Java-based applications on Azure. We learned how to deploy Java-based applications on Azure services like Azure WebApp, Azure Kubernetes Service, Azure Spring Cloud, and Azure Functions. We also learned how to work with Azure SQL, Azure Storage, and Azure Redis Cache. We explored how to monitor, secure, and use Azure DevOps for automated infrastructure creation.

We learned how to build and deploy Java applications to Azure services using Azure DevOps in the last chapter. In this chapter, we will explore the best practices to be followed while designing and implementing a Java-based application on Azure. We will also work on a near-production scenario.

Structure

In this chapter, we will discuss the following:

- Best practices
- Build a near-production scenario

Objectives

After studying this chapter, you should be able to get the following learnings:

© Abhishek Mishra 2022
A. Mishra, *Microsoft Azure for Java Developers*, https://doi.org/10.1007/978-1-4842-8251-9_15

- Learn how to build a Java-based application that can be hosted on Azure.

- Understand the best practices while working on Java applications for Azure.

Best Practices

Designing an application architecture is a crucial activity. You must consider the best practices while implementing the application architecture. Applications targeted for Azure should be planned with very high precision so that the application performs as expected in the Azure environment. Let us discuss a few essential best practices that you should consider while designing a Java-based application for Azure.

- Identify the host options.

- Modernize application and then move to Azure.

- Choose the right Azure services for your application.

- Plan the cloud cost meeting your budget.

- Plan for scalability, availability, and reliability.

- Have a robust debugging and monitoring strategy in place.

- Secure your application on Azure.

- Automate spinning up Azure services and application deployment.

- Have the right backup and disaster recovery strategy in place.

Identify the Host Options

You can use App Service for Java SE, App Service for Tomcat, App Service for JBoss, Azure Spring Cloud, Azure Kubernetes Service, and Virtual Machines to host your Java application on Azure. You need to use the right service matching you need. For example, if you have a Spring Boot application, then you can run it on Azure Spring Cloud, App Service, or Virtual Machines.

Modernize Application and Then Move to Azure

You may sometimes find applications developed on older Java versions using legacy components not supported on Azure. You must ensure that you modernize the older Java applications to at least version 1.8. You must modernize your legacy application to a supported framework and Java version and then migrate it to Azure. Try using modern Java development frameworks like Spring Boot. If you have a Java application running on noncompatible frameworks like WebSphere Liberty, try modernizing it to either Open Liberty or Spring Boot for a smoother Azure migration.

Choose the Right Azure Services for Your Application

You must design the Azure infrastructure to suit the need of your application. If you have a distributed microservices application, try hosting it on Azure Spring Cloud or Azure Kubernetes Service. You can also build distributed applications using Azure Functions. You must use Storage Queues or Service Bus Queues to exchange messages across distributed services. The temporary runtime data should be stored in Azure Redis Cache.

If you have a monolith, a single service, or a single container-based application, you must use Azure WebApp.

Plan the Cloud Cost Meeting Your Need

The total cost of ownership is an essential factor while designing the Azure infrastructure for your application. You must analyze the compute and all necessary needs for your application that can influence the cost of usage. For example, you plan to scale your Azure cluster using serverless nodes. Serverless nodes run on Azure Container Instances and can accommodate a single pod at a time. If you need thousands of pods at a time, you need thousands of Azure Container Instances. Instead, you can check if you can scale using the Virtual Machine Scale Set. A single Virtual Machine-based node can accommodate many pods at a time.

Also, while planning the App Service Plan for your WebApp, make sure that you pick the right plan suiting your application compute and other requirement needs. Plan your service tiers or reserve the compute for the services matching the right needs for your application. Do not reserve a higher tier where you may waste compute or reserve a lower tier where your application will fall short of compute. Right-sizing the compute needs for the Azure services saves a lot of cost for you.

Plan for Scalability, Availability, and Reliability

Your Java application must be able to scale, always available, and fault-tolerant as per the business requirements. The application should be highly available. You must try to leverage auto-scaling mechanisms available in the services where you are hosting your application. You must ensure that you have multiple instances of the services hosting your applications running behind a load balancer or an application gateway or a traffic manager, or a front door to ensure that if one of the instances goes down, the traffic should get routed to other instances. You must have a retry mechanism in place for failed operations. The data that could not be processed should be available during retries so that none of the data fails to get processed. This activity would make sure that the application is reliable.

Have a Robust Debugging and Monitoring Strategy in Place

You must leverage Azure Monitor and Application Insights to collect metrics and logs for your application and the Azure infrastructure. This activity would help you debug failures in the Production environment, monitor your application's performance, and take precautionary measures in case of anomalies. Appropriate alerts should be configured to notify the stakeholders if there is a failure or if something will fail.

You can also leverage other monitoring offerings like Prometheus and AppDynamics provided by third-party vendors.

Secure Your Application on Azure

You must configure authentication and authorization for your Java application running on Azure. You may use Azure Active Directory or any other third-party identity provider. All the application accesses and operations should be monitored and periodically audited.

Automate Spinning Up Azure Services and Application Deployment

You must leverage Infrastructure as Code (IaC) to automate spinning up Azure resources and facilitate application deployments using DevOps pipelines. This strategy will reduce manual errors during infrastructure creation and application deployments. Also, it will help you save time when you deploy your application across multiple environments.

Have the Right Backup and Disaster Recovery Strategy in Place

You must periodically back up application data and make it available if there is a data loss. Storing the backup data can be costly. So you must decide upon for how long you need to retain the backup data and clean up the backups beyond the retention period. You must plan a disaster recovery strategy for your application. If the application goes down, you must be able to run the application from another instance or infrastructure on Azure based on your disaster recovery strategy. And you must recover the application in the failed infrastructure fast and quick. At any cost, the business should be up and running.

Build a Near-Production Scenario

Now let us work on a near-production scenario. We will discuss the use case as the problem statement and understand the requirement for the scenario, and then we will provision the Azure infrastructure and build the solution for the problem statement. This activity will give you an idea of how to use Java with Azure in the production environment.

Problem Statement

We have a student table in the Azure SQL database. The table contains the roll number, name, and marks of the students in a class. Let us build a Spring Boot web application to get the student records from the student table and render it in the browser. The application should be available to authenticated users only. Make sure that you enable logging for the application so that you can debug the application when it is deployed on Azure WebApp.

Implementation: Create Infrastructure

We need the following Azure services for the application:

- Azure WebApp that will host the application

- Azure SQL Database for the student table

- Application Insights for logging and monitoring

- Azure Active Directory Application Registration for application authentication

Let us create each of these services first before building the Java application. We can start with creating Azure WebApp and Application Insights. Azure WebApp will host the application, and Application Insights will be used for logging and monitoring purposes. The application will ingest runtime logs into Application Insights that can be used later for debugging purposes.

Go to the Azure portal and click *Create a resource* as in Figure 15-1. You will get navigated to Azure Marketplace.

Figure 15-1. *Create a resource*

Click *Web* in the Marketplace and then click *Web App* as in Figure 15-2

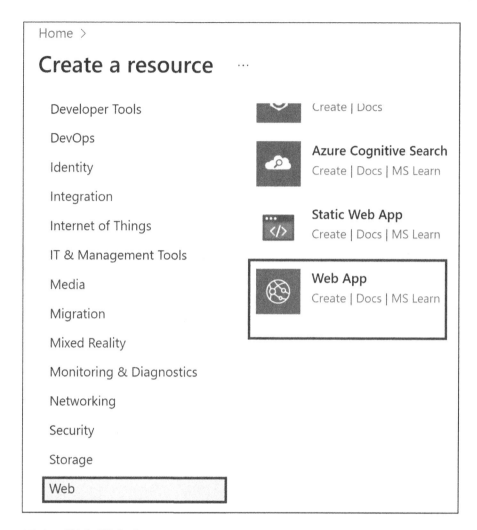

Figure 15-2. *Click Web App*

Provide subscription, resource group, and name for the WebApp as in Figure 15-3.

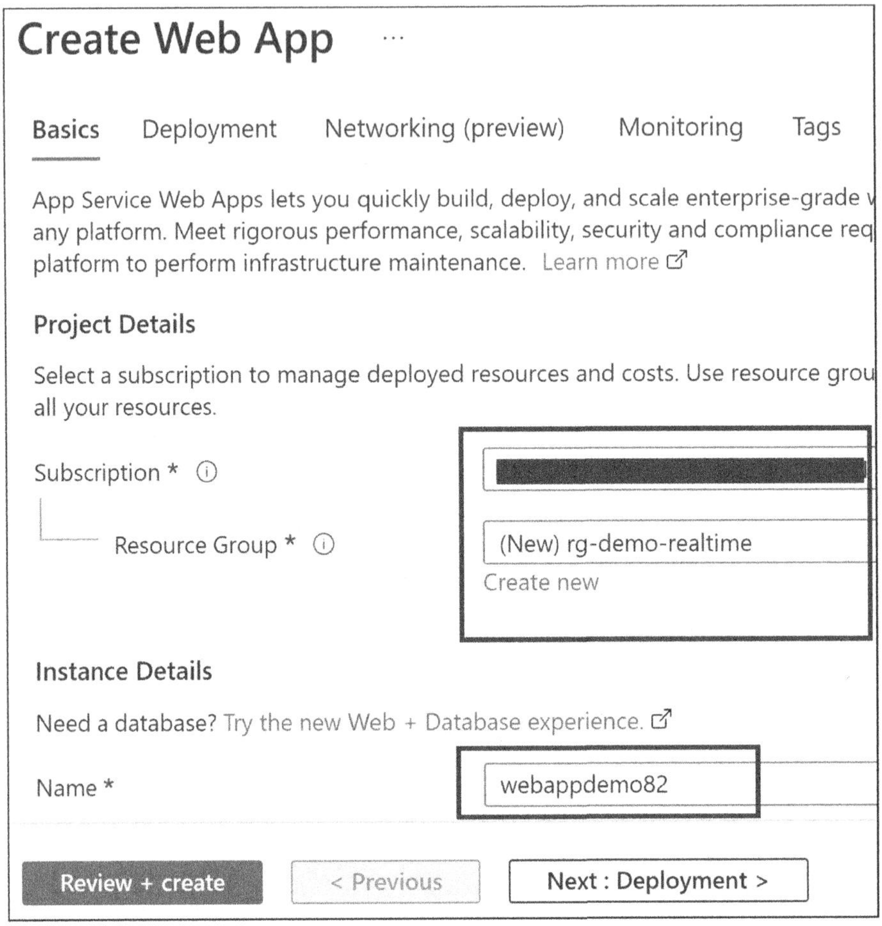

Figure 15-3. *Provide basic details*

Scroll down and provide other necessary basic details for the Web App as in Figure 15-4.

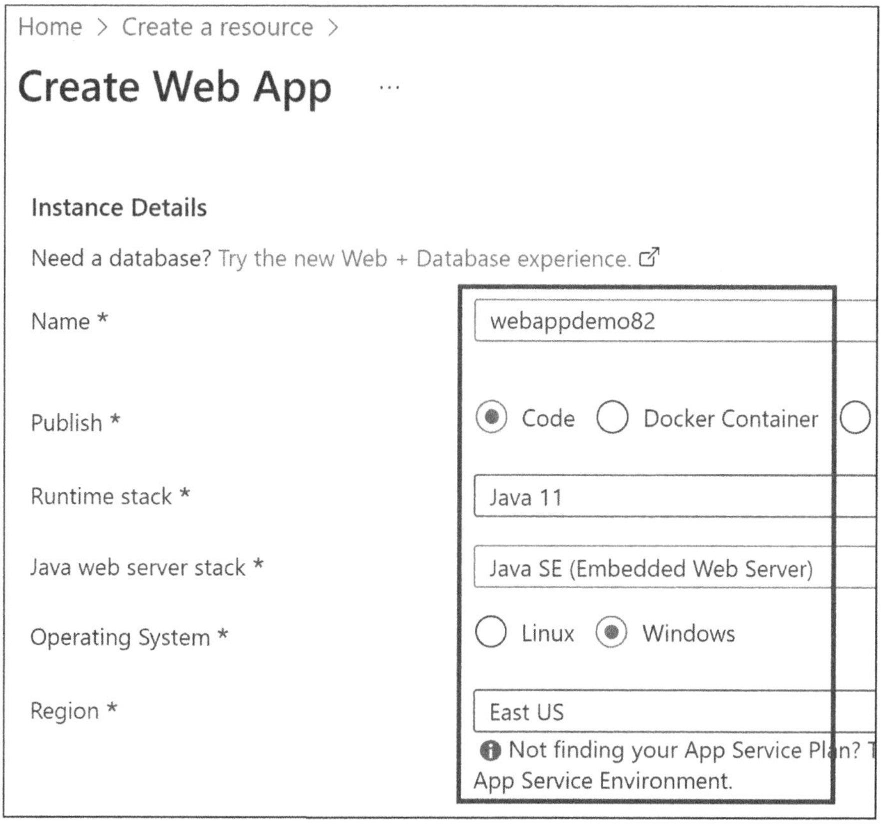

Home > Create a resource >

Create Web App   ...

Instance Details

Need a database? Try the new Web + Database experience. ☐

Name *   webappdemo82

Publish *   ◉ Code ○ Docker Container ○

Runtime stack *   Java 11

Java web server stack *   Java SE (Embedded Web Server)

Operating System *   ○ Linux ◉ Windows

Region *   East US

                                          ⓘ Not finding your App Service Plan? T
                                          App Service Environment.

Figure 15-4. *Provide basic details*

Go to the *Monitoring* tab and enable Application Insights. You need to select an existing Application Insights or create a new one. Click *Review + create* as in Figure 15-5

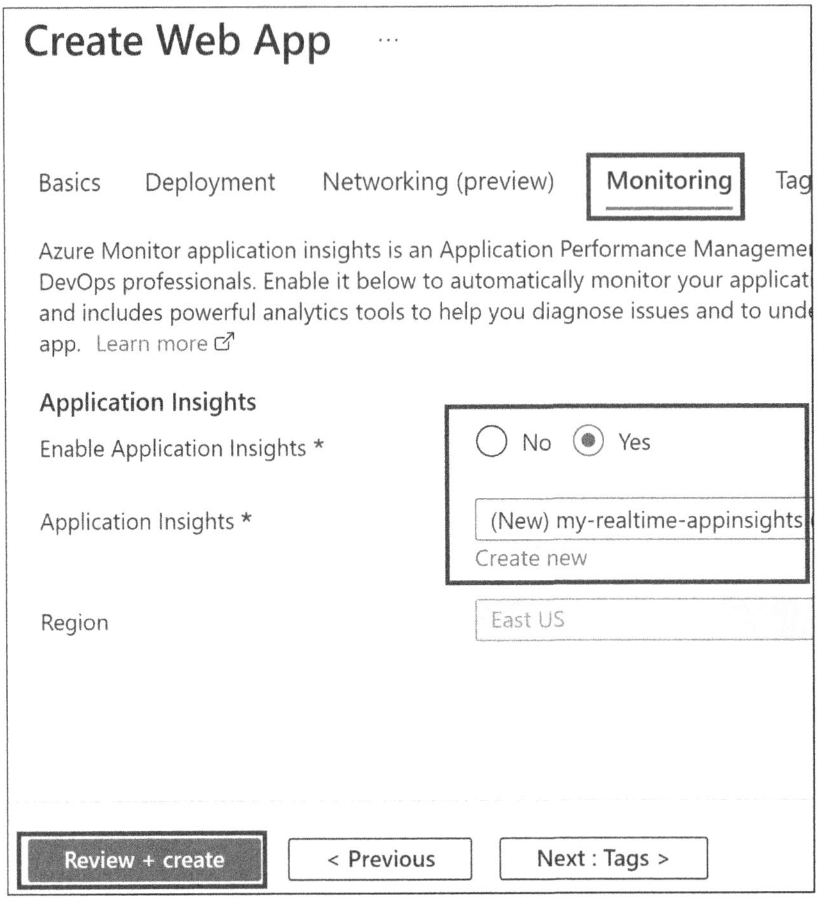

Figure 15-5. *Create Application Insights*

Click *Create* as in Figure 15-6. Your Web App and Application Insights will get created. The Application Insights will get associated with the Web App, and you can ingest application logs to the Application Insights without making any other changes in the Web App.

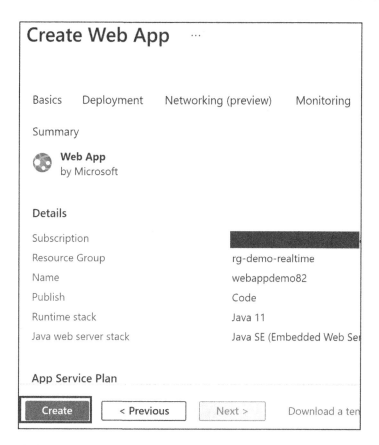

Figure 15-6. *Click Create*

Now let us spin up the Azure SQL database, create the student table and insert some student data. Go to the Azure portal and click *Create a resource* as in Figure 15-7.

Figure 15-7. *Create a resource*

Click *Databases* and then click *SQL Database* as in Figure 15-8

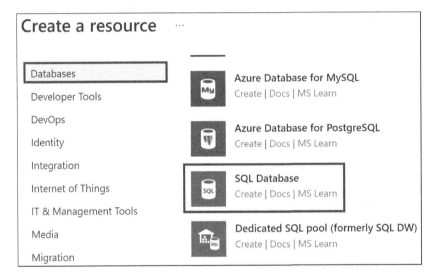

Figure 15-8. *Click SQL Database*

Provide basic details for the Azure SQL database. Click *Next : Networking* as in Figure 15-9.

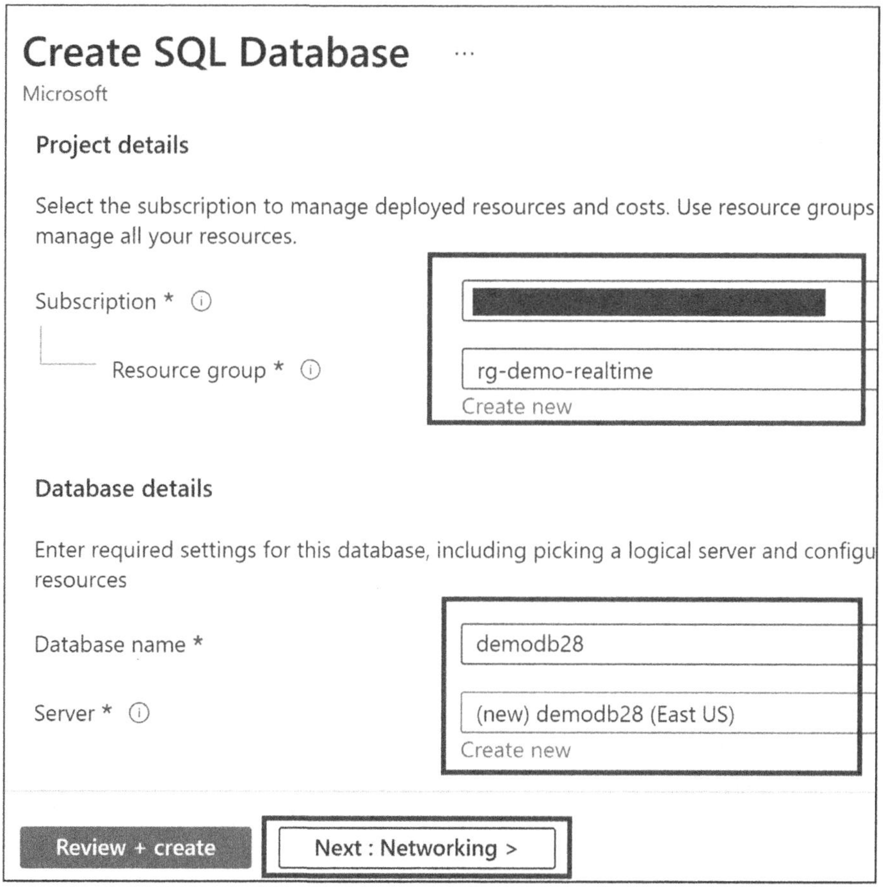

Create SQL Database   ⋯
Microsoft

Project details

Select the subscription to manage deployed resources and costs. Use resource groups
manage all your resources.

Subscription * ⓘ   ████████████████████

└─── Resource group * ⓘ   rg-demo-realtime
                            Create new

Database details

Enter required settings for this database, including picking a logical server and configu
resources

Database name *   demodb28

Server * ⓘ   (new) demodb28 (East US)
                       Create new

[Review + create]   [Next : Networking >]

Figure 15-9. *Provide basic details*

Select the access to the database as a *Public endpoint* as in Figure 15-10. Modify
firewall rules for the database to allow other Azure services to access it, and also, you
should be able to access the database from your local system. Click *Review + create*. And
then click *Create*.

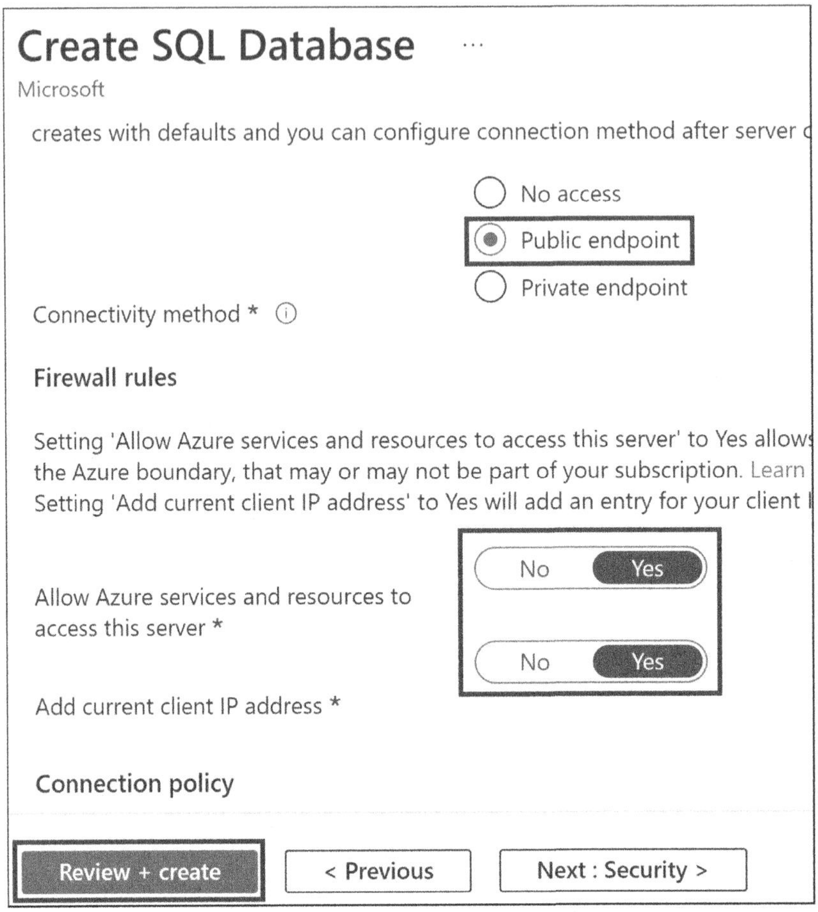

Figure 15-10. *Configure firewall rules*

Once the database gets created, go to the *Query editor* as in Figure 15-11, provide the database credentials, and log in to the database.

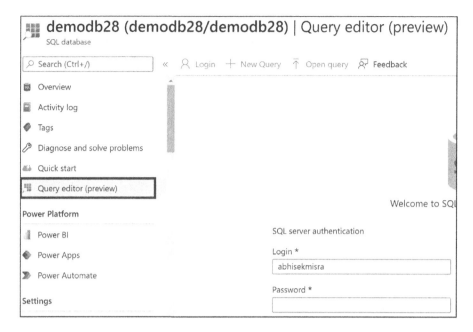

Figure 15-11. *Go to the Query editor*

Run the SQL query shown in Listing 15-1 to create the student table.

Listing 15-1. Create the student table

```
create table student
(
    roll int identity primary key,
    name varchar(100),
    age int,
    marks int
)
```

Insert some student data into the database.

Listing 15-2. Insert student data

```
insert into [dbo].[student] values ('Abhishek M', 18,88)
insert into [dbo].[student] values ('Sam', 16,72)
insert into [dbo].[student] values ('Tom', 18,64)
insert into [dbo].[student] values ('Jim', 19,92)
```

We can follow the same steps as Chapter 12 to create a user in Azure Active Directory and register an application. While registering the application in Azure Active Directory, make sure you provide the following URL as in Listing 15-3 as Redirect URI. Replace {WebApp} with the name of the WebApp we created.

Listing 15-3. Redirect URI

```
https://{WebApp}.azurewebsites.net/login/oauth2/code/
```

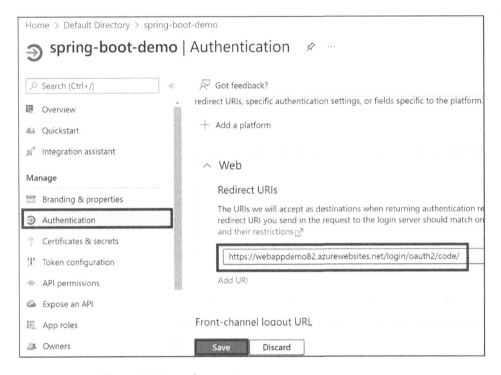

Figure 15-12. *Redirect URI configuration*

Build the Application and Deploy It to Azure WebApp

We have the infrastructure ready. Let us build the application and then deploy it to Azure WebApp. Listing 15-4 is the POM file for the application. You need to add dependencies to work with Azure SQL, Azure Active Directory, and Application Insights.

Listing 15-4. POM.xml

```xml
<?xml version="1.0" encoding="UTF-8"?>
<project xmlns="http://maven.apache.org/POM/4.0.0" xmlns:xsi="http://www.
w3.org/2001/XMLSchema-instance"
    xsi:schemaLocation="http://maven.apache.org/POM/4.0.0 https://maven.
    apache.org/xsd/maven-4.0.0.xsd">
    <modelVersion>4.0.0</modelVersion>
    <parent>
        <groupId>org.springframework.boot</groupId>
        <artifactId>spring-boot-starter-parent</artifactId>
        <version>2.6.3</version>
        <relativePath/> <!-- lookup parent from repository -->
    </parent>
    <groupId>com.database</groupId>
    <artifactId>demo</artifactId>
    <version>0.0.1-SNAPSHOT</version>
    <name>demo</name>
    <description>Demo project for Spring Boot</description>
    <properties>
        <java.version>11</java.version>
        <azure.version>3.14.0</azure.version>
    </properties>
    <dependencies>
        <dependency>
            <groupId>org.springframework.boot</groupId>
            <artifactId>spring-boot-starter-data-jdbc</artifactId>
        </dependency>
        <dependency>
            <groupId>org.springframework.boot</groupId>
            <artifactId>spring-boot-starter-web</artifactId>
        </dependency>

        <dependency>
            <groupId>com.microsoft.sqlserver</groupId>
            <artifactId>mssql-jdbc</artifactId>
```

```xml
                <scope>runtime</scope>
            </dependency>
            <dependency>
                <groupId>com.microsoft.azure</groupId>
                <artifactId>applicationinsights-spring-boot-starter</artifactId>
                <version>2.5.1</version>
            </dependency>
            <dependency>
                <groupId>org.springframework.boot</groupId>
                <artifactId>spring-boot-starter-oauth2-client</artifactId>
            </dependency>
            <dependency>
                <groupId>com.azure.spring</groupId>
                <artifactId>azure-spring-boot-starter-active-directory
                </artifactId>
            </dependency>
            <dependency>
                <groupId>org.springframework.boot</groupId>
                <artifactId>spring-boot-starter-test</artifactId>
                <scope>test</scope>
            </dependency>
        </dependencies>
        <dependencyManagement>
            <dependencies>
                <dependency>
                    <groupId>com.azure.spring</groupId>
                    <artifactId>azure-spring-boot-bom</artifactId>
                    <version>${azure.version}</version>
                    <type>pom</type>
                    <scope>import</scope>
                </dependency>
            </dependencies>
        </dependencyManagement>

        <build>
            <plugins>
```

```
        <plugin>
            <groupId>org.springframework.boot</groupId>
            <artifactId>spring-boot-maven-plugin</artifactId>
        </plugin>
    </plugins>
  </build>

</project>
```

Listing 15-5 is the *application.properties* file. Here in this file, we need to provide the database connection details, Application Insights instrumentation key, and Azure Active Directory details.

Listing 15-5. Application.properties

```
logging.level.org.springframework.jdbc.core=DEBUG

# Specifies Database details:
spring.datasource.url=jdbc:sqlserver://{Provide Database
Name}.database.windows.net:1433;database={Provide Database
Name};encrypt=true;trustServerCertificate=false;hostNameInCertificate=*.
database.windows.net;loginTimeout=30;
spring.datasource.username={Provide Database User Name}@{Provide
Database Name}
spring.datasource.password={Provide Database Password}

spring.sql.init.mode=always
# Specifies App Insights Instrumentation Key:
azure.application-insights.instrumentation-key={Provide
Instrumentation Key}

spring.application.name=StudentApp
# Specifies your Active Directory ID:
azure.activedirectory.tenant-id={Provide Tenant ID}
# Specifies your App Registration's Application ID:
azure.activedirectory.client-id={Provide Client ID}
# Specifies your App Registration's secret key:
azure.activedirectory.client-secret={Provide Client Secret}
```

Let us create a *Student* class as in Listing 15-6. The *Student* class works as a domain model for the *student* database table.

Listing 15-6. Student class

```
package com.database.demo;

import org.springframework.data.annotation.Id;

public class Student {

    public Student(){

    }

    public Student(String name, int Age, int marks){
        this.name = name;
        this.age = age;
        this.marks = marks;
    }

    @Id
    private int roll;

    private String name;

    private int age;

    private int marks;

    private int getRoll()
    {
        return roll;
    }

    private void setRoll(int roll)
    {
        this.roll = roll;
    }
```

```java
    public String getName() {
        return name;
    }

    public void setName(String name) {
        this.name = name;
    }

    public int getAge() {
        return age;
    }

    public void setAge(int age) {
        this.age = age;
    }

    public int getMarks() {
        return marks;
    }

    public void setMarks(int marks) {
        this.marks = marks;
    }
}
```

Now let us add a *StudentRepository* interface as in Listing 15-7 in the same folder where we have the *Student* class and the *DemoApplication* class. The *StudentRepository* interface works as the repository class for the database and the domain model. The Spring Data JDBC manages this repository class.

Listing 15-7. StudentRepository class

```java
package com.database.demo;

import org.springframework.data.repository.CrudRepository;
public interface StudentRepository extends CrudRepository<Student,
Integer> {
}
```

Create the *DemoApplication* Java class as in Listing 15-8 and convert it into a REST Controller. In the REST GET API, we access the Azure SQL database and return an HTML response with the student details. Authentication is enabled, and we are logging traces and exceptions to Application Insights.

Listing 15-8. DemoApplication class

```java
package com.database.demo;

import com.microsoft.applicationinsights.TelemetryClient;
import org.springframework.boot.SpringApplication;
import org.springframework.boot.autoconfigure.SpringBootApplication;
import org.springframework.http.HttpStatus;
import org.springframework.security.access.prepost.PreAuthorize;
import org.springframework.web.bind.annotation.*;

@SpringBootApplication
@RestController
@RequestMapping("/")
public class DemoApplication {

    public static void main(String[] args) {
        SpringApplication.run(DemoApplication.class, args);
    }

    static final TelemetryClient telemetryClient = new TelemetryClient();

    private final StudentRepository studentRepository;

    public DemoApplication(StudentRepository studentRepository) {
        this.studentRepository = studentRepository;
    }

    @GetMapping("/")
    @ResponseBody
    @PreAuthorize("hasAuthority('APPROLE_superuser')")

    public String getStudents() {
        Iterable<Student> students = studentRepository.findAll();
        String html = "<html><body>" ;
```

```java
try{
    for (Student student: students) {
        html = html+"<p>";
        html = html+"<b>Roll : </b>" + student.getRoll()+"<br/>";
        html = html+"<b>Name : </b>" + student.getName()+"<br/>";
        html = html+"<b>Age : </b>" + student.getAge()+"<br/>";
        html = html+"<b>Marks : </b>" + student.getMarks()+"<br/>";

        telemetryClient.trackTrace("Processing Success with Roll :
        "+student.getRoll());
    }
    html = html+"</body></html>";
}
catch(Exception ex){
    telemetryClient.trackException(ex);
}

return html;
    }

}
```

Build the application. It should compile successfully.

Deploy the Application to Azure WebApp

Now let us deploy the application to Azure WebApp. Here, we will use the IntelliJ editor to build the application and then use the Azure plug-in for IntelliJ to deploy it to Azure. You can go through Chapter 2 for using Maven plug-in to deploy the application. However, you can use Eclipse or Visual Studio Code or any other Java editor that supports deployment to Azure. Go to IntelliJ settings, click *Plugins* and search for *Azure* in the *Marketplace*. Install *Azure Toolkit for IntelliJ* plug-in as in Figure 15-13.

Figure 15-13. *Install Azure Toolkit plug-in*

Once the plug-in is installed, right-click on the project as in Figure 15-14.

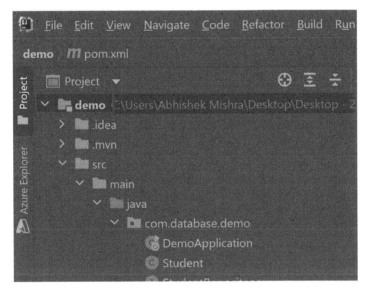

Figure 15-14. *Right-click on the project*

Click *Azure* and then click *Deploy to Azure Web Apps* as in Figure 15-15.

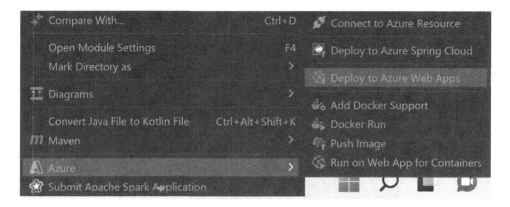

Figure 15-15. *Deploy to Azure WebApps*

Select *Azure CLI* and click *Sign in* as in Figure 15-16. Provide your credentials when prompted.

Figure 15-16. *Select Azure CLI*

Select the subscription and click *Select* as in Figure 15-17.

Figure 15-17. *Select the subscription*

Select the WebApp we created and click *Run* as in Figure 15-18.

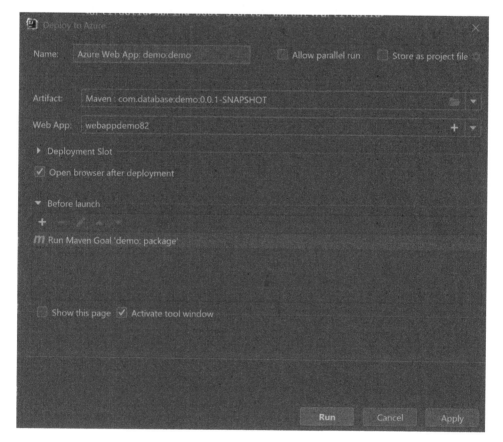

Figure 15-18. *Deploy to WebApp*

Once the deployment is complete, wait for ten minutes for the application to boot up in the WebApp. Navigate the WebApp URL after ten minutes. You will be prompted to provide login credentials as in Figure 15-19. Use the user's credentials you created and authorized in the registered application in Azure Active Directory.

Figure 15-19. *Provide login credentials*

You can see the student details rendered on the browser as in Figure 15-20.

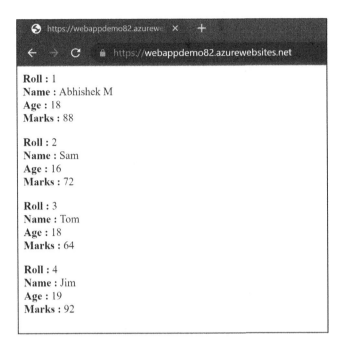

Figure 15-20. *Output on the browser*

The application trace logs get ingested at runtime in Application Insights as in Figure 15-21.

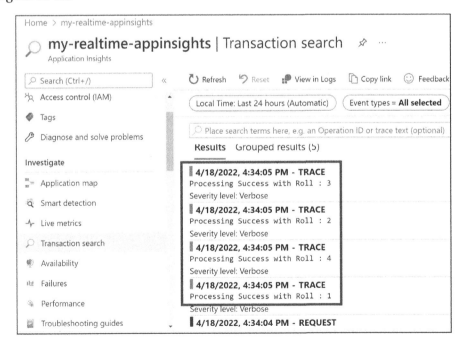

Figure 15-21. *Application logs in Application Insights*

Summary

In this chapter, we used the concepts we learned in the book to design and develop a complex use case. We explored the IntelliJ Azure plug-in to build and deploy Java applications to Azure WebApp. We applied multiple concepts like reading from Azure SQL, authenticating using Azure AD, monitoring applications using Application Insights, and deploying to Azure WebApp in a single Spring Boot application.

Index

A

Application Insights, 223, 247
  basic details, 249
  connection string, 250
  creation, 248
  .json file, 250
  JVM argument, 251
  logs, 251
  search result, 247
Application.properties file, 151, 339
App Service Plan
  dedicated compute, 17
  isolated plan, 18
  Java application
    Azure WebApp, 25–29
    Azure WebApp, deploy,
      29–31, 33, 34
    Java Spring Boot, 18–24
    scaling, 34–37
  Shared Compute, 17
Azure, 10
  Java-based applications, 12
  pricing model, 11
  services, 11
  WebApp, 12
Azure Active Directory, 207, 254
  authentication and
    authorization, 255
  enterprise applications, 267, 268,
    270, 271
  register an application, 258, 260,
    263, 267

  Spring Boot application,
    271, 273, 275, 276
  user creation, 255–257
authentication scenarios, 276
  native application, 277
  Server application, 278
  Single Page Application, 277
  Web Application, 277
  Web Browser to Web
    Application, 276
Azure Container Registry, 67, 71, 73, 79,
  85–88, 91, 92
Azure Cosmos DB, 161–163, 167, 171
  complete code, 173
  concept, 161
  database, 162
  Java application, 161
  Java code, 168
  location, 166
  NoSQL database, 179
  operations, 161
  POM file, 168
  student database, 178
  ways, 162
Azure DevOps, 286
  login URL, 286
  project creation, 286
    Authorize connection, 295
    CLI task, 290, 293, 296
    deploy release, 301
    job template, 289
    login credentials, 295

© Abhishek Mishra 2022
A. Mishra, *Microsoft Azure for Java Developers*, https://doi.org/10.1007/978-1-4842-8251-9

Z

Printed in the United States
by Baker & Taylor Publisher Services